M000304844

MORE BY EUGENE H. PETERSON
FROM WATERBROOK

On Living Well

This Hallelujah Banquet

As Kingfishers Catch Fire

Every Step an Arrival

A Month of Sundays

LIGHTS A
LOVELY MILE

LIGHTS A LOVELY MILE

Collected Sermons of
the Church Year

EUGENE H. PETERSON

WaterBrook

All Scripture quotations, unless otherwise indicated, are taken from the Revised Standard Version of the Bible, copyright © 1946, 1952, and 1971 National Council of the Churches of Christ in the United States of America. Used by permission. All rights reserved worldwide. Scripture quotations marked (KJV) are taken from the King James Version. Scripture quotations marked (NEB) are taken from the New English Bible, copyright © Cambridge University Press and Oxford University Press 1961, 1970. All rights reserved. Scripture quotations marked (NKJV) are taken from the New King James Version®. Copyright © 1982 by Thomas Nelson. Used by permission. All rights reserved. Scripture quotations marked (PHILLIPS) are taken from the New Testament in Modern English by J. B. Phillips, copyright © 1960, 1972 J. B. Phillips. Administered by the Archbishops' Council of the Church of England. Used by permission.

Copyright © 2023 by The Hoiland Group, LLC

All rights reserved.

Published in the United States by WaterBrook, an imprint of Random House, a division of Penguin Random House LLC.

WATERBROOK and colophon are registered trademarks of Penguin Random House LLC.

Library of Congress Cataloging-in-Publication Data
Names: Peterson, Eugene H., 1932–2018, author. |
Christ Our King (Church : Bel Air, Md.)
Title: Lights a lovely mile : collected sermons of the church year / Eugene H. Peterson.
Description: First edition. | Colorado Springs : WaterBrook, an imprint of Random House, a division of Penguin Random House LLC, [2023] |
Identifiers: LCCN 2023012313 | ISBN 9781601429704 (Hardback) |
ISBN 9781601429711 (ebook)
Subjects: LCSH: Church year sermons. | Presbyterian Church (U.S.A.)—Sermons. |
Sermons, American—20th century. | Bible—Sermons.
Classification: LCC BV4253 .P43 2023 | DDC 252—dc23/eng/20230705
LC record available at https://lccn.loc.gov/2023012313

Printed in Canada

waterbrookmultnomah.com

2 4 6 8 9 7 5 3 1

First Edition

Background art by Muratart/stock.adobe.com

Most WaterBrook books are available at special quantity discounts for bulk purchase for premiums, fundraising, corporate and educational needs by organizations, churches, and businesses. Special books or book excerpts also can be created to fit specific needs. For details, contact specialmarketscms@penguinrandomhouse.com.

Contents

✻

Editor's Note   xi

ADVENT

It Is Time to Wake Up to Reality   3
Awake!   10
Christ in Creation   13

CHRISTMAS

God's Last Word Is Jesus   23

EPIPHANY

Being Changed into His Likeness   33
How Worship Shapes Life   40
Love's Strategy   48
Time Is Very Short   55
So Run   65

LENT

Like Newborn Babes   75
Christ in the Christian   82
Christ in Our Conduct   90
Be Holy Yourselves   99

Priest of the Good Things   107

Transfigured   114

EASTER

Raised   125

Raised to Life with Christ   132

Not of Perishable Seed   139

Put on the New Nature   146

What Is Not for Sale in Church   153

Love Lessons: Love Is of God   160

Love Lessons: What Do I Do When It Doesn't Work?   166

Love Lessons: Love One Another, Just as He Has
    Commanded   172

PENTECOST

Suddenly a Sound   181

What Does This Mean? . . . What Shall We Do?   188

Filled with the Holy Spirit   195

Church Burning   199

The Trinity Mystery   204

Angels Long to Look   211

Follow in His Steps   217

ORDINARY TIME

The Most Dangerous   227

The Camel's Nose and the Needle's Eye   233

You Are the Christ   241

You Should Turn from These Vain Things   248

But You Have Come . . . to Jesus   254

What You Therefore Worship as Unknown   260

Contents • ix

This Prior Love   266

Christ in the Church   273

God's Splendor—His Righteousness   280

Getting It Straight, Keeping It Simple   288

Christ in Our Work   293

Editor's Note

Like any good writer, every good preacher is an artist who paints by means of words. But while the writer paints on the still surface of *space* (the page, kept blank), the preacher paints on the flowing surface of *time*.

This time, called a "sermon" and generally lasting between fifteen and sixty minutes, has also been kept blank. It has been set aside by the church for the artist to come humbly, trusting that inspiration and preparation will not fail, and, in prayer, to begin to speak. To encourage, implore, inspire, and remember, as the voice of a particular group of people in a particular place. To paint the songs and stories of the eternal Word freshly across the hours, the days, and the years. The call is not to be an expert but to be a pilgrim. Not firstly to be smart in mind or smooth in speech but firstly to be true in love and to be wise.

This book collects such artistry from Eugene H. Peterson. In it are some of his best sermons preached during his years as pastor at Christ Our King Presbyterian Church in Bel Air, Maryland.

We have chosen to arrange these sermons according to the same logic by which Eugene originally preached them: the traditional Christian calendar of the church year. Whether this historic seasonality is part of your faith tradition or not, it's our hope that by encountering Eugene's preaching in the season in which he delivered it, you'll experience some of the "fit" his words were intended to encourage, as the truth of Christ dovetails with some space you create for it in your daily life. (The only exceptions to this sermon arrangement are found in Ordinary Time, which holds a few that were preached elsewhere in the year but fit well in that location because of their theme.) However, these collected sermons were not all preached in the *same* year, nor are they arranged in the order in which they were originally given.

Forty-one sermons are included in this collection. Advent and Christmas have fewer sermons because these seasons are brief. Other seasons, such as Pentecost and Ordinary Time, have more sermons because those seasons are longer. While each sermon has a stand-alone quality, effort was made to establish a semblance of flow within each season—to be, as Eugene would say, "intently haphazard."

Eugene was keenly aware of the difference between the two old Greek words for time. *Chronos* referred to the sort of time that belonged to calendars and sundials, watches and alarm clocks. *Kairos* was the marker of organic time: the time of planting and harvest; of festival and funeral; of birth, love, and death—and of the inner working of God in the human spirit.

In the rhythm of the church year, those two times overlap. The movement of the calendar syncs with the seasonality of our delicate, unpredictable inner lives, and we find, as weeks pass, that every day becomes an invitation.

Our prayer at WaterBrook, in partnership with Eugene's family, is that you take up that invitation in this book, through the company of a past pilgrim and an artist, who painted with words larger than his own on both space and time.

—Paul J. Pastor, editor

ADVENT

It Is Time to Wake Up to Reality

Why all this stress on behaviour? Because, as I think you have realised, the present time is of the highest importance—it is time to wake up to reality. Every day brings God's salvation nearer. The night is nearly over, the day has almost dawned. Let us therefore fling away the things that men do in the dark, let us arm ourselves for the fight of the day! Let us live cleanly, as in the daylight, not in the "delights" of getting drunk or playing with sex, nor yet in quarrelling or jealousies. Let us be Christ's men from head to foot, and give no chances to the flesh to have its fling.

—Romans 13:11–14 (PHILLIPS)

A few years ago at the University of Michigan, a fantastic movement among the students was dominated by the belief that Christ was coming again very soon. On the surface, it was a Christian group, initiated by a professor who had a remarkable influence over the students. The group interpreted current-event reports as fulfilled prophecies of obscure sections of Scripture and put them together in such a way to prove that the end of the world was imminent. The end would be initiated by the Second Coming of Christ, who would remove all his people from the about-to-be-destroyed world. One of the more spectacular things that many of these people did was go to Detroit and buy the most expensive Cadillacs available: Since they were going to be around only a short time, they knew they wouldn't have to make any payments.

The frequency of such incidents is increasing today. There is an enormous amount of interest in the religious future. Books being sold today—purchased mostly by Christians—claim to show how current history is full of "signs of the end." Popular preachers on radio and television are exploiting this interest and using it as material in their preaching. I know you are exposed to this kind of thing and are either attracted or repelled.

Today is the first Sunday in Advent—a Sunday that initiates a time in the church when we talk about what it means for God to come to us. In an age of intense interest in the coming of Christ, I want to spend some time understanding what Scripture says, especially what Paul said in this classic Advent passage in Romans. The coming again of Christ is a very important doctrine. I want you to understand it and believe it.

I will begin with an affirmation in its simplest form: Christ is coming again. He came once in history: in the first century, in the place of Palestine, and in the person of Jesus. He will come again.

The early church was formed and the New Testament was written with that belief. The belief was vivid and intense. Jesus provided mounds of evidence for expecting his return. You can't read a page of the New Testament without sensing that expectation.

Let me quote a few passages to give some substance to this early belief:

Christ, having been offered once to bear the sins of many, will appear a second time, not to deal with sin but to save those who are eagerly waiting for him. (Hebrews 9:28)

Now may our . . . Lord Jesus . . . make you increase and abound in love . . . so that he may establish your hearts unblamable in holiness before our God and Father, at the coming of our Lord Jesus with all his saints. (1 Thessalonians 3:11–13)

Be patient. Establish your hearts, for the coming of the Lord is at hand. (James 5:8)

You must understand this, that scoffers will come in the last days with scoffing, following their own passions and saying, "Where is the promise of his coming? For ever since the fathers fell asleep, all things have continued as they were from the beginning of creation." (2 Peter 3:3–4)

And our text for today: "It is time to wake up to reality. Every day brings God's salvation nearer. The night is nearly over, the day has almost dawned" (Romans 13:11, PHILLIPS).

The early church believed all that. And the Christian church has continued to believe it. Christ is coming again. History is not an endless repetition of the same old thing. Our Lord will finish his work in history, achieving victory in this creation and concluding his work of redemption.

For myself, I share that belief. I hold it in a rather naïve, unsophisticated way and can tell you very little about what accompanies it. My belief is quite simply that it is going to take place. Jesus said he would return—Paul believed it, the early church believed it, and the great majority of Christians ever since have believed it right down to our own day. And I believe it.

Now, having affirmed the doctrine of the Second Coming, let me point out something about its use that those who seem to talk the most about it rarely mention—yet is the most biblical thing about this doctrine.

When writing to the Romans, Paul told them how they ought to live as Christians. Beginning in chapter twelve, he gave them a series of rapid-fire commands. He told them to be hospitable, to serve, to teach, to contribute money, to feed hungry people, and to be lawful. He then brought these commands to a climax by saying, "Owe no one anything, except to love one another. . . . Love does no wrong to a neighbor; therefore love is the fulfilling of the law" (13:8, 10).

You can imagine Paul sitting back and thinking, *How can I get these people to begin to act in this aggressively loving way to their neighbors? They have heard this so many times; they have gotten*

so used to being told this—what can I say that will get them going?
What he did was talk about the Second Coming: "It is time to
wake up to reality. Every day brings God's salvation nearer. The
night is nearly over, the day has almost dawned."

Quit procrastinating. Love now. Don't be forever putting off
the most important act that is commanded. Don't make plans for
the future love you will give your neighbor. Love your neighbor
now.

Paul used the news of the Second Coming as a jab to wake believers up to the world around them where love needed to be acted
out. He used it to bring an awareness of "crisis as a motive to
ethical seriousness."[*]

When Paul finished this paragraph about waking up to the fact
that they wouldn't have forever to obey the commands of God, he
went right back to the ordinary instructions of everyday life: "As
for the man who is weak in faith, welcome him" (Romans 14:1).
Paul was immersed in working out Christian solutions to daily,
real-life problems. He believed that the doctrine of the Second
Coming gave special urgency to the daily.

In his book *Exile's Return*, Malcolm Cowley talked about his
days in France when he and other American expatriates were involved in the revolutionary movements of the Spanish Civil War.
He said, "There were moments in France when the senses were
immeasurably sharpened by the thought of dying next day, or possibly next week."[†] The Second Coming does this to Christians: It
sharpens their moral/ethical senses. They are pulled out of sludgy
lethargy and impelled to feel and act with intensity—because they
know that the Lord may come "next day, or possibly next week."

I think it is important that you be warned about this. For, in
fact, a great deal of the stuff I hear about the Second Coming is

---

[*] C. H. Dodd, *The Epistle of Paul to the Romans* (New York: Harper and Brothers,
1932), 209.
[†] Malcolm Cowley, *Exile's Return: A Literary Odyssey of the 1920s* (New York: Viking,
1951), 42.

wildly separated from the Scriptures. It is full of sensationalist headlines. It is designed to provoke a kind of panicky fright. It makes its case by a perverse reading of obscure passages in Ezekiel, Daniel, and Revelation. And because people are not familiar with these writings, they accept what such glib, smooth persons say without question. All such teaching reveals a vast ignorance about history—and an irresponsible handling of Scripture.

The result of that kind of teaching is to make people irresponsible. Why go through the patient motions of loving a neighbor if it is all going to be over soon? Why get deeply involved in a nation or community to bring about the realities of justice if there will be a cataclysmic war in the next year or two? Living the gospel is reduced to shouting slogans.

Those kinds of false prophets distract us from the daily living out of the gospel that our Lord and St. Paul so persistently affirmed as the context for experiencing God's presence. They take our eyes off the ball. They substitute fantasy, fears, or wishes for the realities of God's love, the needs of our neighbors, and the plain commands of Scripture.

What a person thinks about the future is very important. It influences in a pervasive way what she is in the present. In a day like ours of great uncertainty, many see the question of the future as up for grabs. In a time of historical transition, people are characteristically obsessed with the future, and their obsessions ruin their present lives.

The Christian gospel says something about the Second Coming to provide God's people with a joyful, mature means of dealing with the present—a way that does not narrow life to a few people who share our point of view, plague us with panicky fear about the end of the world, or give us a manic euphoria unrelated to any present reality.

The Second Coming means the overwhelming fact about the future is that God will accomplish his redemptive purposes. He will get done what he told us he wants to do.

Other people are telling us other things about the future. Some describe it in terms of the "end of the world." Others talk of the dissolution and breakdown of society; some give lurid descriptions of ecological disasters and population explosions; novelists tell us what a nuclear holocaust would be like. Doomsday people project all these possibilities on the screen of the future. And other people who specialize in talking about the Second Coming describe it as a kind of supernatural escape operation in which a few Christians are pulled out of the messy problems of society to enjoy an eternal bliss.

With this kind of rhetoric ringing in our ears, we might respond in a couple of different ways. One is to avoid dealing with the future by planning for it. Rationalizing that the future is a long way off, we work out elaborate insurance plans, retirement plans, and educational plans. We schedule the future on the calendar so that there is always a good deal of distance between us and it. We live in a kind of "preparation complex." As a result, we never give our attention to what is in the present. We subordinate present things— like loving our neighbors, for instance—to those far-off goals.

Another way to avoid dealing with the future is to simply deny it and wallow in the present. With this mindset, I just do what feels good at the time for me, reducing the world to my own pleasures and whims. Since the future is so ominous, so unthinkable, I don't think about it. I immerse myself in presentness—a very characteristic response today.

Yet neither one of these responses is much good. The gospel alternative is to affirm the Second Coming. The overwhelming fact of the future is that God comes—the same God we know about in Jesus Christ.

Knowing this, we can go about our work in the present with calmness, peace, joy, and sureness. We know that the future holds not something foreign to the experience we already share in the gospel but the completion of it. Therefore, it makes sense to love my neighbor, help the hungry, and be generous with the church's mission. The future thus brings an intensity of grace into the present moment. Love, trust, hope, and faith make sense.

We return to Paul's words:

Why all this stress on behaviour? Because, as I think you have realised, the present time is of the highest importance—it is time to wake up to reality. Every day brings God's salvation nearer. The night is nearly over, the day has almost dawned. Let us therefore fling away the things that men do in the dark, let us arm ourselves for the fight of the day! Let us live cleanly, as in the daylight, not in the "delights" of getting drunk or playing with sex, nor yet in quarrelling or jealousies. Let us be Christ's men from head to foot, and give no chances to the flesh to have its fling. (Romans 13:11–14, PHILLIPS)

Amen.

Awake!

You are not in darkness, brethren, for that day to surprise you like a thief. For you are all sons of light and sons of the day; we are not of the night or of darkness. So then let us not sleep, as others do, but let us keep awake and be sober.

—1 Thessalonians 5:4–6

God comes. He is not an object at the center of the universe; he is not a fixed point on an astronomer's map of heaven. He is active and moving. And this movement has direction. He comes *to us*. He does not wander around, window-shopping from galaxy to galaxy, juggling the moons of Jupiter and casually admiring the rings of Saturn. We are his destination.

He didn't simply come once and then return to spend the rest of eternity like an old tourist, telling stories of his trip and boring the angels with slides of his visit. He came. He comes. He will come again. And we know what to expect when he comes and comes again because we know exactly what happened when he came.

God came to us in Jesus. And at his ascension, Jesus promised that he would come again. The Christian life is lived between those two comings: He came, and he will come. To believe and serve a God who comes, to live a life in a world to which God comes—what does that mean? That is the Advent task: to clarify and celebrate this, to live heartily and hopefully in response to the God who comes to us.

Will you live slovenly, with unbuttoned mind and disheveled spirit, thoughtlessly supposing that the same things are monotonously repeated in creation and in history? Or will you live alertly and ardently, convinced that God continues to come to us and will come to us again in Jesus? And will you believe that in receiving his coming and being hospitable to his arrival, we will get the most out of life?

A passage in Paul's first letter to the Thessalonians has been important to Christians for two thousand years now by showing us how to live wholeheartedly between the great fact of God's coming and the sure expectation of his coming again. The word *awake* sums up Paul's counsel.

We Stay Awake (1 Thessalonians 5:1–4)

One unforgettable thing we learned when God came in Jesus is that God comes into the everyday. He is God not merely of the big issues but also of the daily routine: bedding down in village stables, touching run-of-the-mill lepers, lunching with tax collectors, fishing with old friends, and so forth. Therefore, we stay awake lest we miss something significant.

When traveling with my children, it is disconcerting to have them go to sleep and say, "Wake me when we get there." Don't they know that the journey is part of the reality? And they miss so much: antelope, hawks, sunsets . . .

We Are Assertive (1 Thessalonians 5:5–8)

The coming of God in Jesus also convinced us of the reality that God is on the offensive: making persons whole and at peace, healed, and blessed. Living by faith is not escapist; God does not show us a place to hide in a world that is too much for us. Rather, living by faith is a strategy for doing something complete, great, final, and victorious.

We are given armor to live in the rough and tumble of life. We are not defenseless flowers in danger of being crushed by trampling feet. We are protected, and we can take the initiative.

We Are Expectant (1 Thessalonians 5:9–11)

God's coming to us in Jesus demonstrated and convinced us that God's coming is good for everyone: Salvation is his purpose. Therefore we are full of hope, taut with anticipation. The person who is afraid, who feels "destined for wrath," hasn't listened very closely to what God is saying or hasn't observed Christ's coming very accurately. If we are mired in despair, we are missing the great reality of life: God has salvation plans for us.

> Expectation has never ceased to guide the progress of our faith like a torch. The Israelites were constantly expectant, and the first Christians too. Christmas, which might have been thought to turn our gaze towards the past, has only fixed it further in the future. The Messiah who appeared for a moment in our midst only allowed Himself to be seen and touched for a moment before vanishing again, more luminous and ineffable than ever, into the depths of the future. He came. Yet now we must expect Him—no longer a small chosen group among us, but all men—once again and more than ever.*

The Advent candles symbolize the accumulation of light in our darkness. Week by week, the light increases until on Christmas Eve this sanctuary will be ablaze with the lights we hold in an act of praise. There is nothing complicated about living in Advent. It is as simple as waking up. What good is the light to you if you are asleep? Awake to God!

Amen.

---

* Pierre Teilhard de Chardin, *The Divine Milieu: An Essay on the Interior Life* (New York: Harper and Brothers, 1960), 134–35.

Christ in Creation

> He is the image of the invisible God; his is the primacy over all
> created things. In him everything in heaven and on earth was
> created, not only things visible but also the invisible orders of
> thrones, sovereignties, authorities, and powers: the whole uni-
> verse has been created through him and for him.
>
> —Colossians 1:15–16, NEB

Paul is easily the most influential letter writer who ever lived. His letters have been read by more people than any other ever written—and have spoken personally and powerfully to many of these people. With that kind of success, we might suppose that he was some sort of literary genius, giving himself to a life of correspondence and doing it well.

But he didn't write very many letters. He wrote them only when he had to. And even then, they showed marks of haste, marred by a bluntness of style and a complete disregard for literary polish and form.

The circumstance of imprisonment forced him to write letters. Paul had a vital interest in supervising and training congregations of Christians in several cities in the ancient world. His usual practice was to travel between them, spending a few months in each. Then right in the prime of his life, in the full strength of his leadership, he was thrown into prison. So, he did the only thing left to do if he wanted to maintain contact with his churches: He wrote letters. Thirteen letters in our New Testament are attributed to him.

As letters go, they aren't particularly good. The English composition textbooks that include a section on letter writing wouldn't use any of Paul's as examples. A teacher would not want a student to imitate much of them in either form or style. But these letters, written by a man who had no literary pretensions or aspirations, are still the most influential ever written. Clearly, Paul stirred an extra ingredient into them besides vocabulary, grammar, syntax, and style. Something else must account for their power and influence. As mere literature, they are ordinary and even unimportant. As an influence on the minds of men and women, they are without peer.

J. B. Phillips, who translated these letters into modern English under the title *Letters to Young Churches,* says this about them:

> The present translator who has closely studied these letters for several years is . . . continually struck by the living quality of the material on which he is working. Some will, no doubt, consider it merely superstitious reverence for "Holy Writ," yet again and again the writer felt rather like an electrician rewiring an ancient house without being able to "turn the mains off." He feels that this fact is worth recording.*

In light of this kind of testimony and these letters' tremendous influence throughout history, I would like you to join me in reading, listening to, thinking about, and talking about one of them—in other words, trying to let it influence us as it has so many other people. We will take the brief letter Paul wrote to the little congregation in Colossae, a provincial, inland town in Asia Minor.

The letter is dominated by two words: a noun and a preposition. The noun is a most impressive proper title: Christ. To Paul this name consummated two thousand years of history, fulfilled centuries of longing, and brought a completeness to humankind's

---

* J. B. Phillips, *Letters to Young Churches: A Translation of the New Testament Epistles* (London: Geoffrey Bles, 1947), xii.

fragmented life. The preposition, *in,* is a small word in both Greek and English, but it is not insignificant. And in this letter it regularly occurs with the aforementioned proper noun, sometimes before and sometimes after.

The subject of the letter is Christ—not as an abstract study but in relationship: Christ *in,* or *in* Christ. A preposition generally functions by showing the relationship between a noun and another word, and none does it quite so intimately or thoroughly as *in.* *On, around,* and *beside* are prepositions of the same type (locatives), but notice the difference. They all leave their nouns in proximity to each other: The book is on the table; the flowers are around the tree; the car is beside the curb. Yet *in* brings the two words into union: The nail is in the board; the heart is in the body; the seed is in the ground. *In* is a preposition of intimacy, immersion, and penetration.

What we can expect in this letter, then, is an incomparable proper noun (Christ) put into the most penetrating relationships (in) with several other nouns: creation, the Christian, the church, and our conduct, to name a few. Examining these relationships will give us an opening into Paul's preaching, a kind of foot in the door to the mind of this apostle who has helped shape the course of Christian thinking. But focusing on one relationship at a time is enough, and first of all is Christ in creation.

After the greetings and prayer (characteristic beginnings to Paul's letters), we read perhaps the most remarkable passage in the whole letter. One scholar thinks this may be "the most striking of all the Pauline expressions of conviction as to the status of Christ."[*] Here is the passage:

> He is the image of the invisible God; his is the primacy over
> all created things. In him everything in heaven and on earth
> was created, not only things visible but also the invisible
> orders of thrones, sovereignties, authorities, and powers: the

[*] C. F. D. Moule, *The Epistles of Paul the Apostle to the Colossians and to Philemon* (London: Cambridge University Press, 1957), 58.

whole universe has been created through him and for him. (Colossians 1:15–16, NEB)

This description, of course, refers to Christ. Now, the term *Christ* is not really the name of a person but a title. And we must remember that for a long time this title was unattached, floating around loose, waiting to be pinned on some person. For hundreds of years people speculated about who the Christ might be and built a great deal of anticipation and hopeful expectation concerning the time this individual would come. The New Testament Gospels narrate how that title was finally fixed on the man Jesus, who came from the little village of Nazareth in upper Palestine.

People attached the title to Jesus because they became convinced by listening to his words and observing his acts that this was, in fact, God speaking personally to them. God had taken human form and was living a life like theirs. And as he did this, they heard him speaking the eternal words of love and grace. God was there, establishing communion and fellowship with them. The God who had made the universe was now standing among them and making them whole. As they realized all this, they called Jesus "the Christ."

And only some thirty years after Jesus's time, Paul could say this about him: "The whole universe has been created through him and for him." In other words, Paul was not content to see in Jesus of Nazareth simply the culminating expression of God's love compressed into a thirty-three-year life span. He saw the eternal expression of God's grace that, far from being confined to those middle years of the Roman Empire, was determinative in the original work of creation.

I just said that the title of Christ had floated around unattached for several centuries before it was fixed on Jesus. It certainly looks like that historically. But no, Paul said this one called Christ was active from the beginning. This was no late development, no modern solution. Christ is and has been at the center of everything ever created.

Another New Testament writer independently testified to the same thing: "In these last days he has spoken to us by a Son [that is, in the years of Jesus's life], whom he appointed the heir of all things [placing him in the culmination of time and history], through whom also he created the world [confirming Paul's point that Christ was active from the very first]" (Hebrews 1:2).

There is a message in all this that must be spoken personally to us, that struggles out of the past to find practical expression in our lives. There is a word here that can reorient our lives and pour meaning into some of the empty places in our living.

Listen to Paul's words again: "In him everything in heaven and on earth was created. . . . The whole universe has been created through him and for him." What does this mean for us?

Well, it means that God's plan that we should share in his love is built into the very stuff of creation and is demonstrated in Christ Jesus. Christ is the image of God, showing us that God is love and that he is actively engaged in making it possible for us to live in and enjoy that fellowship. And this Christ, the one who shows us these things, is at the very center, at the very beginning of creation. Christ—that is, God acting to win us in love, drawing us to himself, healing us, and forgiving us—is the "primacy over all created things." This is why everything visible and invisible was created: so that we might share in his love and know his grace.

The great thing for Paul about creation was not any theory of how it happened—whether our universe spun out from some other galaxy several billion light-years ago as a set of suns congealed and separated or some other equally plausible theory (and several were current in Paul's day). It was the discovery, the revelation, that at the very center of creation was a good meaning, good news: Christ himself.

The fact that the universe was created through and for Christ means the only reason God created was so that he could love. Creation is a stage on which God engages in loving relationship with his creatures. Creation is the external scaffolding for the internal movements of love and grace. Creation is to Christ what a pail is to water: There was water before there were ever pails to carry it. Pails were devices by which water could be directed, conveyed, and shared. And there was Christ before there was ever a creation. Creation was a device by which Christ (God's seeking love) could be directed, conveyed, and shared.

It follows, then, that Christ is no afterthought. He is not a kind of emergency measure designed to fix things up after the original plan goes wrong. He is not a kind of cosmic fireman called in a panic to try to keep the house (the world) from burning up. He is there from the beginning. The Christian gospel is an original plan, not an emergency provision.

And that means, you see, that we need Christ simply because we are creatures, not because we are sinners. We are sinners, so we need him all the more. But before we were sinners, Christ was there, the "image of the invisible God," the evidence that God's first word was a word of love and grace bringing all creation into fellowship. We are more likely to think of Christ when we are in trouble than when we are at ease. We are more likely to pray when we are sick than when we are healthy. And we are more likely to think of the church when we are confused than when we have things tidily figured out. But in doing so, we miss at least half— and maybe the better half at that—of Christ.

Christ was not intended to be a tool to use when everything else quits working, a kind of last resort. Christ will help us when everything else goes wrong; he is a last resort. But it certainly cheapens his work and minimizes his power to think of him only as that.

Infant baptism symbolizes this truth. Before a child thinks his own thoughts, takes his own steps, or does anything on his own, at the baptismal font we witness that God's grace is on him. We witness that he was created in and through and for Christ, that God's love and grace are the original and primary factors in his life, and that the meaning of his life must be understood from then on in terms of grace—that is, in terms of Christ.

Paul's word here is simply an extension of that symbolism to the whole creation. Everything that exists must be construed and understood in terms of God's love and grace. The meaning of our lives on any plane, of the circumstances we encounter at any level, and of our participation in the events of business, society, and recreation—all these exist through and for the sake of Christ. Therefore, if we are to know meaning at any of these levels, if we are to know love and grace here, we must know Christ.

The little congregation of Colossians to whom Paul wrote was not very different from many congregations in America. Back then, Paul was so insistent on putting Christ in creation, at the beginning, preeminent and sovereign, because some religious teachers were demoting Jesus to a kind of medicinal role. They didn't deny Christ or anything like that. They wanted only to put him in his place. If you had committed a sin and needed forgiveness, it was all right to call on Christ then. If you felt guilty about something you said or had an uncomfortable blotch on your conscience, Christ was very useful in setting you right and cleaning you up. But for the regular business of living, the important ways of thinking, or the rough and tumble business of human relations and commerce, he was out of his depth; they had other gods to take care of such concerns.

After two thousand years, we need to hear Paul's insistent words again because we very easily become involved in a similar attitude toward Christ. What was explicitly taught in Colossae is implicitly communicated today. We readily call on Christ for help in private crises, but when the crises pass, so does our reliance on Christ. We call for aid in personal disappointments, but when time begins to take the edges off our unhappiness, the name of Christ also becomes a dim memory. We acknowledge our devotion to him in worship on Sunday mornings, but in the six days following, he is often conspicuously absent. As a result, much of what we call our lives—maybe the major part of our existence—has no meaning, no love, and no grace in it.

Paul's word—and this has become the word of God for us—is to look around at creation, at all things visible and invisible: our lives and the lives around us; the visible world of people, animals, houses, and food; and the invisible world of thoughts and emotions, ideas and feelings. We must look at all this created world, visible and invisible, and realize that Christ is *in* it. It was all created in and through and for him. If we don't see him at the center, we see it hollow and empty and meaningless.

But having seen Christ there in creation—that is, in everything—we must seek to know him. And as we do, we will participate in the joyful meaning of creation, for he moves in it all as its internal word of love and grace.

Amen.

CHRISTMAS

God's Last Word Is Jesus

In many and various ways God spoke of old to our fathers by the prophets; but in these last days he has spoken to us by a Son, whom he appointed the heir of all things, through whom also he created the world.

—Hebrews 1:1–2

Christmas is the celebration of a conclusion. A baby who cannot yet talk is the divine Word of God spoken to humankind. A child lying in a manger on a dark night in a poor town completes thousands of years of sacred history. Mary's firstborn is God's last word. "In many and various ways God spoke of old to our fathers by the prophets; but in these last days he has spoken to us by a Son" (Hebrews 1:1–2).

God's first recorded speech in Scripture consisted of words of one syllable: "Let there be light" (Genesis 1:3). The first thing we are told about God is that in creating a place for humanity, he provided visibility. He did not leave us to grope in darkness. God let humankind see where they were going. The simplest and most elementary condition of human existence is the subject matter for God's first word. Beyond the satisfaction of her needs, light is the first reality a baby shows awareness of. Before she can see a face or distinguish a father from a mother, she sees and can respond to light. Just so basic is the content of God's first word in creation. He offered no complicated notions on predestination, reconciliation, or sanctification—only the one-syllable words "Let there be light."

The early chapters of Genesis are a primer on God. God spoke using words that everyone could grasp: *day, night, earth, trees, waters, stars, birds, fish, beasts, man.* Before we have read past the first chapter, we have heard God speak a basic and decisive word to us in terms that a child can understand. We turn the pages and hear of sin and murder, war and judgment, music and crafts, building and history. We hear the profound words of God speaking to us of his will and his ways.

We come to the great names of Abraham, Isaac, Jacob, and Joseph. God was still speaking, and his word was expanding. The history and lives of these people became the vocabulary of God's message. There was still no mistaking it for anything other than the word of God, but he filled out the narrative and filled in the details of each life situation. God called Abraham, accompanied Isaac, changed Jacob, and saved Joseph. The message still carried a majestic simplicity, but the context grew more intricate and complex to match the intricacy and complexity of our lives.

The words multiplied in Moses's story. Thousands of people were forged into a new nation. Their lives were placed in relationship and formed countless possibilities for sin, faith, rejection, rebellion, worship, and love. And with each new event came a new word. Moses transmitted the word of God in commandment, regulation, and exhortation to the people of God (Israel). Because many people were living in close proximity, Moses had to render fine judicial decisions. Because long stretches of time separated promise from fulfillment, he had to preach convincing sermons. The word of God found new applications and fresh situations. The primer of Genesis chapter one gave way to an advanced-level textbook.

The centuries passed, and in imitation of Moses, many tried their hands at speaking the word of God. They shouted advice, counsel, rebuke, and guidance to the people. Some of the speaking bore authenticity; some of it was patently spurious. But the net effect was confusion. With so many "words" of God being spoken, who could hear *the* word of God? God restored authority and legitimacy to his word by inaugurating a kingship in Israel: Saul, David, and then Solomon. No longer could people set themselves up to speak to the nation. God had his anointed through whom he ruled and spoke. Credentials accompanied the spokesperson for God. Organization and coherence again encompassed the word of God.

But then, as so often happens, the organization became professionalized. The word of God turned into a formal edict. The institution became dead to its Lord. The kings grew more interested in politics than in prayer, more engrossed in government than in God. And this created a new way of speaking the word of God: through the prophets. Isaiah thundered, Jeremiah wept, Amos denounced, and Hosea pled. Indifference gave way to sensitive response. Deaf ears were traded for alert minds. The prophets were gifted with eloquence and insight. They spoke the word of God with power and clarity. It was an exciting word, a glad word. No human word could stand in comparison to it.

This passage from Isaiah reverberates down to our times:

> How beautiful upon the mountains
> > are the feet of him who brings good tidings,
> who publishes peace, who brings good tidings of good,
> > who publishes salvation,
> > who says to Zion, "Your God reigns."
> Hark, your watchmen lift up their voice,
> > together they sing for joy;
> for eye to eye they see
> > the return of the LORD to Zion.
> Break forth together into singing,
> > you waste places of Jerusalem;
> for the LORD has comforted his people,
> > he has redeemed Jerusalem.

The LORD has bared his holy arm
  before the eyes of all the nations;
and all the ends of the earth shall see
  the salvation of our God. (Isaiah 52:7–10)

As all this was written down and pondered by succeeding generations, it brought bewilderment and confusion. It needed interpretation. A new profession came into being to guide the people through the forest of words. Scribes and rabbis became the people's allies in hearing the word of God. They in turn wrote commentaries and interpretations of what had been written, and their words soon engulfed the word of God in an ocean of comment.

Yet what the people needed was not another commentary but a conclusion—not another book but a last chapter to the book they already had. The process could become interminable, so there had to be a stopping place. The logical search for complete truth would never end. The people needed a revelation.

So, God spoke a last word: *Jesus.* But there is a surprising difference in this word. Jesus is not just a speechmaker for God; he is God. His whole being is a word of God—his presence, his action, and his talk. We complain that the deeds of some people speak so loudly that we cannot hear what they say. Yet we cannot make that complaint of Jesus, for his deeds and words are identical. Jesus became an event. He was a stopping place for sacred history. The birth of Jesus was like arriving at the top of a mountain peak after a long, difficult climb: You can look back and see the whole trip in perspective, see everything in true relationship. And you don't have to climb anymore.

But I have been talking as if everyone has spent years struggling with the meaning and conclusions of the Old Testament. More likely, you have not read it through for years, or maybe you have never read it at all. What does this text say to you who have not pondered the first words, who have not been bothered by the fragmentariness of Scripture? Will the last word have any meaning if you have not read the first word? Will the answer make any sense if you have never asked the question?

A great many Old Testament prophecies had been left unfulfilled. Many things were said of the future that never came to pass. Many hopes were articulated that no reality ever confirmed. And then Jesus was born in Bethlehem. One of the great thrills of the early church was seeing this great mass of unfulfilled detail suddenly come together in fulfillment in Jesus Christ. The Old Testament suddenly had a point to it—and the point was Jesus.

We can see the operations of their excited minds in all the New Testament letters: "This was done in fulfillment of Isaiah . . . of Moses . . . of Jeremiah . . ." (see Matthew 2:17; 4:14; Luke 24:44). All the loose ends were tied together. All the strained interpretations they had been forced to manufacture to hold things together could now be thrown out because Christ held things together in a conclusion. All their labored attempts to explain away inconsistencies and gaps now were done away with because Jesus gave all the words wholeness and integrity.

This is why the church has consistently insisted on the necessity of keeping and reading the Old Testament. There was a strong movement in the first centuries of the church to abolish the Old Testament. Those believers reasoned that since we have everything in Christ, why bother with all the incompleteness and fragmentariness of Israel? Why plow through all those genealogies (such as 1 Chronicles 3:10, which says, "The descendants of Solomon: Rehobo'am, Abi'jah his son, Asa his son, Jehosh'aphat his son.") when one really needed to know only the name above every name—Jesus? But the church didn't accept this reasoning. All of that really is the word of God spoken to humankind in various conditions and times: The word is as true as ever. Although it is old, it is not obsolete. Although it is ancient, it is not antiquated. And if it is not read, the foundation of Jesus is never understood. To skip reading the Old Testament would be to skip the first thirty-nine chapters of a forty-chapter book. *The Confession of 1967*

summarizes the church's stance: "The Old Testament is indispens-
able to understanding the New, and is not itself fully understood
without the New."* This is why it is the usual practice to give an
exposition of the Old Testament during Advent, so that the gospel
of Christmas is seen in its true setting.

But while the importance of reading the Old Testament cannot
be too strongly emphasized, I cannot say that everything depends
on it. If you are one of the many who do not read it or have not
read it enough, you will still find a meaning in the text. The reason
is that God has not confined his speaking to what is recorded in
Scripture. That is where his authoritative word is written, but he
has spoken many other times and in many other places—in places
where we have been and at times when we have heard him.

If each of us were to write a completely honest and thorough
history of our personal life up to the present, that would in many
ways parallel the writing we call the Old Testament. That autobiography would begin with the simplest facts: birth, life, light, food,
parents, disobedience, and rebellion. And as the years increased,
the words would become more difficult and the arrangement more
complex. From the simple elemental realities of infancy would
come the intricate emotional, physical, and mental realities of adolescence and adulthood. Nothing that we would thus record would
be untrue, but we would have to confess that much of it did not
make sense. Many thoughts, events, feelings, and experiences
would appear to be in contradiction and at cross-purposes. The
body makes promises for which there is no fulfillment. The emotions cry out for satisfaction that is never given. The mind asks
questions for which no answers are found. As we look back on
them, our lives quite undeniably happened, but do they go any-
where? Is there any central meaning or any conclusion?

Our private doubts, disappointments, frustrations, and
strangely incomplete joys can fill in the details of such a story.

* The Confession of 1967: Inclusive Language Version (Louisville, Ky.: Presbyterian
Church (U.S.A.), 2002), 9.28, www.pcusa.org/site_media/media/uploads/theologyand-
worship/pdfs/confess67.pdf.

Whatever its specifics, it will echo in a remarkable way the experience of the men to whom God spoke in "many and various ways . . . by the prophets." This experience is the context for the last word of God in Jesus. The word of God conclusive in Jesus gives sense and meaning to every person's life. This gospel is the affirmation to what in W. B. Yeats was only surmise:

What the world's million lips are thirsting for,
Must be substantial somewhere.[*]

For many people, Christmas is a dreary time. Maybe it is that way for more people than we think. The labored and frantic efforts to bring merriment into the holiday lead us to suspect that the good cheer is not rooted in "substantial" joy. The demand for happiness and well-wishing that society and friends impose on one and all pushes some who have hearts full of despair and unhappiness only further into gloom. And all of us—even the relatively happy and optimistic—when we look into our own souls discover great areas of emptiness. We live on the surface; frivolity is characteristic of us. Can joy spring from such a well? Can merriment be structured on such a foundation?

It can, if we have another word to listen to besides the words from our own inadequate, fragmentary pasts.

When the stories about Jesus' birth took form in the early church they emphasized the fact that it was night when he was born. The shepherds were keeping watch over their flocks by night; the wise men were following the star through the night; in Herod's gloomy midnight councils all the little children of Bethlehem were to be slain, and every way it was against encompassing darkness that Christ's coming shone out.

When people now say that these are dour times in which

* W. B. Yeats, *The Shadowy Waters,* acting ed. (London: A. H. Bullen, 1907), 8.

to keep Christmas [the time of the Vietnam War, of world poverty, of secularism, of commercialism, of nuclear terror], they forget this basic fact about the Christmas stories. This is indeed a dark time. . . . In easier times we left the night out of the picture and made of the Christmas season a light-hearted holiday of festival and merriment, but now we are back where Christmas started—with its deep black background behind the Savior's coming, like midnight behind the star.[*]

In many and various ways God spoke of old to our fathers by the prophets; but in these last days he has spoken to us by a Son, whom he appointed the heir of all things, through whom also he created the world. He reflects the glory of God and bears the very stamp of his nature, upholding the universe by his word of power. When he had made purification for sins, he sat down at the right hand of the Majesty on high, having become as much superior to angels as the name he has obtained is more excellent than theirs. (Hebrews 1:1–4)

To us a child is born, to us a son is given. (Isaiah 9:6)

Amen.

---

[*] Harry Emerson Fosdick, *A Great Time to Be Alive: Sermons on Christianity in Wartime* (New York: Harper and Brothers, 1944), 209.

EPIPHANY

Being Changed into His Likeness

We all, with unveiled face, beholding the glory of the Lord, are being changed into his likeness from one degree of glory to another.

—2 Corinthians 3:18

D o you have people in your life who, when they meet you, say, "My, how you've changed. Why, I can remember when you were just a little baby throwing food on the kitchen floor and tantrums in the supermarket"? They usually have a couple of stories they insist on telling. Everyone is greatly amused—except you, to whom it is a great embarrassment to be linked to that messy, dirty creature of thirty or forty years ago.

Embarrassing as it is, though, it is better than its opposite. Suppose you are sitting at dinner with one of these old friends and accidently knock over the water glass, sending a torrent across the table and making a pool in your hostess's lap. And he says, "Why, you haven't changed a bit. Remember that time we were at dinner at the Odegaards' when you were six years old and you spilled the chocolate milk over her best linen and spoiled her best dress? Same old fumbling butterfingers. Ha ha!"

St. Paul had some interesting things to say about change. I don't think you will find what he has to say embarrassing—quite the opposite. His style was not to drag out some old story to humiliate us; rather, he had some insights to give us hope. You will be especially interested in his remarks if, at this point in your life, you are quite sure that nothing can change or that if change does occur, it will certainly be for the worse.

Here is Paul's sentence, taken from a long letter of counsel he wrote to the Christians in the Greek city of Corinth: "We all, with unveiled face, beholding the glory of the Lord, are being changed into his likeness from one degree of glory to another; for this comes from the Lord who is the Spirit" (2 Corinthians 3:18).

The first thing that strikes me about this text is the confident air of freedom—change is possible. Nobody must remain as she is. Yet many of us feel like we are stuck, as though no growth or change is possible. This feeling of stuckness, enslavement, or imprisonment takes many different forms, but it has a remarkable continuity.

A friend recently went to the Baltimore city jail and was taken into a visiting room to see a prisoner. As the warden left the room, he locked the door. After an hour, my friend was ready to leave, but the warden didn't return. The warden was visible through a glass barrier, so my friend motioned to him, waved his hand, and gestured that he wanted out. But the warden was preoccupied, talking with someone, and didn't notice him. My friend simply couldn't get his attention. When this had gone on for some time, the prisoner remarked, "It feels different when you can't get out, doesn't it?"

I don't know in what forms you experience your imprisonment. Perhaps it is a job you can't get out of, a family that you feel has you locked in, emotions and moods that dictate their will to you, or a body that traps you in weakness and pain. You feel lifeless. Existence is stagnant. You are dead inside, and nothing is moving. Or you feel that you are up against a stone wall—progress is blocked, and there is nowhere to advance.

Paul wrote to such persons, saying, "You don't have to be stuck with what you are; you can change." If you don't like what you are today, that is a cause for hope, not for discouragement. If you do not love as you would like to love, that is evidence not of failure but of immaturity, and growth is possible. If you do not hope consistently and faithfully, that is not evidence of fickleness but of incompleteness, and completion is possible. If you do not believe unwaveringly and boldly in the face of every contradiction, that is not evidence that you are unworthy disciples but simply a signpost to eventual maturity, and Christ will be your companion as you make the journey.

Change is part of the gospel. The Christian life is not something we are handed already complete. It begins as a seed, and the seed is the word. The seed grows as Jesus described it in the parable—"first the blade, then the ear, then the full grain in the ear" (Mark 4:28). Or the gospel is inserted into our lives like leaven in a loaf of bread dough and initiates a slow but inevitable process of expansion and rising.

Those who believe in Christ, who have accepted his salvation and lordship, already have the power of change working within them. No matter what you feel, no matter how you assess your condition, no matter how stuck you feel—the feelings are wrong, the assessment is wrong, and God's word is right. For, as St. Paul said, "The Lord is the Spirit, and where the Spirit of the Lord is, there is freedom" (2 Corinthians 3:17). This means that we are free to become what he wills us to be: changed "into his likeness."

None of us is yet whole in Christ. All of us are in the process of becoming. We are not finished products. He has pruning and shaping to do in us. And he has promised that he will continue what he has begun.

The second thing I notice in this text is that the Spirit of Christ brings to us the change of growth, not the change of magic. We are "being changed into his likeness from one degree of glory to another." This is not the kind of quick change that takes place in the telephone booth as Clark Kent morphs into Superman. It is the slow, gradual change of the infant into the adult. For this kind of change, you can' t be in a hurry. We are involved in something that stretches into eternity. You can't see it happen; you can see only that it does happen—just as you can't see children grow but only that they do grow.

Many people quit the Christian church because they are impatient. They quit worshipping, the Christian fellowship, and discipleship. They came to church because they wanted something different and thought they would give God a try. They had tried everything else, so why not religion? They joined the church and enthusiastically entered the life of the congregation. But after six months they couldn't see that anything had changed. They still woke up depressed on Monday. They still had spats with their spouses. Their kids had been in Sunday school every week but still weren't behaving as they were told. These folks had been as good as they could be, and God still hadn't answered their prayers for job promotions. So, they quit the church. They had supposed that the new life would come quickly, suddenly, like a rabbit appearing miraculously out of a magician's hat. But rarely in Scripture do we find illustrations of magical change. The biblical models are mostly analogical to the growth of plants and people: slow, intricate, complex, and sure.

If you are in a hurry, unwilling to immerse yourself in the process of what God is doing—letting grace develop from the inside, letting your spirit age in the Spirit of Christ—you will, I'm afraid, never find out what it means to go from one degree of glory to another.

The third important thing in the text is that this change results from a relationship with Jesus Christ: "We all, with unveiled face, beholding the glory of the Lord, are being changed into his likeness from one degree of glory to another."

Change into the likeness of our Lord is not automatic. It is not something inherent in us. It has a cause: beholding the glory of the Lord.

Change is rooted in a relationship with Jesus Christ. God becomes open, personal, and accessible to us in Jesus. For centuries people had to guess about and grope after God, but they need do so no longer. St. John wrote that "the Word became flesh and dwelt among us, full of grace and truth; we have beheld his glory" (John 1:14). Glory is what you can see of God in Christ: It is that which is visible, tangible. We have, in Jesus, evidence that can be examined in history by our senses.

Now, the word "beholding" that Paul used is based on the word for "mirror."* The person of Jesus is a mirror in which we see God. When we are with Christ, we are in touch with all that we can apprehend of God. In that environment, we are changed by what we see, transforming into his likeness. If we are in an exposed relationship with the sun, our skin changes to a darker hue. If we are in an exposed relationship with Christ, our lives change. The transformation results from our relationship with Jesus Christ. By opening ourselves to him, we come under his influence and are shaped into maturity—changed into his likeness from one degree of glory to another or from one level of maturity or stage of development to another.

In that relationship, our present condition is never an occasion for blame or condemnation. The phrase is not "from a degree of infamy to a degree of glory"; it is "from glory to glory." The bottom step in a staircase is neither better nor worse than the top step: It is good in its own right and a way of getting upstairs. What you are this morning is no occasion for despair, no basis for discouragement. It is the very place God will begin to change you to his likeness, step by step, degree by degree. Or, as Paul said in another place, "There is therefore now no condemnation for those who are in Christ Jesus. For the law of the Spirit of life has set me free from the law of sin and death" (Romans 8:1–2).

Some, I fear, avoid Christ because they feel they have lived sinfully and are afraid of rejection. Others, I fear, avoid Christ because they feel they have lived selfishly and are afraid he will take away what is dear to them, impoverishing them. Both fears are groundless: Our sin and our selfishness are our prisons, and as

* *Blue Letter Bible*, s.v. "*katoptrizō*," www.blueletterbible.org/lexicon/g2734/esv/mgnt/0-1/.

long as we cling to them, we will be stuck. But association with Christ will initiate a process of growth that will accept us where we are, define that starting point as the first degree of glory, and then develop largeness, stature, wholeness, and maturity in us: "We all . . . beholding the glory of the Lord, are being changed into his likeness from one degree of glory into another."

A friend who is about fifty-five years old went to his physician the other day for an annual checkup. Among other things, he was weighed and measured. When he noticed the doctor writing his height down as five feet, ten inches, he said, "I think you have my height wrong. I'm six feet tall." The doctor smiled and said, "Stand up here again." The standard indicated five feet, ten inches. My friend was faced with the undeniable evidence that he had shrunk two inches.

All of us are either on the way up or on the way down. We are growing up into Christ, or we are diminishing toward death. Our bodies are subject to certain laws of growth and decay. Being with Christ will not keep us from shrinking as we age, but it will set us on a growth road that stretches into eternity.

One goal of the Christian life is to remove the distractions and barriers that keep you from looking directly at Jesus Christ in faith, to convince you that you no longer have to be stuck in a life that is inadequate, and to persuade you to permanently associate yourself with our Lord, entering a growth process that will, in the end, bring to maturity the likeness for which you were originally created (Genesis 1:28).

Charles Wesley wrote a hymn that shares Paul's theme in 2 Corinthians 3:18. I don't know of a better prayer than the final stanza:

Finish, then, Thy new creation;
   Pure and spotless let us be:
Let us see Thy great salvation
   Perfectly restored in Thee;

Changed from glory into glory,
    Till in heaven we take our place,
Till we cast our crowns before Thee,
    Lost in wonder, love, and praise.*

Amen.

* Charles Wesley, "Love Divine, All Loves Excelling," hymn 560 in *The Hymnal* (Philadelphia: Presbyterian Board of Publication and Sabbath-School Work, 1912), 414.

How Worship Shapes Life

Present your bodies as a living sacrifice, holy and acceptable to
God, which is your spiritual worship. Do not be conformed to
this world but be transformed by the renewal of your mind.

—Romans 12:1–2

Worship is not a religious performance we sit back and enjoy
but an act in which we participate. As we participate, we
are changed. Because our lethargy constantly threatens to turn us
into mere spectators, it is necessary to emphasize the active part
we play in worship: singing hymns with interest and enthusiasm,
praying silently as the leader of worship prays and responding au-
dibly with an affirmative "Amen," bringing our offerings as an act
of sacrifice and dedication, listening to scripture and sermon to
hear God's Word spoken to our condition ("to listen in order to
act," as Kierkegaard put it*). There must be a personal commitment to the act of worship for it to be alive. "We can never understand it without taking part in it; moving with its movement, and
yielding to its suggestions."†

But however many times we say this and however many re-
minders we need of it to save us from our sloth, we must never
forget that God is more active in worship than we could ever be.
And in contrast to ours, which is all response, his action is creative

---

* Søren Kierkegaard, *Purity of Heart Is to Will One Thing*, Harper Torchbooks ed.,
trans. Douglas V. Steere (New York: Harper Torchbooks, 1956), 179.
† Evelyn Underhill, *Worship* (New York: Harper and Brothers, 1937), 33.

and formative. "In worship the initiative lies with God."* "Christianity recognizes that man needs something done to him which only the action of God can do, if he is ever to be capable of Eternal Life."[†] As we worship, God acts among us and shapes our lives.

St. Paul wrote these words to the church at Rome: "Present your bodies as a living sacrifice, holy and acceptable to God, which is your spiritual worship. Do not be conformed to this world but be transformed by the renewal of your mind" (12:1–2). What Paul was asking for is focused in our common worship. Worship is the presentation of our bodies—our "concrete, observable, historical existence"[‡] —as a sacrifice to God so that he can act upon us. Either the world shapes us or God shapes us. We are either conformed to the world or transformed by God. Conforming to the ways of this world, which is corrupted by sin, is an endless tyranny. God is our maker and preserver; transformation by him is liberty and joy: "This is one way in which the liberty of the Christian man is realized. He is not the slave of the conventional judgments of society."[§] Worship shapes life in God's pattern. It releases in us the creative love of God and the sanctifying spirit of his grace. This love and holiness effect a transformation that every person desires in his deepest soul. "To worship well is to live well."[¶]

Worship follows "the rhythm of human existence from its beginning to its apparent end and beyond."[**] Our regular worship provides a constant leavening, transforming influence on our lives, shaping us to God's will in a multitude of small and daily ways. But we see the divine transformation with particular clarity on four special occasions in each person's life: birth, marriage, sickness, and death. In these times, worshipping Christians see some-

---

* "The Directory for the Worship of God," in *The Book of Order* (New York: Presbyterian Church [USA], 1967), 17.01.

† Underhill, *Worship,* 65.

‡ Karl Barth, *The Epistle to the Romans,* 6th ed., trans. Edwyn C. Hoskyns (New York: Oxford University Press, 1968), 431.

§ C. H. Dodd, *The Epistle of Paul to the Romans* (New York: Harper and Brothers, 1932), 192.

¶ Underhill, *Worship,* 79.

** Underhill, *Worship,* 77.

thing entirely different from what the world sees: the activity of God shaping life to eternity.

The common element in these four quite different moments is sacrifice. Primarily, these are occasions when the worshipping people of God make presentations to God so he can do something with what we give him. "Present your bodies," said St. Paul—so we present a baby at baptism; a man and woman in love at marriage; a sick person at the time of prayer; and the body of a loved one at death. At these four times, we are presenting our bodies in worship. Our emotions range from exhilarating joy to the deepest sorrow. More importantly, we worship in our presentations so that at these four turning points of existence, God transforms our bodies into more of his eternal likeness.

In the Old Testament we read of the Hebrews bringing a sacrifice to God called a burnt offering. It was placed on the altar and consumed by fire. But the "essence of the burnt offering was not destruction, but transformation: God, by his sacred fire, taking, accepting, transmuting that which was offered, so it might enter His very life."[*]

We are little enough inclined to think of weddings and funeral services as worship. And we minimize the worship in baptism and prayer for the sick. But these are the moments of transforming worship: We bring physical life, human love, senseless suffering, and lonely death. God accepts our offering, "transmuting that which is offered, so it might enter His very life."

Baptism is the act of worship marking the beginning of life in God. It may take place in infancy or in adulthood; its meaning is the same in either case. As the water touches the person, the pastor says, "I baptize you in the name of the Father, and of the Son, and of the Holy Spirit," and the grace of God that cleanses us is made visible to all. It shows that the roots of a person's life are in God. God's first word, the word of baptism, is one of promise, not of

* Underhill, *Worship*, 59.

demand. God's first confrontation with a person involves cleansing, restoration, and nurture—all symbolized by the water. And baptism is the church's first word about a person: that we belong to God who created us and cares for us.

Beyond showing the priority of God's grace and love in a person's life, baptism also shows what that life is like as a result. Jesus was baptized at the river Jordan and gave meaning to the act that determines our understanding of it. St. Paul said in Romans 6:

> Do you not know that all of us who have been baptized into Christ Jesus were baptized into his death? We were buried therefore with him by baptism into death, so that as Christ was raised from the dead by the glory of the Father, we too might walk in newness of life. For if we have been united with him in a death like his, we shall certainly be united with him in a resurrection like his. (verses 3–5)

Baptism, then, identifies the life the person is to live from that moment on as the resurrection life imparted by Jesus Christ. It is a supernatural life imparted continually by grace—a life to which sin is alien. Thus, our bodies presented in baptism are defined by two words: love and grace. We begin in the love of God; we live by the grace of God.

Marriage is a second decisive moment in life that is shaped in worship. For the Christian, marriage is not just a legal union of a man and woman performed in church because it is a nicer setting than the living room of the justice of the peace. The Directory of Worship says, "The Christian marriage ceremony is a service of worship before God, normally conducted within the house of God."*

The church worships when a marriage is performed because it sees God's hand working in the union of two lives together in love.

---

* "The Directory for the Worship of God," 22.03.

A prayer in the marriage ceremony says, "As Thou hast brought them together by Thy providence, sanctify them by Thy Spirit."* Love finding its fulfillment in marriage is the result of the call of God—God's providence makes it possible, and his Spirit sustains it in all its complexity and growth. God ordains the union of a man and woman in a lifetime companionship of love for the "welfare and happiness of mankind."†

Because of the divine dimension of marriage, the church expects couples looking forward to marriage to engage in counseling with the pastor, so that they may understand the teaching of Scripture and benefit from the experiences of the church.

Worship shapes our lives by declaring it is God's will that we live together in love. A person's life is most complete when it is shared intimately with another. Marriage is the norm for human relations, and the love learned and the faithfulness experienced there become the central means for interpreting love and faithfulness in our human relations.

The marriage service also shapes our lives by declaring that love is impossible without God. The bare love of a man and woman is not enough for the "welfare and happiness of mankind." Bishop Fulton Sheen's book on marriage is titled *Three to Get Married*. God's direction, sanctification, and sustenance are necessary parts of marriage. The marriage prayer says, "Almighty and ever blessed God, whose Presence is the happiness of every condition, and whose favor sweetens every relation . . ."‡ The frustration, misery, and chaos that plague the marriages of our time seem to be negative documentation of this. The marriage that is contracted in a service of worship looks for God's love and Spirit at its center and God's blessing on its love. Human love is perfected in the love of Christ.

Sickness is the moment of pain and suffering in a person's life.

* *The Book of Common Worship* (Philadelphia: Presbyterian Board of Publication and Sabbath-School Work, 1915), 52.
† *The Book of Common Worship*, 51.
‡ *The Book of Common Worship*, 52.

Few lives are exempted from it. It is not ordinarily viewed as an occasion for worship, but the Directory for Worship has a chapter on it, and we need to include sickness if we are to see the full scope of how worship shapes life.

The Directory states,

> Since the Christian gospel speaks to every human situation, a Church which is faithful to its calling has a responsibility to its members at every moment of their lives. The gospel speaks with particular directness to those who are confronted by illness or death. . . . Prayers of intercession on behalf of the sick shall be a regular part of public worship."*

As we bring the sick into the act of worship, we assure them of the power of God to heal his people, and we affirm the presence of God in the midst of pain. We can do this by going to the sick, bringing them to the church, and regularly engaging in intercessory prayer for them. Intercessory prayer for the sick shapes lives by interpreting our suffering in terms of Christ's suffering, looking forward with him to resurrection health and wholeness.

Many churches have been extending this concern by holding special services for the sick. Realizing that one of our Lord's paramount concerns was healing the sick, the church has sensed its omission and is endeavoring to do something about it. This is not to detract from or minimize, in any way, the work of the medical professions. They are instruments of God's healing in a primary way. But we take responsibility for following in our Lord's footsteps, realizing that no sickness is totally physical, that every sickness has spiritual consequences, and that some sicknesses have spiritual causes. We need to minister to the sick not only through our own individual efforts but also as a worshipping congregation.

In the church, a person's life begins with Christian baptism; it ends with a Christian burial. The Directory for Worship says, "In

---

* "The Directory for the Worship of God," 23.01–02.

the presence of death [Christians] witness to their faith that God, in Jesus Christ, has conquered death and raises his children from death to life eternal. . . . Christians should make of the occasion of death a time in which the hope of the gospel is reaffirmed by them with solemn joy."*

One regrettable tendency of our times is how often funeral services are conducted in funeral homes by morticians rather than in churches by pastors. Morticians should not direct funerals; they do it sentimentally and badly. The funeral service is a worship service of the church. It witnesses directly to our hope of eternal life in Christ. It is a service in which we face death realistically and openly. It is a service where the bereaved may sorrow and grieve with the comfort of God's promise to uphold them and the concern of God's people to surround them.

The service, of course, should be in the church. If a casket is presented, it should be closed—we come not to admire the embalmers' art but to worship the God who receives the dead to life eternal. A pall should cover the casket to eliminate any tendency toward ostentation or needless expense in the purchase of casket or flowers. The emphasis is on readings from Holy Scripture declaring the Christian hope. It is appropriate to sing hymns that declare the church's belief in the communion of saints. Prayer is offered, giving thanks to God for the life he has given to us and taken again to himself.

The funeral service shapes our lives even at its end, enclosing our fragile existence in the eternity of God. In the funeral service of worship, humanity's time is seen from the perspective of Scripture. It is viewed not only in its own pattern of passingness but also in God's time. The broken rhythms of our existence are enfolded within the mightier rhythm of God's eternity:

Lord, thou hast been our dwelling place
in all generations.

* "The Directory for the Worship of God," 24.01.

Before the mountains were brought forth,
>   or ever thou hadst formed the earth and the world,
>   from everlasting to everlasting thou art God.
>   (Psalm 90:1–2)

In these moments we look to God, our refuge and our fortress, our rock and our strength. We look to Jesus Christ, the author and finisher of our faith. We look to the Holy Spirit who has promised to be our strengthener and comforter.

You can be born without being baptized. You can get married without ever entering a church or seeing a minister. You can be sick without thinking or caring about God. And you can die without scripture or prayer, without a word from or to God. Many people live lives like this: Birth is biological, marriage is sexual, sickness is unfortunate, and death is the end.

Yet worship shapes life into a different form. God acts on us in our worship and defines life in its extremities by his love and grace. In worship, our birth, our love, our pain, and our death are surrounded with the grace of God and transformed meaningfully and redemptively.

I appeal to you therefore, brethren, by the mercies of God,
to present your bodies as a living sacrifice, holy and acceptable to God, which is your spiritual worship. Do not be
conformed to this world but be transformed by the renewal
of your mind, that you may prove what is the will of God,
what is good and acceptable and perfect. (Romans 12:1–2)

Let us pray: O God, *thou art the potter and we are the clay. Our past, our present, and our future—our birth, life, and death— need thy hand to shape them into an eternal whole. We present our bodies to thee. Renew us, re-create us, and make us into thy image through him who is able to do exceedingly abundantly above all that we ask or think, even Jesus Christ our Lord. Amen.*

Love's Strategy

Love bears all things, believes all things, hopes all things, endures all things.

—1 Corinthians 13:7

St. Paul, as you well know, wrote in Greek. In the Greek language, there are four words for what in English there is only one. We use the word *love* to cover a wide spectrum of human experience that the Greeks divided into four segments. If we had four words, we might eliminate some of the confusion that surrounds the subject. But at least we can look at the four Greek words and benefit from their analysis and order.

Affection (*storge*) is the first segment. This kind of love is most likely to have parallels in the animal world—the affectionate love of a dog or a cat, for instance, or a person's affection for a pet. It is a warmth and contentment of association and appreciation that makes no demands on the intelligence or the will. A mother's affection for her newborn child is of this kind. There is nothing inferior or low about this love, but it involves a simple relationship that is given to us and makes almost no inward demands on us.

The second rung up the vocabulary ladder of love is friendship (*philia*). It springs from the companionship of two persons who have an affection and respect for one another and pursue a common interest or goal. We see very little of this form of love in our time, though it was the form most prized by the ancients. Adolescence is the time when we observe it functioning at its strongest, but some are fortunate to enjoy deep friendships in their adult years.

Romantic love (*eros*) is on the third rung. Our common usage of the word love in English centers on this area. This is the love of a man for a woman and a woman for a man. It is the love that seeks to possess its object. It is one of the purest and highest of human passions and has been the creative source of the finest art, noble acts, heroic deeds, and civilized achievement. It has also been distorted and spoiled into some of the most sordid kinds of human behavior.

Charity (*agape*), the fourth type of love, transcends the human situation. This is God's love that we see in the life of Christ. It is a new kind of love, not known from human experience. The New Testament writers contributed examples and descriptions of this love to the human language. It is the love that describes God's relationship to humankind and humans' destined relationship to their neighbors. It is the divine strategy for new life.

The first three loves—affection, friendship, and romance—are human loves. The fourth is divine. That does not make the first three less important. They are God given, and as they are expressed, they establish healthy and happy relationships between individuals and the things and people around them. But if we limit our conception and experience of love to these three, we will never understand or participate in our Lord's special work in our lives. It would be proper to examine the divine similarities and likenesses in affection, friendship, and romance and their divinely appointed place in our lives, but today we will consider the fourth love: the love that began in the mind of God and has become the strategy by which all our loves can be redeemed.

The famous description of this new, uniquely Christian love is in St. Paul's first letter to the church at Corinth. Just so you don't underestimate Paul's realism in making the new love the keystone of how a person should live, you should know something of Corinth and its people.

I sense that some people think Christianity was conceived beside a quiet lake with lilies blooming around—a very beautiful, extremely lovely place that is rather remote from the harsher realities of life. To speak of Christian love in the kind of world in which we live is a little like a frock-coated person, bred in the gentle manner and educated in the classical tradition, walking into a noisy brawl in a waterfront saloon and saying in a very sweet, timid voice, "Boys, please be careful. You must love one another." To preach a pious love in that place would be laughable.

The church to which St. Paul wrote was not all that different from a waterfront saloon. Corinth was a seaport. It had a large immigrant and transient population and practically no traditions or social stability. Adventurous Romans, uprooted Greeks, merchandising Asians, and dislocated Jews poured into the melting pot and produced, with the assistance of a decadent pagan religion, a city renowned in the ancient world for profligacy and vice. To live like a Corinthian or "to Corinthianize" was a proverbial expression for promiscuous living.

The Christian church in Corinth didn't seem to be much better than the city itself. Reading St. Paul's letter to the church, we discover him dealing with conditions that seem astonishing. There were open instances of sexual perversion and irregularity among the membership. The church was divided into quarreling groups, each appealing to a different authority. Worshippers came to the Lord's Table for communion and became intoxicated with the wine, turning the sacrament into a drunken orgy. The congregation's leaders were emotionally unstable, and there was chaos and disorder in public worship. Nearly everything that could go wrong with the church did go wrong at Corinth.

Into this crude, harsh, disordered situation, St. Paul strode, talking confidently and firmly about love. And nobody laughed because he was using the new word: the fourth word for love. If he had so much as mentioned affection, friendship, or romance to these Corinthian roughnecks, they would have tuned him out. But he was speaking not of those human loves but of the new love. This love had been defined by the life of Jesus Christ—a life bracketed by a poor peasant birth in a rude stable and a bloody crucifixion on an abandoned hill. The new love of God come down among humankind had faced and conquered every vile act, every weak defeat, every hard pain, every shattered hope, every disappointed belief, every rebellion, every hate, and every indulgence. This was not the love of a gentleman poet written on scented stationery; it was the love that suffers, that faces every adversity, that is all compassion, and that has the strength of eternity in it.

I can see many parallels between the Corinthian situation into which St. Paul injected the doctrine of Christian love and our own modern situation, which needs a power and an ethic strong enough to overcome and redeem social hate, collective evil, cultural immorality, and decadence. We live in a society that has spawned an unbelievable amount of racial injustice. We live in a world that is constantly threatened by the misuse of nuclear power and has become anxious and spiritually impoverished. The poverty, inequity, injustice, and evil in our world are different from that in Corinth only in their extent; instead of being localized in one city, they have spread across a civilization.

It would be sentimental to talk about love in such a world if our only options were the three human loves of affection, friendship, and romance. But happily, we have another love to proclaim and practice—Christian love, God's love, the love that can face the harshest reality and emerge as conqueror.

St. Paul described the new Christian love in 1 Corinthians 13. He listed fifteen specific things about how it acts and gave a four-part summary in verse 7.

One, "love bears all things." The word *bear* means to put a roof over things.* You put a roof over a house to keep off the rain and snow, ward off cold, and protect the inhabitants from discomfort or danger. The idea is not that love suffers all things (takes it on the chin meekly) but that it actively goes into the world to protect the object of its love from hurt.

---

* *Blue Letter Bible*, s.v. "*stegō*," www.blueletterbible.org/lexicon/g4722/esv/mgnt/0-1.

There is much in other people and in the world that displeases us and sometimes is repugnant to us. We often use these things as an excuse to stay away and avoid contact, especially in the cases of cultural crudity or economic misfortune. We don't care to associate with the person. We know there is no possibility of affection, friendliness, or romance, yet we forget there is a fourth kind of love. Irritants, faults, ignorance, immorality, and sin are decisive in blocking the three human loves; they cannot block the new love. The new love puts a roof over those things—doesn't consider these aspects of the situation or the person to be the determining factors. They are no less present or real, but they are not permitted to blunt or deflect the activity of Christian love.

Two, love "believes all things." Love is not gullible. Just because we choose to exercise Christian love, we are not to swallow everything told to us without criticism or discrimination. Love "believes all things" because there is potential in all people—there is good in all people—whether we see it or not. Nothing in all of creation is outside the interest and concern of God.

We cannot bring the mentality of a mathematician to the work of Christian love. We cannot add up the reasons for loving before we do it. Much that needs the penetrating, redeeming influence of Christian love gives no outward evidence of deserving a bit of it. But the new love works where there is no evidence that it will be rewarded or succeed, simply because of God's command to love our neighbor as ourselves.

Three, love "hopes all things." "When Love has no evidence, it believes the best. When the evidence is adverse, it hopes for the best."* Hope is the activity of love that reaches into the future. Love sees in its action the seed of future salvation. The fact that people reject reason, spurn affection, and react violently and senselessly to moderation and justice is not a deterrent to the new love. It sees beyond these contradictions to the final victory of God's

---

* Archibald Robertson and Alfred Plummer, *A Critical and Exegetical Commentary on the First Epistle of St. Paul to the Corinthians,* 2nd ed., International Critical Commentary (Edinburgh: T & T Clark, 1914), 295.

plan and remembers our responsibility to participate responsibly in the just acts that bring men and women closer to their created destiny as sons and daughters of God. It hopes all things.

Four, love "endures all things." "Having done all without apparent success, [love] still stands and endures, whether the ingratitude of friends or persecution of foes. Throughout the Pauline Epistles it is assumed that the Christian is likely to be persecuted."* The word *endure* is often used in a military context to mean "remain instead of fleeing." This is the love that can outlive the feelings of courage, ambition, affection, friendship, and romance. When all these decay and pass away, it still exercises its redeeming influence, still witnesses to its Lord of love, and still works in a committed way in the strategic work commanded by almighty God.

In one of the most moving speeches I have ever heard, Martin Luther King, Jr., who received the Nobel Peace Prize, said,

> We will match your capacity to inflict suffering by our capacity to endure suffering. We will meet your physical force with soul force. And do to us what you will, and we will still love you. . . . And so throw us in jail, and as difficult as that is, we will still love you. Bomb our homes and threaten our children and as difficult as it is, we will still love you. Send your hooded perpetrators and violence into our communities at the midnight hours and drag us out on some wayside road and beat us and leave us half-dead and we will still love you. But be assured that we will wear you down by our capacity to suffer.†

That is a love that endures all things.

In these four instances of Christian love, you will note that its effectiveness or possibility does not depend on any qualities or pre-

---

* Robertson and Plummer, *Critical and Exegetical Commentary*, 295.
† Martin Luther King Jr., speech, Illinois Wesleyan University, Bloomington, Ill., February 10, 1966, www.iwu.edu/mlk.

suppositions we associate with our human loves. It does not rely on affection, that natural kinship between creatures; it does not depend on friendship, the mutual intimacy that comes from common interests and goals; and it receives no assistance from romance, the physical and spiritual desire to possess and be possessed in a personal way. Christian love goes at its work disregarding as much as is humanly possible one's own feelings of like or dislike, probable success, supposed worth, or personal satisfaction. It does its work in obedience to the command of God, with Jesus Christ as an example.

Actually, there is nothing too startling in this description of Christian love. It is not a complicated, mysterious secret that only a psychiatrist probing the inside of a mind could discover. Arthur Penrhyn Stanley once said that "the true calling of a Christian is not to do extraordinary things, but to do ordinary things in an extraordinary way."* These qualities of the new love are all ordinary things, but they are practiced in defiance of human selfishness and desire—exercised in an extraordinary way.

All of us living on the lower levels of love have borne all things, believed all things, hoped all things, and endured all things for those we have had affection, friendship, or romance for. The more excellent way that St. Paul set before us is that we do them for our neighbors: those who, simply because they are right in front of us, are the targets for our responsible activity in the world—objects for the strategy of the new love. "So faith, hope, love abide, these three; but the greatest of these is love" (1 Corinthians 13:13).

Amen.

---

* Arthur Penrhyn Stanley, *Thoughts That Breathe* (Boston: Lothrop, 1879), 58.

Time Is Very Short

I mean, brethren, the appointed time has grown very short; from now on, let those who have wives live as though they had none.

—1 Corinthians 7:29

Paul. Why do I like him so much? An opinionated man, verging on cockiness, quick tempered, and capable of soaring anger. He wrote on subjects that are of surpassing importance to me: God, my eternal salvation, the meaning of my life, how to think of Christ. These are things I very much want to get clear and straight. I read him and realize after a dozen sentences that I am in the presence of a master. Here is a person who has lived these truths and can describe what I am living. At about that time he plunges into a sentence full of excitement and then forgets to finish it. I am left hanging in confused bewilderment. Peter once commented in one of the great understatements of the ages that Paul's letters include "some things . . . hard to understand" (2 Peter 3:16).

But it doesn't matter. I like him all the more. The life of faith was a passion for him. There was nothing conventional, dull, or routine as he pursued the way of Christ—and wrote about it. I meet people all the time who want to reduce God to an argument or who seem to think that being religious means having a discussion. For Paul, it was risking his entire life in an act of love. I meet people all the time who seem to think that being a Christian means being nice and disguising all the unlovely parts of their lives so that they appear smiling, polite, and adjusted. For Paul, it meant plunging into confrontations and encounters that engaged his emotions and his thoughts in a great contest against evil and a great venture into holiness. I open one of these New Testament pages that Paul wrote, and in minutes I am surfing on this thought, tumbled out of my ordinariness by the wild aliveness of his faith.

And Corinth. Why do I like Corinth so much? It was a pastor's nightmare. In that Greek seaport city was a congregation of Christians that not many of you would put up with for twenty minutes. Fiercely antagonistic groups in the church pushily and abrasively claimed to be better than the others. Excitable people disrupted worship services with what they claimed to be direct revelations from God. When the believers celebrated the Lord's Supper, some got drunk on the communion wine. Members were taking each other to court over civil disputes. The pigsty sexual morality of the city had been imported into the church without anybody thinking there was much wrong with it.

All the same, I like these people. The new life in Christ was ablaze in them. They were up to their armpits in problems, but the problems didn't hold a candle to the mystery of the Christ that was ablaze in them. They knew their lives were being shaped for some grand and eternal purpose. The church was a mess, but God was cleaning up that mess, and they were willing to let God do it. Their morality left a lot to be desired, their emotions were adolescent and undisciplined, and they were childish in their thinking. But they were after God with all of themselves. Corinth was not a pretty little stained-glass chapel; it was more like a barnyard. Everything they had been in the world they brought with them into the church: their appetites, their superstitions, their sexuality, and their bungled relationships. With that as raw material the Holy Spirit was creating something marvelous and wonderful. I like these unlikely and unlovely Christians very much because they stood before God, letting him make something out of them that no one would have supposed possible—a church, a people of God, a community of faith.

The Paul-Corinth combination was electric. Put the two to-gether, and sparks flew. Paul wrote to this church more than any other—three letters, two of which we have. They wrote at least two to him, neither of which survived. We learn more about the basic, visceral Paul here than in any other place. And we learn more about how the Holy Spirit shapes and forms and develops Christians into a church.

I think we will find that Christ Our King Church is not so far from Corinth as two thousand years and five thousand miles might indicate. I think we will find ourselves being addressed and under-stood. And as we listen, believe, and obey, we will be shaped in the Holy Spirit's transforming actions of taking the raw material of our lives and making a church out of it.

When we park our cars on a Sunday morning, walk across the parking lot, come through these doors, and find a place in a pew, we do not leave our problems behind. Sometimes I fantasize about having security guards, equivalent to the kind they have in air-ports. They would examine you for contaminating emotions or sinful thoughts that might interfere with the praise of God that we offer, distract you from a childlike faith, or profane the holiness of God's Spirit among us. As you walked through the security system, a little buzzer would go off, and you would go back and empty your pockets—or your heart or your mind—of whatever would mess up our worship. I wonder how long it would take us to get everyone through security. We would probably have to instruct you to arrive two hours early, as the airlines do.

But neither Corinth nor Christ Our King have security checks. Those assembled in worship are the same people who were irrita-ble with each other at the breakfast table, who were trying to make the best of a bad job on Thursday, who spent Saturday night toss-ing and turning in guilt or sorrow or remorse, and who just a few minutes ago looked over the order of worship and groaned at the hymns the pastor selected.

Do you think that by coming here your life will be better? Do you think that I have something wise to say to make things better at the breakfast table? In your work? Help you sleep better? Sing better? Most people expect something like that out of church. The Corinthians did. They had a whole list of problems that they wanted Paul to help solve. Most items on their list are also on ours. I want to look at one item on both the Corinthian list and the Christ Our King list—marriage—and see what Paul does with it.

Marriage is one of those fundamental human conditions that seem to have the power to determine our lives for good or ill. Many people—maybe most—find it to be the single most important reality they must deal with. Think of all the different ways in which we experience marriage.

There are happily married people; others look at them and think, *If I could be happily married like that, then everything would be just fine with me.* There are unhappily married people; they think, *If I could just not be married, everything would have a chance of being all right.* There are unmarried people; they look around for someone who might marry them, believing that life will never be complete or whole until they are a husband or a wife. There are people who have resigned themselves to never getting married but are regretful and bitter about it. There are single people who don't have much interest in getting married. There are people who were married and are now single and finding it difficult to adjust to singleness, feeling sorry for themselves, quite sure that they would be happier if they were not single.

In chapter seven of the first Corinthian letter, we see all these married and unmarried people asking Paul for counsel. "Should I get married?" "Should I get divorced?" "Should I stay married?" Why ask Paul? He hadn't been clinically trained in psychology. He had never read Freud or Jung. He had never been to a Marriage Encounter weekend.

They asked Paul because they knew that God was supposed to make life better and Paul had been their guide to God. If their married or unmarried state was a problem, God would fix their problem so they could live better. "How about it, Paul? What do we do? Give us some answers on marriage."

Being married is one of the most difficult tasks in the human condition. And being unmarried is one of the most difficult tasks in the human condition. In marriage, we are faced with all the demands and complexities of intimacy. Unmarried, we are faced with all the demands and complexities of solitude and friendship. It is no surprise that Paul's very long letter deals with questions arising from being married and unmarried—questions most pastors spend a lot of time dealing with.

Three notable things take place in 1 Corinthians chapter seven. First, Paul took seriously the actual conditions of their lives and gave the best counsel he could come up with. It might not be the counsel that would fit your condition today, but for that time and place, it was wise. He worked hard at helping them. The gospel is never indifferent to what is going on in your life, your work, your emotions, your marriage, or your singleness. Paul did his very best to help with their marriage questions.

Next, Paul said that while he was glad to offer his counsel, it had no divine authority. Four times in this chapter he cautioned them that he was writing out of his own experience and reason. God hadn't given him any direct word on the matter (see verses 6, 12, 25, 40). He hoped to be helpful, but they must understand that this was not the gospel, not the eternal word of God.

Third, in the midst of this careful, patient, discriminating attempt to direct them in the wise ordering of their married and unmarried conditions, he lurched off track and sailed off on one of his brilliant, breathtaking digressions. At one moment, we are moving from one different question to the next; then we are suddenly tumbled into something wildly alive. We are in the atmosphere of gospel—not good advice but good news. The digression is brief (three verses), quickly turning back to the subject at hand. Here it is:

The appointed time has grown very short; from now on, let those who have wives live as though they had none, and those who mourn as though they were not mourning, and those who rejoice as though they were not rejoicing, and those who buy as though they had no goods, and those who deal with the world as though they had no dealings with it. For the form of this world is passing away. (1 Corinthians 7:29–31)

Paul interrupted his problem-solving, advice-giving, people-helping self to say there was something far more important than those questions and answers: God is in our lives, and the invisible God is more real than the visible problems. The way we define our lives as married or unmarried, with a good marriage or bad marriage, does not account for the way things are. The typical ways in which we understand ourselves, get our meaning, and assess our sense of worth are completely inadequate.

Let me quote Paul's three-verse digression again as paraphrase:

Do you think that being married or unmarried is the shaping reality of your life? It isn't. There is something far more important, more determinative, more real.

Do you think that the loss, grief, or sorrow that has plunged you into mourning is the shaping reality of your life? It isn't. Set it aside for the moment. There is something far more important, more determinative, more real.

Do you think the fact that you are exuberantly happy and rejoicing right now is the shaping reality of your life? It isn't. There is something far more important, more determinative, more real.

Do you think that your excellent standard of living that enables you to buy pretty much whatever you want these days is the shaping reality of your life? It isn't. There is something far more important, more determinative, more real.

Do you think that your not-so-excellent standard of living that forces you to scrimp, count pennies, and go without a lot of things that people around you take for granted is the shaping reality of your life? It isn't. There is something far more important, more determinative, more real.

Do you think that your ability to deal with the world in a competent way, make decisions, be successful, and more or less get your way is the shaping reality of your life? It isn't. There is something far more important, more determinative, more real.

Do you think that your failure to deal with the world in a satisfactory way, never managing to get it all together, is the shaping reality of your life? It isn't. There is something far more important, more determinative, more real.

We are in the habit (which our society reinforces in hundreds of ways) of believing that our married state, emotional state, economic state, and success status make us who we are. They don't. They are important, but they don't give us our identity—or rather, the identity they give us is spurious. None of these things is unimportant, but none is of central importance. These are the raw materials God takes to shape his life in us. He takes our married or unmarried condition. He takes our emotions of weeping or laughing. He takes the fact that we have a nice nest egg in the bank or that we are holding a couple of bounced checks. He takes not only the self-assurance that comes from being commended in our work and given a promotion and a raise but also the self-questioning that comes from being criticized and yelled at. God takes all these things and goes to work on them as a creator, as a shaper of salvation in us. All these things that we and everyone else use to assess our lives don't make us what we are. God makes us what we are.

All these things that we think are of central importance are not. Paul said, "The form of this world is passing away." The form is what you see. It is what you have wrongly supposed is the content; but the content is God's loving salvation, his shaping grace, his creating Spirit. The form of this world is passing away. What you see is on the way out. What you don't see is on its way in. In fact, it is at hand right now, ready to be received by faith, accessible to any one of you at this moment.

What is it? In two words: Jesus Christ. In a phrase: the salvation of God entering our present condition. In a paragraph: The unseen God is more real than anything you will ever see. He has more to do with your life than your marriage state, your money state, your emotional state, or your success state. He loves you. He has come into our world in Jesus Christ and has accomplished our salvation. And from that moment on, absolutely everything in your life—marriage or unmarriage, mourning or rejoicing, affluence or poverty, competence or incompetence, the way you spend your money, and the way people treat you in your work—is raw material that God is using to create the new creature, the Christian, you.

Salvation is not some fragile, invisible thing going on in some secret part of your soul. It is an immense visible thing that involves every part of your life. He is the creator. He is the savior. And you are the one he is creating and saving.

Paul began his digression with these words: "The appointed time has grown very short." I want to look at these words carefully. *Appointed time* is a distinctive term, very important in understanding the way our life of faith operates. The Greeks had two words for time: *chronos* and *kairos*. Chronos is calendar time, clock time, and is important for getting through the day or week.* The other type is kairos, meaning the opportune or the ripe time, the time when things come together.† A man says to a woman, "It's time we got married." And she replies, "Yes, I agree; it's about time." Those two people weren't looking at their calendars or watches when they said that. Many things much more personal and complex— emotions, desires, purposes, maturity, and commitments—all converged into a sense of the right time, the appointed time.

Kairos is Paul's word for gospel time: the right time for your life and God's life to converge in a faith life. The right time to quit trying to define your life by the conditions of marriage or emotions or money, instead offering all these conditions to God for blessing. The right time to move from being totally preoccupied with solving your life's problems to entering the mystery of grace and love in Jesus Christ.

For, said Paul, the time "has grown very short." This is an un-

* *Blue Letter Bible,* s.v. *"chronos,"* www.blueletterbible.org/lexicon/g5550/esv/mgnt/0-1.
† *Blue Letter Bible,* s.v. *"kairos,"* www.blueletterbible.org/lexicon/g2540/esv/mgnt/0-1.

fortunate translation because it makes it sound like clock time—that if we don't hurry we will be late. Something quite different is intended. This word is used only twice in the Bible, and a look at the other use will help us see Paul's meaning here. Acts chapter five shares the story of Ananias lying to the apostles and then falling dead on the spot. In telling that story, Luke wrote that after the death the young men "wrapped him up and carried him out and buried him" (verse 6). And here is our word: "wrapped him up." Paul wanted to show us the nature of this time in which we live, the time in which God is here to create new life in us in the midst of our present conditions, whatever they are. This time, this right time, is "wrapped up." There is nothing else to wait for. All the work has been done; the time is at hand.

When something comes to you wrapped up, what do you do? If it is a corpse, like Ananias, you bury it. If it is food, you prepare it for eating. If it is clothing, you put it on. If it is a tool, you use it. If it is a game, you play it. If it is Christ, you live it—God's time for shaping his new life in you is all wrapped up; now unwrap it, and enter into life.

On Tuesday morning I got up a little before six o'clock, went into the living room, and opened the drapes a few inches. The world outside was very cold and dark. As I set about dealing with the conditions of my life, getting ready to function as adequately as I could through the day, I turned on a lamp so I wouldn't stumble or run into furniture. I let the dog out, put on the coffee, found my slippers, and glanced over the newspaper. Then I went downstairs to my study. An hour or so later, I came up. Our living room faces the east. While I had been in my study, the sun had risen. Through the opening in the draperies, the sun was blazing across the snow, pulling all the colors of the spectrum into our recently dark house, warming the world. The lamp, still on, was directly in the sun's path. The lamplight that had been so important only an hour before looked pathetic and artificial. I turned it off. I didn't throw it away; I will need it again in the pre-dawn darkness. But the sun is far more glorious in my life than the lamps.

First Corinthians 7 is a lamp, Paul lighting his way and ours the best he could with the wisdom available. Verses 29–31 are the sun, pouring the word and presence of God into our lives, showing us the wide and wonderful world in which God is at work, and pulling all the colors of salvation into our lives. What will we do? Close the drapes and sit by the lamp figuring out how to deal with the conditions of our lives? Or throw the drapes wide and, for right now, turn off the lamp? Paul didn't despise lamplight, but he loved sunlight and the gospel—God pouring light and energy into our lives. Marriage and money and emotions and job don't disappear or become less important in that light, but they become less central and not at all definitive. I will give any of them the attention they need when they need it, but for right now it is God we must attend to. This is the right time to accept him, praise him, and follow him.

Amen.

So Run

Do you not know that in a race all the runners run, but only one receives the prize? So run that you may obtain it.

—1 Corinthians 9:24

This should be enough. We have all these people meeting Sunday after Sunday to hear what God says to us. We freely assemble together to be directed by God, hoping that we can do a little good in the world. What more is there? We are well-motivated people, coming together in a place where God's Word is honored. It seems ideal. What can go seriously wrong with such people under such conditions?

Surprisingly, a lot can happen. It turns out that it is not enough to put up a church building, place a sign out on the road announcing the time for services, get a choir and organist together, remember to turn on the heat each Saturday night, and arrange for someone to lead in prayer and preach a sermon and administer the sacraments.

The unadvertised fact is that we find a lot of pettiness and an enormous amount of prejudice in church. The signs identifying this as a place of worship post no warnings that people are often hurt in churches in deep and crippling ways. I know a considerable number of people who give the church a wide berth in their travels. Their avoidance is not out of ignorance or based on hearsay or gossip; they themselves have been hurt, misunderstood, or rejected in life-damaging ways. They are limping or aching or bereft because of something that took place in a church where scriptures were read, God's praises sung, and invitations given to receive the salvation of our Lord Jesus Christ.

One reason we are reading Corinthians together is so that we will not be naïve innocents in these matters. We need to know how many different ways the church can go wrong and never be smug or complacent in our own churches. But there is more than warning in the Corinthian letters; there is Paul's health and joy and sanity in the middle of what goes wrong, as well as his skill as Christ's servant in bringing peace out of the noisy squabbling and love out of the selfish jostling.

In chapter seven we see that you cannot reduce the church to a problem-solving institution. We can expect our problems to be taken seriously and even find some direction in dealing with them, but our problems do not define our being. The primary reason for being the church is not to solve problems but to cultivate the life of faith, to submit ourselves to the love that shapes something deep, eternal, and energetic in us.

In chapter eight we see that the church is not a standard-setting and standard-enforcing institution. It is not the place where a correct belief is set forth that forces everyone to know the right answers to all the God questions. Nor is it a place that defines the moral questions so that everyone knows exactly what is proper for Christians to do in our daily lives and what kinds of dress, language, or associations are forbidden. Nor is it a sorting-out place where weak and useless people are cut from the roster so that we can have a winning team and make a revolutionary impact on the world. No, we are the church not because of our answers or rules or strategy but because God is forming new life in us, shaping his will in us. It is slower going for some of us than for others, so we need to protect each person's free space where the creative work of grace and mercy occurs. What God is doing in you and in me is far more important than anything we are doing for God or for each other.

And in chapter nine we come up against another negative: The church is not where we get understanding and affirmation. Because the church is the arena in which God is doing his great work of salvation, forming a people who are whole and in love and courageously hopeful, not all the people are finished products yet, and they are often doing a quite different work. As God is making a good salvation for us, we are making life difficult for one another.

I would like this congregation to be perfect; I really would—a place and a people that would draw unsolicited exclamations from people: "My, how those Christ Our King Christians love one another!" I hope that every person who enters this place feels accepted. I hope that as you receive God's word in scripture and sermon and sacraments, you will know not only the affirmation of God in the way of faith but also the appreciative encouragement of everybody here. I hope that you will sense in the spirit and atmosphere of this place that we are all in the serious business of following Christ and are not just a bunch of sloppy sentimentalists who get together and hold hands once a week as a kind of solace against the world's indifference. I want this congregation to be full of energy, sharp in its purpose, with nobody feeling criticized or misunderstood or left out.

There are stretches of time when I am quite sure that we are almost there—the perfect congregation! I especially feel that way when I go away from here and speak to other congregations and with other pastors and realize how ragged and contentious it is in so many places. I return here and breathe fresh air, proud of you and glad to be your pastor. All the same, I remind you and warn myself that just because we have taken the trouble to get out of bed this morning and know that we are the church of Jesus Christ, that is no guarantee that the worst will not happen to us. Something unwelcome, maybe even evil, may occur—an unkind word, a misunderstanding, criticism, a malicious act. It might even happen this morning! Then what will you do? Go shopping for another church? Quit the church completely? Worship before a television screen where all the music is flawless and the preacher has hair on his head, where no babies cry and nobody disturbs you and you are the only hypocrite in the room?

Or will you do what Paul and his Corinthians did, along with millions upon millions of Christians ever since: learn how to survive in the holy place in a crowd of sinners? This ideal is what 1 Corinthians 9 exhibits.

You would think that by immersing ourselves in the Scriptures, discovering God in Christ, realizing that we are saved by grace, and living under the mercy as we do, we would all be considerate, courteous, understanding, friendly, energetic, grateful, and well motivated. It isn't so—not in the early church, not in Corinth, and not at Christ Our King.

But somehow, we never quite get used to this. Out in the world, we rather expect to be treated badly. We have our defenses up. We know that people will lie to us and cuss us out and rip us off. We try to be prepared. But in the Christian place, in the church, we let our guard down, expecting the best out of people. Often, we get what we expect. But not always. Sometimes we are treated in a decidedly unchristian way in the Christian place. Then what do we do?

All of us will be in this situation sometime or another. When that happens, we will feel less lonely and less bewildered if we have 1 Corinthians 9 under our belts.

Some of the Corinthian Christians were critical of Paul on two counts. One, they said he was incompetent. Two, they said he was inconsistent. The criticisms had to sting. No one wants to be called an incompetent bungler, and no one relishes having the reputation of a fickle opportunist.

The first criticism went something like this: "All the other apostles were companions of Christ Jesus and were trained by him and have a diploma to prove it. When they come to visit us, they all wear three-piece suits and have their wives with them. They all draw good salaries. They have a good appearance and make us proud of them. But you, Paul—you never saw Jesus in the flesh and can show us no credentials of your authority. You are a bachelor, traveling around in a shiftless, irresponsible way. Why is that? Why can't you find a woman to marry you, or are you afraid of the responsibility? And since people don't value your ministry enough to pay you lecture fees when you speak, you do it for nothing? You can't be worth much: no wife, no contract, and no apostolic degree. Why should we listen to you or take you seriously?"

The second criticism went something like this: "Paul, you are the most inconsistent person we have ever met. You are totally exasperating; we never know what you are going to do next. One minute you are in the synagogue arguing with the Jews over the Scriptures, and the next thing we know, you are over in Athens talking pagan philosophy in the streets. One week you are cozying up to all the devout people in prayer, and then reports start coming in that you are hobnobbing with slaves and prostitutes, treating them like long-lost relatives. And isn't it about time we got a clear statement of condemnation on some of the moral issues in the empire? And another thing—why are you always letting people see your weak side, your failures, your faults? We don't need that in a leader. We want somebody we can look up to and admire. One day you are telling people to keep the law, and the next you say that they don't have to keep it. We need a role model who is consistent, someone we can depend on to show us how to live the Christian life. And what happened to that hair dryer we gave you last Christmas? Why don't you ever use it?"

Those were the criticisms. Was there any basis for them? As a matter of fact, there was. The Corinthians had the facts right.

First set of facts: Paul had not seen Jesus in the flesh; he did not have a wife; he did not take a salary or accept fees for his ministry. The Corinthians took those facts and criticized Paul for being unqualified, unattractive to women, and incompetent to command a good salary.

Second set of facts: Paul did conduct his ministry one way with Jews and another way with pagans, and he did make special effort to identify with the weak and the down-and-out. The Corinthians took those facts and criticized Paul for being wishy-washy, inconsistent, and opportunistic without character or backbone, a poor excuse for a leader.

Both sets of facts show Paul at his very best: Paul was willing to work in the shadow of the apostles and to set aside marriage to give himself greater freedom in his dangerous travels. He refused to take money for his preaching and teaching lest it be misunderstood as an obstacle to the free gospel. And Paul inventively and selflessly identified with the people to whom he was serving the Word of God, entering into their condition instead of arrogantly demanding that they come to him on his terms.

The Corinthians understood the facts accurately, but they didn't understand Paul at all. They saw the facts out of context, outside the gospel. What can you do when you are trying your very best to do the right thing—to love the Lord, to serve his people—and people fail to understand your actions and make a quick judgment, calling you bunglingly incompetent or a canny opportunist? What can you do when you are misunderstood and unfairly criticized?

What Paul did was give a feisty, spirited defense. He did not submit to letting them malign him at will. He did not take a lofty stance far above all such petty criticism and arrogantly refuse to answer from his perspective. He accounted for the facts they had observed in terms of his commitment to the gospel of Christ. He refuted the charges, and he clarified his life of ministry to them. Taking their misunderstandings seriously, he then openly and honestly tried to clear them up. He didn't change his life to make it easier for them or alter his ministry to make it congenial to their expectations. While he wanted their affirmation, he couldn't get it while staying true to his Lord. He was convinced that he was doing the right thing, so he didn't cave to their criticisms.

There is wisdom here. Misunderstandings need to be dealt with. They are inevitable. Just because we are people of faith doesn't mean that we are perfect people with sensitive discernment. It is all right to criticize; it is all right to defend. The give-and-take is part of the life of the community. In the cross fire of the Corinthian criticism and the Pauline defense, we learn some things about Paul that give us all the more cause to respect and admire him.

But then, as so often in Paul's writings, there is a spurting explosion of energy, an unexpected turn that puts us in a new territory—which is, in fact, gospel territory. It takes us outside the atmosphere of criticism and defense, of misunderstanding and clarifying, of misaligning and explaining motives and goals, and it puts us in the middle of one of Paul's surging cascades of words that pull us into a deeper, livelier participation in the faith:

> All the runners in the stadium are trying to win,
> but only one of them gets the prize.
> You must run in the same way,
> meaning to win.
> All the fighters at the games go into strict training;
> they do this just to win a wreath that will wither away,
> but we do it for a wreath that will never wither.
> That is how I run, intent on winning.
> That is how I fight, not beating the air.
> I treat my body hard and make it obey me,
> for having been a preacher myself,
> I should not want to be disqualified. (1 Corinthians 9:24–27,
>   my paraphrase)

Do you see? Suddenly we are no longer with Paul and his critics trying to sort out motives and goals and meanings. We are in a race. We really don't have any more time to spend talking about this. We are going somewhere together, and the act of going requires all our attention, all our discipline, and all our energy. We are not kibitzers watching what other people do and making comments on it. We are runners. And if we are running the race, we don't have breath left over to talk about the other runners.

Paul was saying, in my paraphrase, "I don't want to spend any more time talking about this. It doesn't matter that much. I want you to understand me and accept me and affirm me, but not at the cost of dropping out of the race. The big thing for me, and also for you, is running the race of faith—not sitting around talking about the faith, not sauntering down the boulevard of faith window-shopping, but running the life of faith." Running is a good metaphor for this: It requires training and concentration; it implies a goal. It excludes spectators, gathering the participants into a camaraderie that overcomes differences. You don't have to understand or like or affirm the other runners to run with them. It is the goal that defines the race and your act of running that defines you as a runner. That is what we are doing.

Paul told us that we are runners. Do you know how tragic it would be if we quit running so that we could make each other better runners? Do you want to be a club of former runners? The church is not a club for either former, dropout runners or aspirant runners. It is not a club that depends on us working out the rules of understanding or getting along with each other. It is not a club at all. It is a race. And if we are in the race, we have precious little energy left over for the kinds of discussions that we insistently seem to engage in. Let's get on with the race. It is worth the best.

> Run the straight race
> Through God's good grace,
> Lift up thine eyes, and seek His face;
> Life with its way before us lies,
> Christ is the path, and Christ the prize.*

Amen.

---

* John S. B. Monsell, "Fight the Good Fight with All Thy Might," in *Hymns of Love and Praise for the Church's Year* (London: Bell and Daldy, 1863), 163.

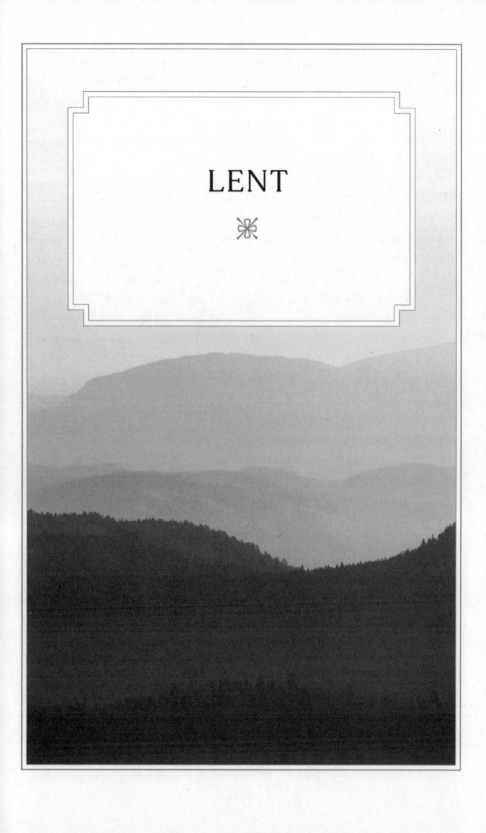

LENT

✳

Like Newborn Babes

Like newborn babes, long for the pure spiritual milk, that by it you may grow up to salvation; for you have tasted the kindness of the Lord.

—1 Peter 2:2–3

G. K. Chesterton, in one of his essays from *Tremendous Trifles*, divides individuals into two types: vertebrates and crustaceans. Chesterton complains that our age is dominated by the crustacean type—people who are hard, brittle, and impressive on the surface but are cowards and weaklings behind that shield. What we need, he implied, is a new race of vertebrates—men and women who are soft and kind and gracious outwardly but who have a bone structure of conviction and integrity to support this grace.*

St. Peter dealt with a similar problem in his epistle. The Christians to whom he was writing were growing their bones in the wrong place—on the outside. Their lives had hard, brittle, bony surfaces. They were becoming crustaceans.

Now, it is true that they needed protection. They were living in a hostile world where the virtues of faith, hope, and love were scorned and sometimes even punished. Martyrs were not uncommon. When a person lives day in and day out in such a world, it is

* G. K. Chesterton, "The Prehistoric Railway Station," in *Tremendous Trifles* (New York: Dodd, Mead, and Co., 1909), 267.

wise to develop some protective device. But they were building the wrong defenses.

Peter mentioned five "crustaceous" features that were inappropriate: malice, guile, insincerity, envy, and slander. The one thing all these have in common is that they are antisocial. They are responses to human society that express the negative attitudes of mistrust and hostility.

It is not at all surprising that these tendencies developed in the Christian community. In fact, in retrospect, it was predictable. A clinical psychologist would describe them as "defense mechanisms." Society treated the Christians with an enormous amount of slander, persecution, and discriminatory behavior. To survive, they had to defend themselves. They did so by reacting in kind, but because they did not have the power to react openly, they resorted to the more hidden, but no less effective, retaliatory ploys of guile and insincerity.

The problem was one of survival. How do you survive an adversary's attack without developing that adversary's traits? How do you learn to exist in a hard-shelled civilization without becoming hard-shelled yourself?

I don't know how much biology St. Peter knew, but his choice of illustration in responding is perfect biologically. He tells us to grow up into vertebrates. What we need is to develop a strong, inward skeletal structure of bones. Everyone knows vertebrates are a far higher form of life than crustaceans. A crustacean may wound a person in the flesh (as crabs occasionally do to swimmers at the beach), but the versatility and intelligence of the vertebrate will far out-survive the lowly crustacean. A giant crustacean is a fearful thing to look at. Who would not shudder at meeting an Alaskan king crab or a large lobster while swimming? But the human race is in no danger of being defeated by them.

Actually, Peter didn't say it just like that. He said, "Drink milk." But as a parent who has said times without number to our children, "Drink your milk so you will grow up to have strong bones," I couldn't resist having Peter say the same thing. Milk is the great bone builder. Milk is the first food of vertebrates. As newborn babes, we all drank milk, and that milk gave firmness to those baby-soft bones, gave strength to that inward skeletal structure.

What is this milk a symbol of? It was the "milk and honey" of Israel's hope in the promised land. Later in the church, this milk was seen in the word of God as it came in scripture, sermon, and sacrament. Here God shared his inner life with us. Here he provided the means by which we could assimilate his grace. The response of obedience at baptism; our faithful, believing listening to the written and preached Word in scripture and sermon; and the thankful, sacrificial offering of ourselves and receiving of Christ in the Lord's Supper—these are all the milk.

In light of this tradition, some translations have rendered St. Peter's phrase as "the milk of the word." But Peter simply wrote "milk." Still, if you see the substance of the word of God in this threefold way of scripture, sermon, and sacrament, you come close to Peter's meaning. He told us what the milk is in the next sentence: "You have tasted [already] that the Lord is gracious" (1 Peter 2:3, NKJV)—it is the grace of God they have already tasted; therefore, they are to desire even more of this milk. God's grace is the milk that we are to receive, digest, and assimilate into our bodies. We receive this through the word of scripture, sermon, and sacrament. And by receiving it, we "grow up to salvation," or, as we have developed it, into vertebrates with strong bones.

Peter then employed another, entirely different, illustration. He wrote, "Like living stones be yourselves built into a spiritual house, to be a holy priesthood, to offer spiritual sacrifices acceptable to God through Jesus Christ" (verse 5). In the first illustration where the believers were likened to newborn babes desiring milk, the emphasis was on strong development and growth. In this second one where they are likened to building stones in a house, the emphasis is on the function of their acquired strength. The images are not related, but the meanings are—growth must be growth into something; development must develop into something.

Several Old Testament passages (in the Psalms and Isaiah) refer to the Messiah as a stone, a rock, and a cornerstone. This long-standing tradition and expectation were fulfilled in Christ who became the rock of salvation and the cornerstone of existence. Peter drew from these passages to illustrate that our lives derive their essence from our Lord's—we, too, are to be stones built into the structure of the house of God, in which he is the cornerstone.

But Peter intended something even more specific here. He connected the imagery of the Christian as a stone with references to being priests and offering sacrifices. In the life of Israel, the altar was the place where priests officiated and sacrifices were offered. And the altar was made of stone. In the early church, the altar was changed into a table where the Lord's Supper was celebrated. It was around this table that the Christian community offered up its life in sacrificial devotion, and it was from this table that they ate the memorial supper that turned them all into priests—Christ living in them. And this table, whenever possible, was also made of stone.

Our lives, Peter was saying to us, must be like the stone of this table—a solid, eternal place where sacrifices are made to the glory of God and where grace, love, life, and strength are shared in glorious banquet to all who come to it.

Do you see how personally St. Peter was speaking? This is practically pure autobiography. He wrote of these truths with such ease because he had lived them himself.

No one was more of the crustacean type than Peter. He was a hard man, but this hardness was all on the surface. A fisherman who lived his life on the whim of wind and sea, he was inwardly as capricious, unstable, uncertain, and moody as the elements he served. He was also a Jew who learned to accommodate himself to the Roman rule by being adaptable and even servile when the situation demanded it. On the outside he looked like the indomitable, indestructible man of action—but on the inside he was weak, uncertain, and full of fear.

Two illustrations: on the night of Jesus's arrest, Peter and the other disciples were with our Lord. When the crowd came from the high priest to arrest Jesus, Peter boldly drew a sword and, swinging it wildly, cut off the ear of one of the men—and then ran as fast as he could. The bravery was all on the surface. After that brief, momentary, dramatic show of boldness, he forsook Jesus to the mob (Mark 14:50; John 18:10).

On that same night, while Annas was questioning Jesus in the court of the high priest, Peter was standing outside, a safe distance away. One of the maids stationed at the door asked whether he was not one of Jesus's disciples. Here was a chance for bravery. Here was a chance to stand up for the one who had changed the meaning of life for him. Peter, the spokesman for Jesus's band of followers, one of the first whom Jesus had chosen to be with him on earth, had a chance to speak again. It was in an out-of-the-way corner, to an obscure person, but it was an important word. Yet it never came. Peter still played the strong man. He cursed and blustered, but it was weakness and cowardice that spoke. He denied he ever knew Jesus.

But if that were the end of the story, we would not still be hearing about Peter or reading a letter he wrote to the Christian churches of the first century. The marvelous thing is that he was changed from a crustacean to a vertebrate—from a man with all his hardness outside and softness inside to the apostle of strength who was renowned for his compassion.

Peter became a shepherd in the early church, a man with tremendous internal strength that was fused with an amazing tenderness and compassion. He was the one who heard the words of our Lord "Feed my sheep" and obeyed them (John 21:15–17). Jesus had declared him to be the apostolic rock on which the church would be built, and the confidence and stability of Peter's faith and witness did, in fact, become the rock of the early church's life. His leadership was the focus for the early development of the church's sacrificial life and faithful witness.

And in his epistle, he described the process of transformation. "Like newborn babes, long for the pure spiritual milk," meaning the grace of God that comes in baptism, the word of God that brings new life to us day by day. And "like living stones be yourselves built into a spiritual house," meaning a place where sacrifices are made and life is shared—a place like the Lord's Table where we place ourselves in obedient, sacrificial service to Christ and find sustenance for life rooted in the eternal love of God.

Just as Peter spoke from his own life experience, we must listen to what he said in a very personal way. The word of God that comes through his epistle is a word spoken directly to each of us. I can think of no word that is more relevant or more in need of personal response.

Many of you confide in me as your pastor, sharing with me the pressures under which you live. I am regularly made aware of how difficult it is to live the life of Christ as a businessperson, a professional, a spouse, or a student. A hundred years or so ago, Charles Spurgeon wrote, "The world is no friend to grace."* And times have not changed since he said that. The Christians to whom Peter wrote were not the only ones who lived in the midst of hostility and intimidation and had to devise ways to survive—you and I also face survival problems. The hostility has changed its form, but what we call the "pressures of modern living" amount to the same thing. Grace, love, hope, faith, sacrifice, and prayer seem like fragile products in our secularized society. Not for a minute do I minimize the difficulty, the precariousness, the struggle involved in obeying the word of God.

But even as Peter observed inappropriate defenses against the pressures of his society, so I cannot help but observe inappropriate defenses among us. These almost always consist of using the name of Christ as an external shield. Each of us does this in our own way, but all of us externalize the Christian virtues. We construct a shell of righteous indignation against the world, develop a mask of pious superiority toward the world, or practice a good neighborly affability with the world—but in every case, we overdo it because

* C. H. Spurgeon, *All of Grace* (Springdale, Pa.: Whitaker House, 1983), 119.

there is no inner life to sustain it. And in time, it develops into a hard, brittle, meaningless shell hiding our inner emptiness.

There is a better way. Desire the pure spiritual milk of God's grace. Receive the word of God through careful listening and faithful obedience. This will develop a strong bone structure that will let us be ourselves as God has created us and redeemed us. Our defenses will be inside, and we will be able to face the world, speak to it, and serve it with all the assurance and confidence of a vertebrate over a crustacean.

By God's grace we will become living stones like St. Peter and our lives will reflect that ultimate symbol of solidity and strength: the rock of Christ. If it could happen to St. Peter, it can happen to us—to you and to me.

Like newborn babes, long for the pure spiritual milk, that by it you may grow up to salvation; for you have tasted the kindness of the Lord.

Like living stones be yourselves built into a spiritual house, to be a holy priesthood, to offer spiritual sacrifices acceptable to God through Jesus Christ.

Amen.

Christ in the Christian

It is in Christ that the complete being of the Godhead dwells
embodied, and in him you have been brought to completion.
—Colossians 2:9–10 (NEB)

I n reading Paul's letter to the Colossians with an eye for seeing
Christ in creation, we could grasp something of the long-range
purposes that God has for us in Christ. We could see creation as an
external structure specifically designed to house the internal movements of saving love and grace. And through creation, we could
view the love of God and his purposes for us, prepared "before the
foundation of the world" (Ephesians 1:4).

But what we saw macrocosmically through Christ in creation
we can see microcosmically as we look at Christ in the Christian.
All those plans and purposes have a focus in humankind. It will be
a little like moving from the great telescope at Palomar Mountain
to the electronic microscope in a biophysicist's laboratory. Our
purpose is to see something of what it means to bring all God's
redemptive activity behind the term *Christ* into intimate association with the creatures of God who have opened their lives to his
love and grace—the people we call Christians. The text is Colossians 2:9–10: "It is in Christ that the complete being of the Godhead dwells embodied, and in him you have been brought to
completion."

The term *Christian* does not occur in this text. Neither does it
occur in the letter as a whole. In fact, it is found only three times

in the whole New Testament (Acts 11:26; 26:28; 1 Peter 4:16) and not once in Paul's letters. So, who are these individuals we call Christians, those whom Paul showed to be in relationship with God's fullness of love?

At the outset of this letter—before Paul said anything else—he wrote two phrases that give us a kind of outline introduction to these men and women: They are "in Christ" and "at Colossae." In each case, the subject of the phrase is the same: this letter's recipients, those whom we are used to calling "Christians." A single subject but a double predicate describes the Christians. Under the rubric of these two phrases, we recognize the individuals we are after.

"In Christ" means that Christians are those who have heard the call of God's love and grace, responded to it, and consequently entered into a union of fellowship with God. They no longer maintain themselves in an objective, spectator position before God. They can no longer stand off and talk about God. They have heard a summons, and their active response to it has involved each of them in a spiritual relationship. They are in the arena of God's working love, redeeming grace, and delivering power. They are in Christ.

But they are also "at Colossae." They were quite unmistakably citizens of this little town. Unpretentious even by the more modest standards of the ancient world, this town had no skyscrapers, no famous politicians, and no big temples. The mail came only once a week; we would describe it as "a little on the back side of things." But these Christians called this town home. They lived in houses, bought food in the marketplace, bickered over dyed woolens in the bazaar, sent their children to the academy, and worked at their trades. They were very much involved in Colossian living whether they liked it or not.

Christians, then, are simultaneously "in Christ" and "at Colossae." They are in Christ participating in the plans of God for their lives, open upward to grace; and they are in Colossae with their feet on the ground, living as creatures in a world God created and making no attempt to escape it. Their being "in Christ" does not make them into mystical, heavenly-minded recluses who have nothing to do with the world. But at the same time, their living "at Colossae" cannot be construed as any kind of adequate existence in itself. No, it is precisely because you live in Colossae that you need to be in Christ. The Christian's life is open in both directions. This letter was written to those who were "in Christ at Colossae."

What does it mean for Christ to be in the Christian, to be "embodied"? Well, first it means that the complete being of God, which is what Christ is, has invaded the Christian's sphere. This describes the "at Colossae" part of our Christian existence. *Embodied* means put in a body so we can see it—put in Jesus Christ. It means that the fullness of God, seen in Christ, has entered our history. It means that God has given "a full and complete expression of himself (within the physical limits that he set himself in Christ)" (Colossians 2:9, PHILLIPS) and that expression is in a language we can understand.

It doesn't just mean that two thousand years ago this stupendous, unbelievable thing happened where the eternal God became a man in history and was born, killed, and raised up again. It doesn't just mean that we have a historical record of what God was like and of his will for us. Of course it means that history was invaded, but it means more than that. It means that our history was invaded. Our thoughts, our acts, our feelings, our beginning and our end, our ambitions and frustrations, our loves and hates, our hopes and our fears—everything that a biographer, medical doctor, or psychoanalyst could ever find out about us has been invaded by the fullness of God, by Christ. In the lively phrase of Karl Barth, it means that humankind "is reached and pierced by God however much he may wriggle."*

It means that in Colossae, lives are inundated by God; they are flooded by him. The fullness of God, his completeness, has entered our sphere, and we simply cannot escape him any longer.

Recently, we had a tremendous downpour of rain. Most of us

---

* Karl Barth, *Church Dogmatics*, vol. 3, *The Doctrine of Creation*, part 2 (Edinburgh: T&T Clark, 1960), 141.

were in favor of having rain, but in the middle of the storm I couldn't help wishing that it might come in more modest install-ments. It was impossible to carry out the normal movements of shopping, visiting, getting to and from the car, and such without becoming uncomfortably dampened, if not soaked, by the rain. There was no escaping the rain; it fell on the just and the unjust alike. It flooded basements, clogged drains, ruined shoes, elimi-nated creases in suits, and crumpled hats. While theoretically it was a very good thing, in actual experience, because we were un-prepared for it and because it was so inexorably present, it became an irritation and in some cases a severe discomfort. Everyone agreed that rain was good and needed. But such large buckets of it for such an unpredictably long time and right at the busiest time of day—that wasn't good and needed!

Right in the middle of all this, while you and I were suppressing curses, two little girls from a nearby apartment house came to our backyard and had a wonderful time playing in our plastic swim-ming pool. They were dressed in bathing suits and had no hairstyl-ing to worry about, and instead of begrudging the torrents of water from above, they generously contributed to the wetness by filling the swimming pool from the garden hose. They loved the rain, the water, and the wetness. Of course, they were dressed for it, and they had no previous plans or schedules that were being disarranged. But that can hardly detract from our admiration (and envy) of their joy and excitement in the rain, which all of us would agree was a good and needed thing.

Paul's word that the completeness, the fullness of God, was embodied in Christ means that we now live in a God-drenched world. There is no possibility of keeping him far-off in the heavens or using his presence at our own convenience like we use the water from a tap. He has flooded our sphere. The completeness of God, the fullness of Deity, is here.

And though we all would readily agree that God is good and needed, who can deny that there is too much of him sometimes? The presence of God, which our parched souls need so desperately, makes us uncomfortable. It is because the fullness of God has invaded us, because the completeness of God has penetrated our histories, that we find ourselves so dissatisfied with the way our self-run lives are going, so unrelaxed in our achievements, so uncomfortable in our successes. We live what all the external standards of measurement would classify as good and happy lives, but the restlessness and disorientation at the center seem to threaten the whole business. So, we try for distractions. We try to shore up our lives against disaster. We buy boots, raincoats, and umbrellas. But somehow, they are never quite adequate to keep us dry. Somehow the presence of God leaks through and threatens to ruin our selfish, private, keep-God-in-his-place lives. In other words, it is not possible to live satisfactorily only "at Colossae," as if Colossae were the whole world.

Some, of course, enjoy the rain. They are dressed for it, and their lives are not so cluttered with plans that God's being and action spoil everything for them. They are the ones living simultaneously "at Colossae" and "in Christ." They are the ones who realize that in the very nature of our world and of our lives, the completeness of God confronts us at every point, that we have been invaded by the fullness of God—we are God-drenched. And realizing this, they live openly and joyfully in it. This is the "in Christ" part of the Christian life.

This anticipates the second thing to be said from this text. Not only are we in unavoidable contact with the fullness of God, "reached and pierced by God however much [we] may wriggle," but we can also be "brought to completion" in him. This is what defines us as Christians. Not only do we live in Colossae, where it rains every day with the love and grace of God; we also live in Christ, with God's fullness being poured into us and making us complete. The fullness of God has invaded not only our world but also our life experiences and is perfecting a completeness. And this means that Christ, who embodies the fullness of God, is also particularly concerned that we should be filled by it. In other words,

Christ is for us, working to fill us, engaged in securing openings in our lives to his love and grace, getting us to become like "little children" who will enjoy the obvious and exult in the ever-present presence of God.

This is put in a clear-cut statement right at the outset of Christ's advent into the world: "To you [humankind] is born this day in the city of David a Savior [i.e., your deliverer]" (Luke 2:11). This is his whole purpose: to bring fullness and completion to us. He is concerned with and interested in nothing else. He is here simply to bring us into completion.

And for that reason, the New Testament finds "no room for a portrayal or even an indication of the private life of the man Jesus." It doesn't deny that he had one. We know certainly enough that he was born, was hungry and thirsty, and had family relationships, temptations, and sufferings. But "it discloses His private life only by showing how it is caught up in His ministry to His fellows," which is the "concrete form" of his function in the Godhead. So, the private life of Jesus can never be the theme of the New Testament, and it cannot profitably be our interest. We are curious, of course, but our curiosity really has no relevance. The New Testament writers' tireless aim is "to show that the man Jesus is for others, near and distant, disciples, Israel and the world, and to show what He is for them"—that is, that he is breaking into their lives with the fullness of God so they may be brought to completion.* And He is for you too.

Christ is a thoroughly public person. So, we have passages like this in the New Testament:

Who, though he was in the form of God, did not count equality with God a thing to be grasped, but emptied himself, taking the form of a servant, being born in the likeness of men. (Philippians 2:6–7)

* Barth, *Church Dogmatics*, 209.

Though he was rich, yet for your sake he became poor, so
that by his poverty you might become rich. (2 Corinthians
8:9)

Since therefore the children share in flesh and blood, he himself likewise partook of the same nature, that through death
he might destroy him who has the power of death, that is,
the devil, and deliver all those who through fear of death
were subject to lifelong bondage. (Hebrews 2:14–15)

And all of this is summarized in the Nicene Creed, where it says
of Christ, "For us men and for our salvation he came down from
heaven." Christ is in Colossae so that every Colossian can be in
Christ. Christ is in White Plains, so that every White Plains resi-
dent can be in Christ. Christ did not come just to show us that God
was present and that God loved us; this was not just a spectacular
show of Deity, a kind of parade of heavenly fireworks. The completeness of God descended to this world that it might invade us,
penetrate us, and make us complete. Paul put the whole truth in
one of the most profound phrases in the whole New Testament:
"Christ in you, the hope of glory" (Colossians 1:27).

Twice in this letter Paul warned the Christians in Colossae
about those who (in the translation of Ronald Knox) would
"cheat" them out of the fullness that is in Christ by offering inferior goods under false claims (2:8, 18).* Instead of bringing people
into the fullness of God, the religious ways they offered would lead
people off into the desert. They made attractive presentations of
things like worship of angels, ascetic forms of self-discipline, and
theosophical types of religious teaching. They made a big display
of their expertise and secret inside knowledge of the divine, posing
as specially endowed teachers who could guide a person inside
eternal things.

* *The New Testament,* trans. Ronald Knox (Springfield, Ill.: Templegate, 1945), 208–9.

Paul bluntly called them phonies and cheaters. Persons and movements that hide behind a facade of mystery and secrecy usually are spurious. It is iniquity that hides in the mist of mystery; righteousness has nothing to hide. Christ is the mystery of God, but he is displayed openly. He is the secret of God, but he is that secret made known.

Paul did not live as long ago as we might think, and Colossae is not as far away as a map might lead us to believe. Today we still have soothsayers—psychics, crystal gazers, palmists, and tea-leaf readers in our communities.

We should be concerned by modern-day psychics misleading the people around us. But Paul was worried about a loss that is even more tragic: the loss of lives that were being led into the desert, lives separated from completion, lives diverted from fullness, lives trying to live in isolation from God.

Day by day, we face a host of alternatives to Christ, all of them made attractive by imaginative claims and impelling promises. But if we can take Paul's word as God's Word (and we can), they are all cheaters and phonies who would lead us astray. What they offer will end up hollow and meaningless in the end.

Jesus said, "The thief comes only to steal, to kill, to destroy; I have come that men may have life, and may have it in all its fullness" (John 10:10, NEB).

Paul repeated both the warning and the promise. And on the highest authority he declared to us that "it is in Christ that the complete being of the Godhead dwells embodied, and in him you have been brought to completion."

All of us who live in Colossae, let us also live in Christ and live life completely, in all its fullness.

Amen.

Christ in Our Conduct

Were you not raised to life with Christ? Then aspire to the
realm above, where Christ is, seated at the right hand of
God. . . . Put to death those parts of you which belong to the
earth. . . . Put on the garments that suit God's chosen people.

—Colossians 3:1, 5, 12, NEB

To get a glimpse, however faint, of the purposes of God for us
in and even beyond creation is exciting and exhilarating to the
spirit. To become aware of the presence of God that surrounds us
and attempts to fill us is a welcome development in our experience.
Christian doctrine accurately perceived carries a real exhilaration,
and biblical truth personally apprehended carries a pleasurable
sense of fitness and completeness. But there comes a point in the
discussion of doctrine and in the reading of the Scriptures when
the cantering rhythm of poetry diminishes into plodding work-
horse prose, when the bright and flashing world of the imagination
is submerged in the heavier, grayer world of conduct and exercise
of the will.

Christian thought is awesome and beautiful (theology was once
called the "queen of the sciences"), and the Christian gospel is
dramatic (Dorothy Sayers called it "the most exciting drama that
ever staggered the imagination of man"*). Yet when you get to the

---

* Dorothy L. Sayers, *The Greatest Drama Ever Staged* (London: Hodder and Stoughton,
1938), 6.

realm of conduct, the glamor fades and the drama dulls. One man said that the trouble with being a Christian is that "it is such a daily sort of thing." But if Christianity means anything at all, it finally has to get into the world of what we do between waking and sleeping, into the realm of the routine—of ordinary speech, habitual responses, and casual reactions. We cannot sustain the adventure-on-the-high-seas emotional pitch too long; we cannot think "big thoughts" all day. We are not Hamlet, surrounded by intrigue and murder and plunged into profound soliloquies three or four times a day. We are much more characteristically T. S. Eliot's Prufrock, who says:

> No! I am not Prince Hamlet, nor was meant to be;
> Am an attendant lord, one that will do
> To swell a progress, start a scene or two,
> Advise the prince; no doubt, an easy tool,
> Deferential, glad to be of use,
> Politic, cautious, and meticulous.*

So, we must finally talk about Christ in our ordinary "Prufrock" lives; we need to think about Christ in our conduct. For if he doesn't get finally into our conduct, observers will begin raising serious doubts whether he even exists at all. And we ourselves, in all honesty, will not be satisfied for long with talking and imagining a doctrine that doesn't filter into the ordinariness of our living.

Paul, you will notice, did not begin by talking about conduct, but before he was halfway through the letter, he got to it. And we must get to it too.

The text consists of parts of three verses in the third chapter of Colossians: "Were you not raised to life with Christ? Then aspire to the realm above, where Christ is, seated at the right hand of God. . . . Put to death those parts of you which belong to the

* T. S. Eliot, *Prufrock and Other Observations* (London: The Egoist, 1917), 15.

earth. . . . Put on the garments that suit God's chosen people" (Colossians 3:1, 5, 12, NEB).

Paul provided us with a rhetorical question that serves as a transitional link with all that has gone before, followed by three imperative commands. If we take these statements seriously and reflect on them prayerfully, we can be led a long way along the road of Christian conduct. But before we obey the commands, it is essential that we listen to the question.

The question "Were you not raised to life with Christ?" assumes a "yes" answer and puts us into a positive relation with what has gone before. We recall Christian creation; we recall Christ in the Christian; and we recall the tremendous history of God's redemptive activity, the numberless instances of his love and grace, the whole world of salvation. And then we recall how individuals found themselves incorporated into that activity and were made a working part of it, all summarized here in the words "raised to life with Christ."

If Paul was right (and he usually was!), the question is a reminder that in any discussion of Christian truth, the first word must always be about God and his work in us. If we fail to maintain that priority, everything gets hopelessly distorted and out of order. And Paul never failed to establish the priority. In the letter he wrote to the Romans, he gave eleven chapters to the activity of God before he wrote four on the conduct of humankind. In Galatians, the first four are oriented toward God's plan and the last two toward humanity's response. Ephesians is split exactly in half: the first three describing God's purposes, the last three humanity's part in them. These are the obvious examples, but not once did Paul fail to observe this priority (although not always in such a clean division).

So, it is not possible to begin a discussion on Christian living by talking about conduct. It would be like talking about the performance of a new sailing vessel before the ship was even in the blueprint stage. It would be like talking about going to the moon before you were even sure the moon existed. It would be like making plans to write a great new novel in Chinese before you knew a single word of the language.

Paul's question, then, reminds us that we have been participants in a great saving event—we have been raised with Christ. It reminds us that all the redemptive activity of God has been focused on us, that our lives have been radically altered and charged with new meaning so that we are no longer mere creatures but new creations in Christ. And only by realizing that we are already at this point far advanced in discussing the Christian life is it safe to talk about conduct. But realizing this and recognizing that even here it is primarily Christ we are interested in, we must go on from the question ("Were you not raised to life with Christ?") and listen to the commands.

The first command is to "aspire to the realm above, where Christ is, seated at the right hand of God." It is a command that deals with our ambitions and goals. It is a command that concerns itself with the things we dream about, our long-range hopes for our lives.

But we would be far off the mark if we saw in this only an invigorating call to a higher life, an idealistic challenge toward better things. The area of our aspirations is specifically defined as the realm where Christ is seated at the right hand of God. It is the place, therefore, where Christ exercises rule and authority, where redemption is in the ascendancy, where love is operative in power, where grace is dispensed to needy humankind, where mediation takes place between God and humans. In other words, our aspirations are directed not to a generalized upward, high-minded realm but specifically to Christ as he rules in our lives.

If we obey this command, it is bound to have a deep effect on our conduct, for it will mean that the ruling Christ will become vigorous and alive in our goals and purposes and will inevitably affect our actions. Christ will be in our conduct.

We can see the process working at almost any level. Imagine a young man starting off on a two-mile walk across town to see a girl. Seeing her and spending the evening with her are the purpose and goal of his walk. She is very much alive in his imagination; he can't keep her out of his mind. And so, what happens as he makes that two-mile walk? Passing a delicatessen, he remembers her favorite candy and buys a box. Passing a flower shop, he is inspired with the thought of how lovely she would look with flowers on her shoulder, and he buys a corsage. Passing old acquaintances, he misses seeing them entirely. Passing a church, he looks particularly long at it, for he once heard her remark that she would like to be married there. Nearing her home, he glances at his reflection in a store window and straightens his tie and fixes his hat. And by the time he arrives at her door, we could list at least a dozen specific actions he took in the course of the two-mile walk caused by the girl in his imagination. She was in his conduct.

The image put before us is the ruling Christ—Paul told us to aspire to "the realm above, where Christ is, seated at the right hand of God." If this ruling Christ is alive in our aspirations and dreams, we will do things we never dreamed of before, we will spend our money for things we never thought of before, we will see things we have never seen before, we will miss seeing other things we had always seen before, and we will alter our personal attitudes and actions unconsciously. Christ will be in our conduct because he is in our imaginations, in our purposes, in our goals.

The second command is nearly macabre by contrast: "Put to death those parts of you which belong to the earth." The logic of the movement from the first command to this was well marked by George MacDonald:

> We are and remain such creeping Christians, because we look at ourselves and not at Christ; because we gaze at the marks of our own soiled feet, and the trail of our own defiled garments. . . . Each, putting his foot in the footprint of the Master, and so defacing it, turns to examine how far his neighbor's footprint corresponds with that which he still calls the Master's, although it is but his own. Or, having committed a petty fault, I mean a fault such as only a petty

creature could commit, we mourn over the defilement to ourselves, and the shame of it before our friends, children, or servants, instead of hastening to make the due confession and amends to our fellow, and then, forgetting our own paltry self with its well-earned disgrace, lift up our eyes to the glory which alone will quicken the true man in us, and kill the peddling creature we so wrongly call our *self*.*

Lift up your eyes . . . and "kill the peddling creature." Paul called for not only that primary set of the soul, fixing our imaginations on the rule of Christ, but also this ruthless dealing with what could sabotage the whole enterprise. We must root out that which could make our conduct a sham performance and a laughingstock charade.

St. Anthony the Great, an Egyptian desert hermit of the fourth century, is the most celebrated instance in church history of those who took this command as literally as possible and "put to death those parts which belong to the earth." As a young man and already fairly well-to-do as a farmer, he was sitting in church one day and heard the gospel lesson read as if personally to him: "Sell what you possess and give to the poor . . . and come, follow me" (Matthew 19:21). So, he sold everything, gave it to the poor, and went out into the desert, where he stayed for many years, making only brief returns to the city. His athletic encounters with the devil and demons, his vivid temptations, his extreme efforts to deny himself, and his single-minded pursuit of God have marked him as the greatest of all the desert fathers.† As literally and as completely as he could, he put to death the things that belonged to the earth. His only companions were the jackals that roamed the desert and the scorpions that lived with him in crumbled tombs. In his own

* C. S. Lewis, ed., *George MacDonald: An Anthology* (New York: Macmillan, 1947), 16–17.
† Steven Jonathan Rummelsburg, "St. Anthony the Great: Spiritual Hero of the East," Catholic Exchange, January 17, 2023, https://catholicexchange.com/st-anthony-the-great-spiritual-hero-east.

day he attracted many imitators so that when he finally died at the age of 105, the desert was swarming with hermits weaving mats and baskets and emulating Anthony's ascetism and devotion.

Anthony is the most colorful of the saints who tried to obey this command, but every Christian who has taken the call of Christ seriously has had to grapple with this negative side of it. George Meredith (who was no puritan) said, "Spirit must brand the flesh that it may live."* And fifteen hundred years earlier, Dorotheus the Theban said in blunter terms, "I kill my body, for it kills me!"†

Among many of the desert fathers, there was a tendency to publicity-oriented austerity, a kind of pride in denial, that may have missed the Christian point completely. So, we do better to take Jesus Christ as our interpreter in understanding this command. In him we see no denial for its own sake, no conspicuous rejection of the world, no trace of asceticism. Rather, we see the elimination of everything that would either distract or encumber his service of God; we see the complete death of anything that would interfere with obedience; we see the disciplined rejection of any interest that might dissuade him from laying down his life for others. In other words, in Christ we see the putting to death of self, the killing of self-centeredness, the crucifixion of the ego. And this is what we are to put to death.

The third command is to "put on the garments that suit God's chosen people." It is a positive injunction to dress in clothing that openly demonstrates what we are within.

We live by symbols. We arrange all our relationships on the basis of signs. Not one of us can look inside another, discerning the development of thought in her brain or the change and movements of emotions in her heart. But that doesn't mean we are consigned to ignorance. We have ways of finding out what is inside. Expressions on the face, words in the mouth, the manner of a walk, the

---

* George Meredith, *Diana of the Crossways: A Novel* (Boston: Roberts Brothers, 1893), 11.

† Helen Waddell, *The Desert Fathers: Translations from the Latin* (Ann Arbor: University of Michigan Press, 1957), 10–11.

choice of clothes, the gestures made. Each of us shows our internal realities in any number of ways. We do it by "putting on garments"—that is, by giving signs or outward evidence of what is inward.

Now, Paul already said that our lives are "hid with Christ in God" (Colossians 3:3). No one can see them. A person in Christ and a person out of Christ look exactly the same. A cardiograph would not discern any Christian difference in their heartbeats; an IQ test could not separate Christian from non-Christian brains; a customs inspector examining passport photographs could never sort out the saints from the sinners. Our lives are "hid with Christ in God."

But that doesn't mean we are doomed to blindness. We can "put on" many different things to demonstrate what the inward realities are. We can dress in the "garments that suit God's chosen people." Paul suggested "compassion, kindness, humility, gentleness, patience" (verse 12, NEB). These are words, acts, attitudes, approaches, and voice intonations that will reveal Christ in us. We may choose them quite deliberately to give a sign, to provide a symbol for what we know is the central reality of our lives. Just as a woman chooses a certain dress for a particular occasion and a man carefully picks out a certain suit for a special interview, so Christians can put on garments that suit their new station as the chosen of God.

This is not an imitation of Christ for its own sake but an attempt to give signs and symbols of one's inward reality. Putting on these garments is a reference to grace. It is a witness not of our own goodness (for so many times those garments do not reflect our own feelings on the matter at all) but of that hidden reality of Christ within us.

Having been raised to life with Christ, then, we are commanded to do these three things: to aspire to the realm above, where Christ rules; to put to death those parts of us that belong to the earth; and to put on the garments that suit God's chosen people. These are the things that will enable Christ to be made manifest in our conduct.

These three things will provide Christ an area of activity in our external lives.

If I read Paul rightly, I see little or no interest here in Christian performance as such. He was not concerned that we make a good record. Christianity is no cheap legalism, no grim custodian of the rules of God. Paul wanted us to let Christ live in us so that even our conduct will be a witness to that life—so that even the daily round will be blessed by the freedom and liberty of the movements of grace.

Thomas à Kempis, in the greatest of all devotional writings concerned with Christ in our conduct, *The Imitation of Christ*, challenged us:

> So many people are kept back from spiritual growth, and from tackling their faults in earnest, by one single fault— running away from difficulties; we don't like a tussle . . . The Devil takes no sleep, and the flesh is not dead yet, so don't stop getting in trim for the fight; you have enemies to left and right of you, and they're always on the watch . . . Lord, let what seems impossible for me to do by nature become possible by your grace.[*]

Amen.

---

[*] Thomas à Kempis, *The Imitation of Christ*, trans. Robert Knox (New York: Image, 1955), 57, 74, 112.

Be Holy Yourselves

✻

Therefore gird up your minds, be sober, set your hope fully upon the grace that is coming to you at the revelation of Jesus Christ. As obedient children, do not be conformed to the passions of your former ignorance, but as he who called you is holy, be holy yourselves in all your conduct.

—1 Peter 1:13–15

I saac Watts, the greatest hymn writer of the Christian church in my opinion, wrote the words to the hymn "Holiness and Grace." The first stanza reads:

So let our lips and lives express
The holy gospel we profess;
So let our works and virtues shine
To prove the doctrine all divine.*

The concern to express in "lips and lives" the gospel of Jesus Christ is an essential part of the Christian life. It is discussed by theologians under headings of "sanctification." It is encouraged by devotional writers as "holy living." And it is dismissed with contempt by many others, calling it "puritanism" and "petty moralism."

---

* Isaac Watts, "Holiness and Grace," hymn 132 in *Psalms and Hymns of Isaac Watts,* Christian Classics Ethereal Library, www.ccel.org/ccel/watts/psalmshymns.I.132.html.

As we listen to what St. Peter wrote about holy living, try to shed all the associations our culture has built around the words *holy, sanctity, holiness,* and *holier-than-thou.* Take a fresh start in understanding the meaning. Let St. Peter be our teacher. If we give him half a chance, we will emerge with a vigorous, life-affirming, challenging view of what it means to be holy. The haloed saints, the black-robed monks, and the ancient ladies with loose-fitting dresses and tight-fitting bonnets have dominated the imagery around the word long enough. Let us give it back to St. Peter, who knew how to use it properly—and let him give it back to us that we might experience it joyfully.

The first word in this passage is "therefore" (1 Peter 1:13). That throws us back to what has gone before. Because of what has thus far been stated, this follows. What had been stated? First, the gospel. In Peter's wonderfully compact introduction, we saw the whole gospel in microcosm. The trinitarian balance of truth in which the Godhead provides for our choice, our active lives, and our forgiveness in Christ was all focused in Peter, the man who was given a new name, a new work, and a new master.

Then conversion was stated: the event of being "born anew" (verse 3). We saw that the possibility of new birth provided the hope for everything that was done in the church—that this miracle of a fresh start was what brought us to baptism, gathered us to the Lord's Table, and kept us faithful and attentive to the preaching of the Word.

Third, salvation was stated. The elaborate and centuries-old operations of grace created a salvation history and then, in Jesus Christ, concluded with each believer having a personal, deeply intimate confrontation with God's grace, so that we became grafted individually and carefully into salvation history. St. Peter portrayed salvation as the historical, living drama in which each of us is involved by God's grace and that carries such an abundance of excitement, variety of action, and originality in plot that angels lean over the balustrades of heaven wanting to get a look.

This is what precedes the "therefore." And on this basis, we can make a positive statement about holy living: Holy living is rooted in the great acts of grace.

Peter, you see, did not begin talking about holy living as if he were beginning a completely new, unrelated subject. The new subject, holy living, was rooted in what has gone before. Because of the gospel, conversion, and salvation, holy living is a possibility. It would be impossible to reverse the order and put it first. It is all result. It is the life lived after the mighty acts of grace have occurred.

It is important to insist on this relationship because disaster follows in the wake of their separation. The classical biblical instance, one in which Peter himself was involved, is the case of Ananias and Sapphira in the early church. In a burst of compassion for those who were needy, the Jerusalem Christians sold all that they had and put it in a common fund, actually creating a communal society—no one owned anything, they shared everything, and they were visibly one in Christ. Ananias and Sapphira were attracted by this holy living; it must have been an exciting, appealing community that was living in this daring new way. And in an attempt to share in the adventure, they imitated the action, but they did it out of sequence. They had no rootage in the gospel, in conversion, and in salvation. They imitated the outward form of holy living, which was giving all their possessions to the church, but because they had no inward understanding, they held back a little for an emergency. And death was the result.

The result of that kind of thing is always death. Every one of us is familiar with the deathly pallor that characterizes the person who imitates holy living but in whom there is no life—the person who gives money to the church but does it grudgingly, who sings praises to God but does it with great mournfulness, who is faithful in church attendance but only to maintain a kind of moral superiority, who loves his neighbor but whose neighbor is quite aware that it is only because God makes him do it. The life cord has been cut in all such cases; there is a form that might be called "holy," but all the living has ceased. Holy living must be rooted firmly, and at all times, in the great, previous acts of grace.

St. Peter moved from the "therefore" to specific instructions for holy living through four specific commands. First, he said, "gird up your minds." This is illustrative speech that Peter learned from Jesus. In Luke 12:35, Jesus admonished the disciples to keep their loins girded and their lights burning to be prepared to meet their Lord at the end of the wedding. "Girding one's loins" involved pulling up and tightening together the long, wide outer garment so it would not cause the wearer to stumble while working or running a race.* Christians face a journey, and preparing their minds is part of their overall preparedness for it. In less colorful but more contemporary speech, we might say, "Be alert; use your head. Holy living involves the use of your intelligence."

Second, Peter said, "be sober." Again, it is figurative speech, but this time from the world of the carousing drunk. Under the influence of alcohol, people can become confused, rash, and self-indulgent. They are sometimes pleasant enough, and they certainly seem to be enjoying themselves, even if their associates aren't—but they are so removed from the real world that they become a burden on everyone. And as time goes on, the confusion, deterioration, and escape from reality become more pronounced so that life itself is threatened. This identical escape from reality can occur in the religious life too—even without the help of alcohol, self-indulgence leads to rashness and results in confusion. The enthusiasm and the excitement break with God's reality and become forms of self-indulgence where private feelings and individual egos are indulged. It might even look holy (we often remark that such people are so "zealous," so "sincere"), but it is not the holy living Peter was admonishing. Holy living involves the exercise of self-control over self-indulgence.

Third, he said, "Set your hope fully upon the grace that is com-

---

* Albert Barnes, "Luke 12:35," *Notes on the Bible,* Bible Hub, 1834, https://biblehub.com/commentaries/barnes/luke/12.htm.

ing to you at the revelation of Jesus Christ." Setting your hope on grace and grace alone means refusing to put an ultimate hope in anything else. I find this much more difficult to illustrate, probably because I find less experience of it. We do not hope for great things, do we? We live on the outer fringes of what is described as hope in Scripture. Our lives are filled with trivia and nonessentials. And if someone suddenly confronts us with the question "What is your greatest hope?" we stumble around through various responses: the impatience we feel at waiting for the next paycheck, the home mortgage we would like to pay off, the job promotion that will get us off the shelf, the pressure of getting our children through the "perils of childhood and the temptations of youth." We hope for such small things that we have no imagination or faith left to hope for large ones, to set our hope only on grace. But it is essential to holy living. Holy living demands a large imagination encompassing the world from the perspective of divine action—it sets its hope on the grace revealed in Christ.

Fourth, he said, "Do not be conformed to the passions of your former ignorance." The word *conformed* is an interesting one—it carries the idea of being poured into a mold and looking just like the mold once the material has cooled and hardened.* Life previous to the great acts of grace has a few standard forms into which everyone is poured. It has no real individuality, no pure personality. But now with the operations of grace, those molds are no longer needed. True freedom is a possibility. We can really be ourselves. There is no necessity to fit into those molds that the world has decreed for success or normalcy; we can live under the creative influence of grace. Holy living rejects the world's standards and forms in order to live freely under grace.

Those are the four components of holy living as Peter gave them. After that qualifying division of parts, he said, "Be holy yourselves." One thing struck me about that listing: the proportions of it. Out of the four items, three are stated positively and

---

* "Interlinear Bible Search: 1 Peter 1:14," Studylight.org Study Desk, www.studylight. org/study-desk/interlinear.html?q1=1%20peter+1:14.

one is stated negatively. Gird up your mind, be sober, and set your hope are all positive; do not be conformed is the one negative. And that leads to a second formulation about holy living: Holy living is three parts positive to one part negative.

How often do we see that reversed, and how often do we get it reversed in ourselves? Holy living has a reputation for a great deal of negation. But that is not Peter's fault. And if we had time to examine all of Scripture, we would find that it is not the Bible's fault. Holy living is tremendous life affirmation. There is some negation to it, of course; some things must be avoided. But there is a three-to-one ratio of positive statements.

This is well illustrated in our usual attitudes toward chastity. Perhaps no other aspect of morality is so hedged about with negative counsel as this one. G. K. Chesterton captured the biblical perspective when he said, "Chastity does not mean abstention from sexual wrong; it means something flaming, like Joan of Arc."*

Finally, Peter dealt with the problem of motivation in holy living. And it may be the biggest practical problem for us to meet. In the first twelve centuries of the church, much aspiration was focused on holy living. Young people grew up with ambitions to be saints, much as our young people grow up with ambitions to be professional athletes, glamorous entertainers, and space scientists. Not many actually do it—but it is a common ideal. There may be no fewer saints today than a thousand years ago, but it is a way of life for which interest has waned and whose hero qualities have disappeared. The pragmatic American asks, "Why live a holy life? What's in it for me? What difference will it make? How will it help me be successful?"

I doubt whether Peter heard lack of motivation expressed in just the terms we hear it, but he certainly faced the same problem, because he tried his best to produce motivation by what he said. And this is how he did it: He reminded them that God the Father is an impartial judge, that they were ransomed by the precious

* G. K. Chesterton, "A Piece of Chalk," in *Tremendous Trifles* (New York: Dodd, Mead and Co., 1909), 14.

blood of Christ, and that salvation history took place for their sakes.

Where is the motivational element in reminding them that God is an impartial judge? It throws the details of common life into an eternal perspective. Everything we do is important and will be examined by God. It is not just the big moments and crucial events of life—whether or not we are baptized, faithfully receive the sacrament, regularly listen to the preaching of the Word, or are married and buried in church—but also our day-to-day routines that reflect eternity. God the judge looks at all the evidence, not because he wants to find material to damn us, but simply because all the evidence is part of his gift to us. All of life, even what we consider unimportant and trivial, is God's creation. This should lend itself to a healthy respect for the divinity in all of life.

The ransom by the precious blood of Christ is additional motivation. It is a reminder of the tremendous cost involved in providing life and grace. The freedom we have, the forgiveness we enjoy, the confidence we rest in—these are not discount-store bargains. They all involved the crucifixion of Christ. Being reminded of this moves us to holy living, because we realize our lives are tremendously valuable. A regular complaint of parents is that their young people do not realize the cost of things. They spend their parents' money with great ease and lack of concern. The complaint is valid. I remember leaving my father's toolbox outside in the rain and, when he discovered it there with the tools all rusted, hearing a lecture on how I had no sense of value and no appreciation of the money involved and that if I'd had to earn money to buy those tools, I would have some respect for them. That is true enough. Yet we are all in a similar position before God. For here, our lives are given to us in totality, and we can be very slipshod, treating the great gift of life cynically and casually, if we are not reminded of the great cost at which it was given to us. Holy living is motivated by the knowledge and appreciation of our Lord's sacrifice in making life possible for us.

Peter did not indulge in cheap gimmicks to get us fired up for the holy life. He neither appealed to our self-interest nor exploited our fears. But he was honest. And his principles of motivation provide steady and sure impetus for us as we waver in our commitment to holy living.

"Be holy yourselves in all your conduct." It is no optional extra that Peter gave us. It is the direct consequence of grace. We must take it seriously, whether we consider ourselves the "religious type" or not.

But that should not depress us. For holy living is a "flaming thing" in Chesterton's phrase. We can discard the gloomy associations that have collected like cobwebs around the word and embrace it like Peter himself did—with a lusty exuberance, with an enthusiasm of free adventure.

Amen.

Priest of the Good Things

When Christ appeared as a high priest of the good things that
have come . . . he entered once for all into the Holy Place.
—Hebrews 9:11–12

S ome think the letter to the Hebrews is the most difficult of all
New Testament books to read. It is a tangle of argument and
obscurity. In the middle of it, though, a phrase leaps out with clarity—a phrase that needs no explanation, only attention. It is a
phrase that you need only to hold up to the sun to see it gather and
reflect light. The phrase is a description of Jesus Christ: "priest of
the good things" (Hebrews 9:11).

It's not hard to find the meaning of "good things." It is a reference to the highest and best of creation. It has to do with the highest and best of which humankind is capable—knowledge, love,
and moral purpose. It has to do with God in his love and redemptive action.

Few people would doubt that humans are capable of good
things. We get distracted and sidetracked. But when we are faced
with decisions, there is a pretty good chance we will make the right
choice. I don't know anyone who would trade a baby for a new
car. I don't know anybody who would exchange a marriage for a
corporate presidency. I don't know people who would consciously
barter seventy years of good health for forty years of gluttony and
self-indulgence. I don't know many individuals who in cold delib-

eration would rather have a Sunday morning all to themselves than a time of clarified relationship with God in worship.

I don't mean that no one is actually making those exchanges. But I don't think most people who are making them do so consciously. The success of the transaction depends on them not bothering to examine it—engaging in some denial that anything of importance is being traded and not thinking about it until the terms are set and the exchange is irrevocable.

The "good things" are the things that have to do with creation, with human beings, with God. And it is not hard to agree on what they are. Interestingly, we nearly always refer to the good things in terms of connections—relationships that are set up between them and us. We use words like *enjoyment, praise, forgiveness, love, peace, satisfaction,* and *achievement.* The good things are things that can be shared, that have the capacity for being in relationship. And the deeper the relationship, the more we realize the goodness of the "good things."

When I was a small boy, I and a group of friends used to retreat to a secret "club" cave. One scene is vivid in my mind. About four of us huddled in this cave with a sputtering candle for light. We had a sharp knife, and with solemn ritual each of us in turn cut our fingers and then pressed our blood into one another's incisions. We made some kind of covenant and promise to one another as we did it. From that time on, we were blood brothers. We gave and received blood—the clearest sign of life.

This childish experience illuminates a basic transaction. I have a basic need to share the best that is in me with another person—and to receive the best that is in another into myself. When that happens, I know that I am most alive, most fulfilled, and most in touch not only with the world as it actually is but also with myself as I was created to be.

But there is another experience we routinely participate in that contrasts sharply with the sharing of blood: the exchange of "good things." Frequently I find myself giving others the most unlovely aspects of myself—such as ill-formed opinions, undigested information, and immature emotional responses. I throw these at other people as a substitute for giving myself. And as a result, they are cheated in the human exchange. I have slipped inferior goods to them. Here I am, a being created by God to love, to think, to forgive, to praise and exalt, yet when I am thrust into contact with another, I slip in counterfeit material instead. A pasted-on smile in substitute for honest praise. A cool indifference in substitute for some authentic emotion. A hastily formed prejudice in substitute for a rational exercise of my mental abilities. As it turns out, what I have done is neither given nor received blood. I have treated the other as a mechanical screen on which to project my fears, my dislikes, or my fantasies.

I find other people doing it to me too. Sometimes when someone comes into my study and starts to speak, I feel like saying, "Hey, you're not talking to me. You're talking to someone over my shoulder—someone who is more like your father, your mother, or your rival. Look at me. Deal with the real me. I'm not a blank that you can fill in with whatever you wish. I have content. I have individuality. Look at me, and then talk to the reality that is inside my skin."

We all have a basic resentment and resistance to being treated as something less than human, something other than the unique person that God created and redeemed. We don't like to be treated as a potential sales prospect devoid of taste and culture. We don't like being treated as a worker in isolation from our feelings and aspirations. We don't like being treated as a stand-in for someone else.

It takes neither a poet nor a saint to know that life is full of good things. But by the time they get to us, they may be turned into bad things. They might be scattered into fragments. The problem is not in knowing that good things are there but in getting into some kind of sustained and whole relationship with them. The problem is in establishing the blood relationship between the good things and myself.

Daily, many people invite us to share ourselves and to let them share themselves—to mix blood. The feeling that it isn't happening enough or at all is strong. Yet many individuals are trying to do something about that. One of those persons wrote the letter to the Hebrews.

We have to do a little reading between the lines to reconstruct the situation of the Christians to which this letter was written. But it was something like this: disorganized. Traditions had been disarranged. Life was filled with good things: God, angels, priests, rituals, and memories of the heroes of the faith. But disorganizing elements were in the foreground: persecutions, trials, and some people who had seemed dependable but were traitors to the faith. Compounding that were doubt, fatigue, depression, pride, hate, and listlessness.

And within this whirlpool of material was great confusion. How does one make sense out of one's life in the midst of all this? How do you find the center? How do you coherently establish some kind of living relationship with all the parts that are worth anything?

The answer? You get a priest. A priest is a connector, one who establishes living connections between persons and their meanings. A priest puts things together for a person—things that have to do with the world, with humanity, and with God. A priest acts as a kind of repairer of relationships. Where there have been mangled connections, short circuits, and ill-fitting joints, he tries to get everything to fit and connect again.

Wherever people have lived in any kind of community, they have had priests. It is one of the oldest vocations. Wherever individuals have experienced any kind of relationship, there has been the consequent experience of broken relationship, as well as some attempt at healing the break and restoring the deepest kind of shared life. The priest is the person prominently figuring in all these attempts. One of the most frequently used symbols for getting such relationships established again—restoring the flow of good things—is blood. It represents the innermost aspect of life flowing out and making living contact with our problems, hopes, and desires.

Yet a major difficulty with priests is that they become specialists. One priest will say that a person's major relationship is with God. "You have offended God; I will show you how to get right with him. Offer these sacrifices and do these acts and everything will be fine again." Another priest will say that one's major relationship is with other people. "I will teach you some moral precepts and train you in some ethical behavior. When you learn how to relate to other people, you will be all right."

But I, as a person, have a basic objection to being faced with such alternatives. In either case, half my life is left out. I don't deny that a lot is wrong with my relationship with God, but I want a lot more in my life to be fixed up too. And I don't deny that my relations with other people need some tending to, but there is something ultimate and deeply personal—something about God—that I want addressed too. If I am forced to choose between God and other people, I'm thrown into an impossible situation.

The situation becomes even more impossible as we observe individuals who have made such choices. We see those who are expert in the God relationship. They know a great deal about God, pray much, and engage in a pious life that is supposed to please him. But they aren't much fun to live with. They seem to have a great talent for offending people. And they have a fantastic ability to ignore things that need to be done that are as close as their front doorstep.

We also see those who are expert in human relationships—they seem to care a great deal about others. They engage in many acts of service and helping. They are alert to need and are active in mobilizing aid. But we can't help noticing a certain flatness to their lives too. They have reduced life to functions and needs. They have established relationships, but not much passes through them. The blood has been watered down.

In this impossible place the gospel is declared. And the declaration is that Jesus is the priest of good things. Jesus takes up the ancient job of priesthood—establishing connections, gluing the fragments of existence together so that we are living in touch with everything that matters to us.

But Christ is no specialist. He does not tell us that we first have to deal with God. He does not tell us that we must first deal with other people. He tells us that basically we have to deal with him: God-man. He pulls together in his own existence the highest and the lowest, the divine and the human, the heavenly and the earthly. When he becomes priest, nothing is distorted, unbalanced, or eliminated. Everything that is essential to the related life is restored and healed.

The Hayden Planetarium in New York used to have a sign that directed people to the SOLAR SYSTEM AND REST ROOMS up the staircase.* That is the kind of direction Jesus's priesthood offers. He is the center for everything that seems most ordinary, everyday and unexceptional, along with everything that seems remote, exalted, aspiring, and ideal. The sign to both is upward—to Christ.

The letter to the Hebrews is an elaborate demonstration that Christ does connect everything in living relationship. The letter presents an intricate argument that carefully puts everything that had been disorganized in the community's lives together again. Jesus Christ is priest of the good things. He mixes his blood with ours. The blood that poured from his body at the Crucifixion becomes, by faith, the living exchange that puts us into relationship with all good things.

There is an immediate extension of this truth: Christ lives in the Christian. Paul's phrase is "Christ in you." Christ's priesthood is reproduced in the person who confesses his lordship. The great Reformation exposition of this came under the phrase "the priesthood of all believers." This never meant "everyone his own priest" but "everyone a priest to every other one."

How long has it been since you have looked at another person

---

* Richard Nilsen, "Properly Viewed, Everything Is Skewed," *Richard Nilsen* (blog), March 19, 2014, https://richardnilsen.com/tag/hayden-planetarium.

as your priest—one in whom Christ lives? Your assessment of the quality of another's Christian life has little to do with her capacity for priesthood. God does not wait for perfection before he begins to work in us. And if God is not waiting for perfection, you had better not wait for it either. You must let the other person be your priest because God has chosen her for your priest. Your personal criticism of her effectiveness has little to do with the matter. Your likes or dislikes in the matter have little weight. This is the way that Christ has chosen to share his priesthood—through the persons who confess his name. Only by accepting these priestly acts can you be put together again in the complex of relationships that mix the life of God and the life of humankind in a new unity.

I am not, you will note, urging you to be priests to other people—although that is worth urging and is certainly part of the gospel. I am trying to clarify the other side of that: You must let others be Christ's priests to you. You must receive their ministries. You must let them give you what Christ has given them to give you.

You must not slip into the arrogance of saying, "I accept Christ as my priest of good things, but I won't accept anything from his messengers. They don't talk my language. They don't understand me. They have the wrong color skin or the wrong style of hair."

We are (and this is a diagnosis of our spiritual condition rooted in the letter to the Hebrews) overcommitted to activism in helping, in evangelizing, and in healing. We need to nurture a deeper ability to receive, to accept, to be healed, to be cheered, and to be blessed. Relationship is always mutual. Sharing is always reciprocal. Christ stands at the center of all relationships to give you his life and receive your life—he is priest of the good things. And he stands in every Christian to give you a chance to particularize and experience in your own terms this mighty priestly act. It is all down on your level, being worked out among the people you know. There is no escaping it. No avoiding it. There is only refusing it. Or accepting it.

Amen.

Transfigured

✳

After six days Jesus took with him Peter and James and John . . . and he was transfigured before them, and his garments became glistening.

—Mark 9:2–3

What is the Christian life for you?

Is it mostly hard, disciplined responsibility, doing what you're "supposed" to do? Or is it a kind of carefree freedom, celebrating love and life? Do you fall on one side or on the other? If you do, you've fallen off the road. Because both of those—the legalistic and the libertine—are ditches. Neither one is the Christian way. Yet it is easy to fall into one of them or the other. And sometimes both, in quick succession.

It's easy to say, "Well, God has given me the commandments; he's given all these things he wants me to do, and I've *got* to *do* them. I want to be a good person." And so you get up in the morning, resolving to do what God wants and obey his will. It's hard work.

Or you can do precisely the opposite. You can say, "Well, *God* has done everything there is to do. He runs the universe; he's saved me from my sins; I can be carefree! I don't have to do anything because he does it all." And in this boundless freedom you can trip your way quite irresponsibly through life, putting all the blame on God when things go wrong and giving him all the glory when things go right.

Both of those ways have their appeal. Sometimes we feel responsible. We feel like we really do need to contribute something to this life, and we fill ourselves with resolve. At the same time, we know that there is a lot more to life than that. There's simply the vitality of being a person, and we get impatient with all that other stuff and say, "I'm just going to be a butterfly, enjoy beauty, live, and love."

These dynamics of the Christian life can also be seen in the Christian church as a whole. As we gaze down two thousand years of history, we observe that Christians have weaved through moral responsibility a bit like a drunk driver swerving down the road: first careening into *this* ditch, then going back into *that* ditch, and then going into *that* one, with brief periods of straddling the middle line, but then not being able to stay in any lane or even on the pavement for long and driving right back off the road. The predictable results are dented fenders, blown-out tires, and once in a while having to call someone to help pull us out and repair us and get us going again. And I'm afraid that often our individual lives are a little bit that way too—going from ditch to ditch.

Growth in Christ largely consists of getting in the middle of the road and staying there—balancing between responsibility and freedom, between understanding that God *has* done it all but that our work is to do it too. Life as a Christian means to cease the swerve, to stay out of those ditches that tempt religious and spiritual people. It means moving down a highway that's bounded by those two things but that doesn't dump us into them.

Let us go back to the wider context of our Scripture lesson from St. Mark. Jesus was with his disciples. They were walking down the road to Caesarea Philippi, and he said to them, "Who do men say that I am?" (Mark 8:27). He had been with them for probably a couple of years at this point, teaching, healing, acting out his ministry. They'd had a lot of discussions. They had watched him do many things—even prophetic ones. They answered, in my paraphrase, "Some people say you are Elijah. Some people say you are John the Baptist." The disciples began telling Jesus what the polls were saying about him, but Jesus didn't want to hear that. So, he asked, "Who do you say that I am?" And Peter remarkably (because Peter didn't seem all that bright sometimes) spoke the truth: "You are the Christ, the Son of the living God" (Matthew 16:16).

That's it. Peter saw what Jesus was doing. He finally plowed through all the camouflage that people had put around the identity of their Messiah. He saw through it to understand Jesus for what he really is: *Christ*. This is God's anointed. This is God in their midst. That confession—that discovery—is at the center of the Christian life. When we see that, we're home. We've found what God wants us to know. Our life is centered.

But immediately after Peter made his confession, Jesus kept on teaching them, moving into a difficult subject he'd never taught them before. "The Son of man must suffer many things," he said, "and be rejected by the elders and the chief priests and the scribes, and be killed, and after three days rise again" (Mark 8:31). Remember, that's the first time in the Gospels where he said this. The disciples had never heard that kind of talk before. I don't imagine they even had a category for that last phrase about rising in three days. They were so overwhelmed, so *dismayed*, by this sudden talk about suffering, persecution, and death. That was not for them— and certainly not for the Messiah.

What a disappointment! Here they had identified the Christ, and Jesus had accepted their identification. Here was God with them in power to do something great, and suddenly he started talking about this way of suffering? Peter—understandably and patiently—remonstrated. "No, you can't do that," he essentially said. "That's not the way to do it." And Jesus, very *impatient,* whirled on him: "Get behind me, Satan!" (Mark 8:33). And so, we are left with the hard fact that Peter, the one who was the first to recognize that Jesus was the Christ, also became the first to misunderstand what "Christ" means.

After the brief altercation, Jesus patiently went back to where he started, talking about the way of suffering, the way of denial.

"If any man would come after me," he said, "let him deny himself and take up his cross and follow me. For whoever would save his life will lose it" (verses 34–35). He elaborated on those images. He talked about the necessity for the hard way of the Cross.

Geographically, they were way up in the north; Jerusalem was in the south. Shortly, they would start the trek down and quite directly go to Jerusalem where, in fact, there would be a crucifixion. They needed to know how to be disciples. They needed to know how to take responsibility. They needed to learn how to do the hard things that came with being a follower of Jesus Christ. It was a difficult way—not quite what they bargained for—and so before they started out on the trip, Jesus took three of them up to a high mountain.

That mountain was probably Hermon, a nine-thousand-foot peak in the lower Lebanese range, usually snow-covered even in summer. He took Peter, James, and John along as witnesses, six days after Peter's confession. We can assume that for six days Jesus had been talking to them about denial and discipleship, about taking up their cross. Then he arrived with his chosen three on the slopes of the high mountain. After six days, the seventh is the Sabbath—you work six days, and you rest just as God did. The Sabbath is a day of joy, of contemplating God's work, of surveying the past and rejoicing in it, of worshipping God, of enjoying his presence.

The high mountain in the north might have brought to the disciples' minds expectations of something great, because there were stories among the Jews that when the Messiah came, he'd bring in his kingdom on the mountains of the north. And so, despite the discouraging talk about denial and cross bearing that these three had heard for the last six days, as they approached the seventh day and went up the mountain, they might have thought, *Something great could still happen.* And in fact, it did.

As they arrived on the mountain, Jesus was transfigured before them. He was changed. Mark didn't try to tell us what he looked like, although Matthew and Luke did. All Mark said was that Jesus's garments became dazzling white, glistening, far whiter than any bleach could make them. What the disciples saw was an investiture of royalty. Here was God robing Jesus as king. Many psalms in the Old Testament looked forward to this: "The LORD . . . is robed in majesty; the LORD is robed" (Psalm 93:1); "The LORD sits enthroned as king" (Psalm 29:10); "He rules for ever by his power" (Psalm 66:7, NEB).

There were famous psalms that people for years had been assigning to the Messiah:

> I have set my king
>   on Zion, my holy hill. (Psalm 2:6)

> The LORD sends forth from Zion
>   your mighty scepter.
>   Rule in the midst of your foes! (Psalm 110:2)

The three disciples must have recalled those things as they saw the supernatural robing of Jesus, his investiture as a king. Now on the high mountain, they saw this one that they had identified as the Christ being robed by God as the ruler of the world. They saw Elijah and Moses join him: Moses representing the Law and Elijah representing the prophets—these two great figures from the past who, between them, caught up everything that had gone before.

The kingdom, you see, was being inaugurated in Jesus, but it wasn't starting all over again. It was including everything from the past—all that kingdom talk and experience that had been with the Hebrew people. When God inaugurates his kingdom, he doesn't leave anything out. He doesn't start all over again. He takes all that's been and incorporates it into the new. We don't knock the old thing down and clear the rubble out with a bulldozer. God is conservative. He does not waste anything. While Moses and Elijah were inadequate to rule the kingdom, they were not useless. And now, with Jesus, they became part of the heavenly court.

So, the disciples were in on a witness: God robing Jesus as king.

Peter, our representative responder in all these stories, said, "Master, it is well that we are here; let us make three booths, one for you and one for Moses and one for Elijah" (Mark 9:5).

Now, in the back of Peter's mind was an experience that he was used to participating in: the Feast of Tabernacles. The Jews celebrated this feast every autumn. It was supposed to do two things. First, it recalled to their minds the wilderness wanderings when they lived in tents and how God protected, cared for, and led them. Second, it was a renewal of the covenant; that is, at the time of this seven-day feast, they re-read the Law and re-committed themselves to it. It was also a harvest feast, something like our Thanksgiving.

Through the years, the feast grew, developed, and took on trappings; and by a hundred years before the time of Jesus, it had become the feast of cosmic expectation. The Jews believed that in the last days this would be the final feast when God would gather everything together, and as his people put their booths together to dwell in, he would then come and dwell with them. There would be a new temple, a new dwelling, a new tabernacle. So, Peter was just trying to rush it a little bit and say, "Lord, let's do it. The time has come. You're the Christ. Now I know you're the king. Let's make the booths."

And Jesus completely ignored him.

Peter's mistake was not that bad really. He got the point of what was going on. He saw what Jesus was doing and what was being done to Jesus. It wasn't like the remonstrance after his confession when Jesus rebuked him. He knew what was happening, but he made an inappropriate response—maybe because he was incapable of making any other kind of response at the time.

But then a cloud enveloped Jesus, Moses, and Elijah. We're to imagine a light-filled, dazzling cloud like the one in the wilderness that represented the presence of God and led the people. Maybe you've heard the Hebrew word *shekinah*—the Jews talked about the *shekinah* of God, the glory of God that was manifested in visible light, enveloping his people. And that's what happened on the mountain. Instead of the flimsy little tabernacles that Peter wanted to build out of twigs and leaves, the presence of God came down and enveloped the three. His answer to Peter was something like "I know you would like to build tabernacles for these people to dwell in, but you can't make them. Nothing you could construct would be adequate. I'll build my own." And in this way, on the slopes of Hermon, Jesus became the visible presence of God, tabernacling among the people.

St. John had the same idea. When he began his gospel, he said, "The Word became flesh and dwelt [using the same word—'tabernacled'] among us" (1:14). Jesus set up his dwelling right here. And then at the end of the book of Revelation, he uses the same word in describing the temple of God descending from heaven and tabernacling on earth, when a voice from heaven declared, "The dwelling [tabernacle] of God is with men" (21:3). The point of that imagery is put together in the story of the Transfiguration. What it took John a long discourse to recount is here brought together in a picture so that we can see it all at once: God is present. His dwelling is with humankind in power and glory.

The disciples needed to know that. We need to know that. And then at Jesus's transfiguration, a voice came from heaven, saying, "This is my beloved Son; listen to him" (Mark 9:7). It's the same word that was heard at our Lord's baptism—God identifying Jesus as his own. But this time, he added to it the command "Listen to him," which must refer to the teaching the disciples had heard on the way about cross bearing, denial, and suffering. "Take him seriously. What he is saying is really true. You can't get away from that." And then, immediately, the thing was over, and they saw only Jesus. And they descended the mountain.

Two things are important for us to know about this story. First, we can't restrict talk about the Christian life simply to the area of denial and cross bearing and suffering, being responsible people. There must be a participation in this glorious, celebrating, happy, ruling God. There must be some initiation into an area where we don't do anything and God does everything. Peter and the disciples were prevented from doing anything on the mountain. God was doing it all.

We *must* learn to know that, because left to ourselves, we can take the Christian life much too seriously. We can grind it down into simple, grim responsibility, and it can't be that. At the same time, Jesus didn't let them stay on the mountain very long. We don't know how long that took, but presumably it didn't take more than a day. And then they went down and were back on the road to Jerusalem.

The rhythm of that Caesarean road and Jerusalem road with the Mount of Transfiguration in between has to be maintained in the Christian life, and I can tell you how to do that. You simply come here every week and worship God with all your heart and soul and mind and strength. And you let God speak to you and show you what he is doing, how he is ruling, how he loves you, how he cares for you. Once a week in your lives, you don't do anything. On Monday you start doing something again, but on Sunday you don't.

The ideal church, as far as I'm concerned (which is rooted in my understanding of Scripture), would be one where *nobody* came near the church for six days and *everybody* came on Sunday. The best kind of church would be one with no committees or organizations—nothing happening here between Sundays. Not because we have nothing to do but because we have everything to do. During the week we're out carrying crosses, denying ourselves, following Jesus, making our witness, helping our neighbors, serving God, working responsibly and as hard as we can to be the people of God in the serving and suffering the way he's called us to do it. We work. We do.

But then, on the "seventh day" (the first day for Christians), we come here and leave all that behind. And we enjoy everything that God is doing. We become carefree. *Free.* We become children again. We let God do it all, and you sing and adore and become aware of his presence.

Some churches try to perpetuate that, saying, "Lord, let us build three booths. Let's have a service tomorrow night too. This is so good, the singing's so great, and the preacher's so wonderful; let's come back and do it again. Let's come back on Monday and on Tuesday." And pretty soon you're neglecting your family and neighbors and the strangers on your street. And that doesn't work any more than Peter's tabernacles would have. There has to be the rhythm. We must go down the middle of the road.

We can't fall into either ditch: the *denial* ditch or the *celebrating* ditch. We must stay on the road, and the way to do that is to keep rhythm. It is to move *intentionally* between work and worship, between witness and adoration, between coming together as the people of God and letting God be all the fullness of himself for you and going out and serving him with all the fullness of your soul, heart, mind, and strength that you can offer.

St. Paul did a great job of responding to these verses by saying, "Do not be conformed to this world but be transformed [transfigured] by the renewal of your mind, that you may prove what is the will of God, what is good and acceptable and perfect" (Romans 12:2). We have the same word here as we have about Jesus being transfigured. And, in 2 Corinthians he said, "We all, with unveiled face, beholding the glory of the Lord, are being changed [here is the same word again, 'transfigured'] into his likeness from one degree of glory to another; for this comes from the Lord who is the Spirit" (3:18).

We are called to do that right here. It is simple—we contemplate our Lord in worship; we are changed from one degree of glory to another.

The repetition of that through faithful worship equips us to do the kind of work, between Sundays, that God wants us to do and releases us to come here and enjoy who God is and sing his praises in great joy.

Amen.

EASTER

Raised

If then you have been raised with Christ, seek the things that
are above, where Christ is, seated at the right hand of God.

—Colossians 3:1

We stand in one corner of a resurrection triangle. The first
corner is the resurrection of Jesus Christ that took place
two thousand years ago. John 20 tells the story. Another corner of
the triangle tells the story of the general resurrection of the dead in
the future; the promise of that is in Revelation 20. The third corner
is the resurrection that takes place now—in you. The announcement of that is everywhere in the Bible but focused at this moment
in Colossians 3:1: "You have been raised with Christ."

Resurrection is a fact of the past. The God who made Adam
out of dust raised Jesus from the dead. On the first Easter morning,
there was an empty tomb. There were bewildered and disappointed
and weeping women. There were clear-sighted and quick-thinking
apostles who put two and two together to get four—and this four
was *resurrection*.

The risen Christ appeared to numerous persons. The reality of
his presence was subjected to strenuous testing—it was doubted,
examined, and accepted. The evidence has satisfied sane, rational,
mature people for centuries. The verdict has held up in courts of
appeal before juries in every generation. Resurrection is what God
did in Jesus in a suburb of Jerusalem around the year A.D. 33.

Also, resurrection is what will take place in the future when there will be a general resurrection from the dead. This is not a historical fact of the past but a reasonable hope about the future. We cannot assemble evidence for the future resurrection like we can for Christ's resurrection—it is a belief based on what has been promised and supported by what otherwise appears reasonable. It is true that in the modern age people do not spend a great deal of time thinking about or preparing for the future; they are much more interested in the here and now. Belief in a future resurrection has been secularized into science fiction or psychic research. The Christian belief is not in fashion at the present. But then, Christian beliefs are often out of fashion. We don't take a vote every year on what beliefs are in vogue and modify our creed accordingly. The belief in a general resurrection from the dead in the future retains its place in our creed. For thoughtful Christians, it is as essential as ever in providing a complete account of our relation with God.

The third resurrection is a reality in the present. It is what takes place now. This is the corner of the resurrection triangle on which I want to concentrate. I don't want you to be unaware of the other two corners, but I want to put the spotlight on this one—for in some ways it is the most overlooked and unstudied part. We stand between two great resurrections: the resurrection of Christ that gets popular attention on Easter and the general resurrection of the dead that throws the significance of our lives on the vast screen of eternity. The third resurrection is not as dramatic, but it is just as important. It is the resurrection that involves you, requiring your assent and participation.

Paul is the authority on this aspect of the resurrection triangle. The gospel of John is the convincing evidence for the first resurrection, the revelation of John is the great monument to the final resurrection, and the letters of Paul are the insistent witness to the present resurrection. John 20 and Revelation 20 are great mountain ranges—Colossians 3 is between them like a valley. If it isn't quite as breathtaking, it is at least practical: a place to walk and do things and act and speak in everyday ways.

"If then you have been raised with Christ" is the phrase that gets our attention. It is not actually a conditional, raising doubts about his readers being raised with Christ, for Paul made it clear earlier that they have in fact been so raised: "You were buried with him in baptism, in which you were also raised with him through faith in the working of God, who raised him from the dead" (2:12). Have you believed in Christ and accepted his lordship? And have you made a public confession of that in baptism? All right then, you are raised. The resurrection has taken place in you. Paul knew all about the resurrection in Christ; no one knew that story better. He had it in his head, his heart, and his bones. He thought it, meditated it, pondered every detail for meaning, weighed the words, and tested the actions. Paul had immersed himself in that resurrection life so much that he could say things like, "I have been crucified with Christ; it is no longer I who live, but Christ who lives in me." (Galatians 2:20). There was no detail that he had slighted or missed. He had examined it, mulled it over, and prayed it through.

And from years of doing that, he was convinced that every detail in Jesus's life was livable in the Christian's. The first step in that living was resurrection. Always resurrection. Everywhere resurrection. "Raised with Christ." Resurrection is not only what happened to Jesus and not only what will happen in the future after death. Resurrection happens now. The empty tomb is not only a historical fact of the first century, but it is also a personal experience in this one.

The important phrase here is *raised with*. Another way to translate it is "co-raised." What happened to Christ happens to us. Being a Christian means being raised from the dead. We don't have to wait until we die to experience resurrection. Paul refused to leave the resurrection as an inert fact of the past or to be content with it as a promise for the future. He was not a meticulous historian proving Christ's resurrection, nor was he a cheerleader whipping up enthusiasm for a coming resurrection. He was involved in a present resurrection. He insisted on participation. In his writings, he had a great fondness for prefixing words that involved key items in the Christian life with *co-* or the preposition *with*. In the King James Version, these are translated as "fellow," so we have fellow citizens (Ephesians 2:19), fellow heirs (Ephesians 3:6), fellow helper (2 Corinthians 8:23), fellow laborers (Philippians 4:3), fellow prisoner (Philemon 1:23), fellow servant (Colossians 1:7), fellow soldier (Philemon 1:2), fellow workers (Colossians 4:11). And in this case, fellow of the resurrection, raised with, co-raised.

Everything that took place in Jesus can take place in me.

Paul's entire ministry was an exploration of the ways in which that takes place and a commitment to include others in the exploration. He was a stubbornly practical person. As a little boy he was probably always taking clocks apart to find out how they worked and always tearing down motors to find what made them run. As an adult he ransacked Christ's life to find out how it worked, and having found out, he spent his days going from city to city, from church to church, showing that the Christian faith was something to be lived now. Resurrection was not what you remembered; it was not what you hoped for; it was what you lived—"raised with Christ."

Paul had an absolute genius for making persons realize that the present moment was God's moment. He was one of those important individuals who can make us forget the past, be oblivious to the future, and concentrate on the present—to be alive in the present, to be filled with Christ's life in the present, to experience the present deeply.

Much of what Christians do between Easters is to follow Paul in his explorations of the resurrection life. There are things to seek, to think, to do, and to not do; there are relationships to develop. Paul is an excellent guide and teacher. Very often, in this place of worship through the year, we benefit from his teaching. And you yourselves, between Sundays, study his writings and are trained in the details of living as persons raised with Christ.

Those who live this way find that resurrection is not the kind of thing that removes us from "the tears and sweat and dirt of our humanity" into some paradise "where the gritty quality of our

ordinary daily life is left far behind and can be forgotten."* We
would like that. Sometimes we think that is what happens to other
people, but it doesn't. When people describe it that way, they are
not telling the truth. When people talk as if being raised with
Christ removed them from doubt, pain, difficult responsibilities,
and trying relationships, they are only fantasizing out loud. Paul
never did that.

When he wrote about being raised with Christ, he was talking
about a miracle, but the miracle is not that we are delivered from

the unevenness and turmoil and fragmentariness of being
human. The miracle is to be found precisely within the ordinary round and daily routine of our lives. Resurrection occurs to us as we are, and its coming is generally quiet and
unobtrusive and we may hardly be aware of its creative
power. It is often only later that we realize that in some way
or other we have been raised to newness of life, and so have
heard the voice of the Eternal Word.†

Resurrection is a celebration. We come to this service in a cel-
ebratory air. We fill our ears with the sounds of victorious music
and our senses with the sight and smell of lilies. Ordinarily, the
creation has the good sense to join in—birds sing, the sun shines,
snows melt, and the rain takes a vacation. Christ has risen!

Resurrection is also anticipation. We remember those who have
died—people whom we loved, who were important to us. It is a
tradition in many families to visit the graves of the dead on Easter.
We recollect our hope for a heavenly reunion; we savor a future
blessing. And nature encourages us: A cold, desolate ground produces a crocus. Trees stripped of life are, overnight it seems, full of
buds.

And resurrection is an act of commitment. We worship today
because of a resurrection today: raised *with* Christ. Resurrection is

* H. A. Williams, *True Resurrection* (New York: Holt, Rinehart and Winston, 1972), 10.
† Williams, *True Resurrection*, 10.

an act in which you participate. It is something you can experience. It is an event in which you are a partner. We meet here every week in worship not just because Jesus was raised but because we are raised with him. If it were only Christ's resurrection that concerned us, we would not have a church but a historical society and a lecture hall. If it were only the future resurrection that concerned us, we would not have a church but a cemetery, perhaps with a psychic research center on the side. But because we are involved in a present resurrection, we have a church so that we can participate in praise, believe together, and encourage one another in living resurrection words and actions.

Christ was raised from the dead. There will be a general resurrection of the dead. You are raised with Christ.

That is what I set before you today to believe and live. If someone asks you on Wednesday what happened in church today, I hope that the first thing off your lips will not be the history or the doctrine of the Resurrection but the way in which belief in God through Christ as your personal lord and savior has made all things new.

"Epictetus [a Greek philosopher] said with a certain vivid crudity that sheep do not vomit up the grass to show the shepherd how much they have eaten. They turn it into wool and milk."*

That is the aim of Easter preaching—not to put ideas into your head that you can parrot to someone else but to start a faith in your heart that makes all things new for you in Christ. The Resurrection is not so much something to be explained or proved but a great fact to be used. When we receive Christ that way into our lives, "we shall no longer have to ask where and when this happens, for we shall have first-hand experience of it as we live as ordinary folk in the ordinary world."†

Do you know the name Brendan Behan? He was an Irish writer in the mid-1900s. As a teenager he was recruited into the IRA,

* William Barclay, *William Barclay: A Spiritual Autobiography* (Grand Rapids, Mich.: Eerdmans, 1977), 42.
† Williams, *True Resurrection*, 13.

caught by the British police with explosives in his luggage, and put into a borstal (a prison for youth). With his career as a political fighter stopped, he became an author and wrote *Borstal Boy*—a great story of his adolescent imprisonment that became a bestseller on both sides of the Atlantic. In an interview a few years before his death, he made a comment that I don't think I will ever forget: "I don't know what life is . . . I'm a very confused man. But I'm all for resurrection. There should be resurrection every week for the dead."*

There is resurrection every week for the dead.

Amen.

---

* Arthur Gelb, "Brendan Behan's Sober Side," *New York Times,* September 18, 1960, in *Brendan Behan: Interviews and Recollections,* vol. 2, ed. E. H. Mikhail (London: Macmillan, 1982), 161.

Raised to Life with Christ

Were you not raised to life with Christ? Then aspire to the realm above, where Christ is, seated at the right hand of God, and let your thoughts dwell on that higher realm.

—Colossians 3:1–2, NEB

The text in St. Paul's letter to the Colossians begins with a rhetorical question: "Were you not raised to life with Christ?" (3:1). It assumes a "yes" answer, of course. No question about it. The Resurrection is the root of all Christian existence. Nothing else shares this foundation. Resurrection is at the bottom of everything.

Other words and concepts try from time to time to elbow themselves into the center—things like "Love your neighbor." That sounds foundational. If everybody did it, the world would be great. But love is terribly hard to understand and even harder to get good at. Not a bad ideal, but not much good as a basis for a new life. It is better as a goal than as a foundation. Another favorite is "In the beginning God created the heavens and the earth" (Genesis 1:1). That sounds fundamental. When you push things back to their origins, you find God. When you can't understand something, you reach for the concept of God to plug the gaps. But as a basis for actual living, it seems remote. It is a fine theological truth and a wonderful framework in which to think through ultimate relationships. But I am a philosopher only occasionally and rarely stay awake nights bothered about the vast gaps in my knowledge. The truth "God created" is more like a framework.

The root word for the Christian has to be *resurrection*. God acted in a clearly defined, historically verified, personal way to bring life out of death, salvation out of crucifixion, triumph out of tragedy. Resurrection is God's characteristic action. It is the word that describes the center of God's relationship with humankind. It is the point at which humans share the action of God most personally, most dynamically.

The resurrection of Christ is far more than the addition of a new doctrine concerning the future to the doctrines held in the past. "It was an act that summed up God's purpose in history, conquered sin and death, wrought a new principle of life for this world no less than for the next, and vindicated the righteousness of the God of the Bible." When people believe in the resurrection of Christ, they embrace "not just a new idea about immortality but a belief in . . . the salvation" that God accomplished for humankind. Resurrection is the means of our release from sin and death into life unto God "both in this age and in the age to come."[*]

But when you have said that, what more is there to say? When you have stretched your hyperboles and plundered all the poets, what more is there to be done?

A group of pastors were talking about the difficulties of preaching on Easter Day. We agreed that it is on the order of standing at the rim of the Grand Canyon and saying something like "Isn't that pretty?" or "Oh boy!" One pastor's wife analyzed his Easter preaching by saying that he did the same thing he did on all the other Sundays of the year except that he talked a little louder.

There is something to do besides talking a little louder. Paul did it. And I am going to try to imitate him. He assumed that the people to whom he wrote knew that Jesus's resurrection had taken place. I am making the same assumption about you. He then pro-

* Michael Ramsey, *The Resurrection of Christ: A Study of the Event and Its Meaning for the Christian Faith* (London: Collins, 1961), 24.

ceeded to say, "Were you not raised to life with Christ?" Clearly, he was trying to get them to see the Resurrection as a present factor in their lives. He wanted them to grasp the fact that resurrection is the way in which God has chosen to work in life today, not just the way he operated in Jesus.

The Resurrection is not just a showcase of the power of God. It is the invasion of the life of God into every person's life. The task of the Easter proclamation is to make the truth of resurrection in us as clear and as prominent as it is in Christ.

I am not going to dwell on the first Easter morning or describe the resurrection appearances or try to convince you of the validity of the Resurrection. It is the present reality of the Resurrection that needs proclaiming and acknowledging. The first stage in this process is simply recognition, being able to see the resurrection of Christ as a present reality. The task of the gospel is to proclaim not only what God has done but also what he is doing. This requires the kind of insight that sees God working in human lives—a working that is hidden to all but the eyes of faith.

Paul said in this passage, "Your life is hid with Christ in God" (Colossians 3:3). This resurrection life is not the kind of thing you find described in special reports in *Time* magazine. It is not the kind of thing that becomes current knowledge in your neighborhood through the grapevine of gossip. It is "hid with Christ." To see it, you have to see, by faith, God working in your life.

One of my favorite mystery novel detectives is Hercule Poirot, the fussy Belgian sleuth created by Agatha Christie. A typical mystery in which he is featured is filled with masses of obscure detail. Many characters are introduced, almost any one of which could have committed the crime. Ordinarily the readers know everything there is to know, but they usually can't make much sense of it. All the evidence is there, but it is hidden, obscure, unseen. In the last few pages, Hercule Poirot gets everyone together in a large room in an old country house and locks the doors. He then begins to describe the events surrounding the crime. He talks of each person as he has come to understand them. And he reveals the identity of the murderer to the surprise of everyone.

Christians are engaged in an activity very similar to that of Hercule Poirot. They are immersed in a scene where a great, ultimate event has taken place. It is not a murder but a resurrection. The circumstances are not understood, the identity of all the people is not clear, and relationships are obscured. Christian witness is an exposition of the hiddenness of the Resurrection, a declaration of where it took place and how it affects my life. It exposes who has been an accomplice (wittingly or unwittingly), who has been a protagonist, and who has been an antagonist. Resurrection is the event that holds the plot of every person's life together. But we are ordinarily ignorant of it—we need it explained, and we need to see just how it touches our existence.

If I were smart enough and knew each of you well enough, I could turn this room into the last chapter of an Agatha Christie novel and give a detailed exposition of the event of the Resurrection, showing how each person here is related to it. I could act as a "resurrection detective." The one thing I am quite sure of is that the Resurrection is the most important thing that has happened in your life. I am not quite so sure that each of you knows that or exactly in what ways it is central to you. I would love to be a resurrection detective and use my insight and knowledge in a personal way with each of you. But I am not smart enough, and I don't know enough. However, that doesn't mean that it can't be done. All it means is that I can't do it. If you become active participants in this sermon—if you search out your own heart and feelings and history, let me direct you to the word of God as it has been given to us in Scripture, and then trust the presence of God whom we know is active today—then some recognition will take place. "Were you not raised to life with Christ?" Gerard Manley Hopkins expresses the sudden recognition of those who see the Resurrection as something done in them:

In a flash, at a trumpet crash,
I am all at once what Christ is*

Recognition leads to an obedient and glad participation. Paul
made the transition by saying "therefore." He had said it earlier:
"As therefore you received Christ Jesus the Lord, so live in him"
(Colossians 2:6). Now he says it again: "Put to death therefore
what is earthly in you" (3:5). "Therefore" was one of Paul's favorite words. It is the glue that keeps doctrine and experience together.

Samuel Chadwick, a renowned Methodist preacher in the early
twentieth century, recounted the story of a converted burglar who
attended his church. When the ex-burglar mentioned that he was
going through Romans in his private Bible study, "Chadwick suggested that he must find some parts of the apostolic argument
rather difficult. 'Yes,' said the other, 'it is difficult; but I stumble on
till I come to a "therefore," and then I get a blessing!' "†

The two polar events recorded in Scripture are creation and
resurrection. The making of the world in creation and the redemption of the world in resurrection are the boundaries of human history. Everything else falls in between. Much of it is not pleasant.
There is suffering, confusion, depression, unhappiness, bitterness,
and death. This is all the material that the "therefore" seeks to
make connection with. Every detail of existence that we experience as being without meaning, without purpose, without love, or
out of touch with God—all of that is brought into connection with
the Resurrection by Paul's "therefore."

Paul was an inveterate list maker. He made three lists in this
passage to the Colossians, marking things that need to be put to-

---

* Gerard Manley Hopkins, "That Nature Is a Heraclitean Fire and of the Comfort of the
Resurrection," in *Poems and Prose of Gerard Manley Hopkins*, ed. W. H. Gardner
(Harmondsworth, Middlesex, U.K.: Penguin, 1953), 66.

† E. K. Simpson and F. F. Bruce, *Commentary on the Epistles to the Ephesians and Colossians* (Grand Rapids, Mich.: Eerdmans, 1957), 264.

gether by the Resurrection. He moved through the fields of destroyed hopes and burned-out lives and listed the casualties. And then he related them to the Resurrection with his great "therefore."

His first list itemized five actions: immorality, impurity, passion, evil desire, and covetousness. The second list cataloged five feelings: anger, wrath, malice, slander, and foul talk. The third list set down five relationships: Greek and Jew, circumcised and uncircumcised, barbarian and Scythian, slave and free, and Christ (3:5, 8, 11). Paul was a stickler for details, a great man for inventories. These lists reveal his sharp observation of the items of life that need to be put together again by the Resurrection: items of action, of feeling, and of relationships.

Why don't you make your own lists? You see what Paul was doing; do it for yourself. Examine the disasters of life, the failures, the disappointments, the areas where you think there is nothing to do, and the situations that seem hopeless. Then place them in the context of the Resurrection where "Christ is all, and in all" (verse 11).

Sometimes in our house the children get involved in helping to serve meals. In the kitchen, everything is placed on a plate for a well-rounded meal: balanced proportion of protein and carbohydrate. Vitamins and nutrients are carefully accounted for. It is not only good; it looks good. The arrangement of food is pleasing to the sight. But somewhere between the serving table and the dining room, something happens. The plate slips from the child's grasp and smashes on the floor. Now it is a mixture of broken china, mashed potatoes, and peas spinning off into orbit. It is a bad scene, very unappetizing to look at and impossible to eat, except for the dog, who goes at it with gusto. He discovers a feast.

That is a picture of life when it breaks away from a relationship with God. Everything that was put together in right proportion and beautiful creation is suddenly scrambled, disarrayed, unattractive, base. There seems to be no putting it together again. Some wallow in it, of course, but there is something subhuman in their response. For those who had a good look at it before the disaster, there can be no enjoyment of such a state of affairs.

It is to this kind of disaster that the Resurrection is the great event. We have found no good way to restore the wrecked meal in our home, but the gospel declares that the Resurrection takes all the items of your life, of the world's life, and carefully, lovingly, and powerfully puts them back together again so that they are attractive and beautiful. As Paul described, the Resurrection is at work in your life when you "have put on the new nature, which is being constantly renewed in the image of its Creator and brought to know God" (verse 10, NEB). The Resurrection puts life together again, in God's way, in you.

Amen.

Not of Perishable Seed

You have been born anew, not of perishable seed but of imperishable, through the living and abiding word of God.

—1 Peter 1:23

Have you ever played the game of "first causes"? Aristotle played it on a philosophical level. He traced everything observable in the world to a previous cause, back in a cause-effect chain to what he called the "unmoved mover": the first move in the game of life that was itself unmoved by anything. Darwin played it on the biological level. He observed that every form of life derived from a previous form of life and that there seemed to be a progression from lower to higher. He moved back through the forms to the simplest form of all and guessed that some unknown X factor was the first cause that produced minimal life. Freud played the game on a psychological level, tracing the neurosis of the adult back to the fears and guilts and desires of infancy and childhood. On a less sophisticated level, you can find the game played by children trying to fix the blame for a quarrel or fight— "He started it!" or "She hit me first!" The first cause is somehow very important.

The first cause in Aristotle is mechanical; in Darwin it is chemical; and in Freud it is personal. All those views have a great deal of demonstrable truth to them. They all tell us something about the world as we find it. We have all grown up with such formulations of first causes and accept some aspects of them more or less as a matter of course. It is not uncommon to find religious people Christianizing these ideas by making them over with new words, so that Aristotle's mechanical unmoved mover becomes God setting the universe in motion, Darwin's X factor becomes God creating the first life and setting the evolutionary process in motion, and Freud's discovery of the unconscious mind is translated into a God defined by a person's ultimate hopes and desires.

We are so used to such thinking that it is something of a surprise to read Holy Scripture and find none of it there. What we find instead is that the mechanical, chemical, or psychological first cause is the idea of the "word of God."

Uniformly throughout the Old and New Testaments, it is the word of God that gets things started in the first place. It is the first cause.

In Genesis 1:1, we read that "In the beginning God created the heavens and the earth." In verse three, when it launches into a description of the program this involved, we find that creation in every case resulted from the word of God. "And God said . . ." is the formula used to describe it.

In Isaiah, the prophet was commanded to comfort the people of God in extremely adverse conditions (40:1). They were in harsh exile, far from the signs of their faith and persecuted because of their faith. The exile had been in effect for over a generation, maybe two, and all the memory of Israel was fast fading. When Isaiah inquired of God what he should do to comfort this people, what was possible in creating new hope, providing comfort, and instilling faith in such poor conditions, he was told to cry out that while everything else fades and withers (which was obvious to Israel by then anyhow), the "word of our God will stand for ever" (verse 8).

In St. John's gospel, the most philosophical book of the New Testament, the first sentence is "In the beginning was the Word, and the Word was with God" (1:1).

It is not the preacher but Scripture that identifies the word of God with preaching. We cannot deny or deemphasize the identification without doing violence to Scripture. No, it is the very nature of the word of God to identify itself with the sermon.

The word of God in the sermon is a surprising word. It comes through a person whom you know and in words that are familiar to you. All the visible parts are common and earthly, but in the midst of this, God's word is communicated. How it happens is his miracle; that it happens is the common testimony of twenty centuries of church experience. It is not too different from what took place in the Incarnation—that God should choose humanity to reveal his fullness. For this reason, we can never sit back and say that we have heard the word of God for all time; the word of God preached is always a new, surprising, fresh word. And we can never make the word of God a museum piece, something to be looked upon and polished and engraved in gold plate. It is invariably carried in an earthen vessel and so inevitably resists such well-meaning exaltation.

The other way in which Peter described the word of God was with the adjectives "living and abiding." (1 Peter 1:23). While the word of God as it comes to us in preaching has a surprising, ever-new quality and a contemporary ring to it, as the "living and abiding word of God," it also has another side: It is unchangeable, eternal, and uncontaminated by weakness and decadence.

The sacraments are the signs of the living and abiding word of God in the church. Where the sermon is always new, the sacraments are always old. They never change. They are administered today in the same way they have been for twenty centuries. It is always water that is used in baptism, always bread and wine used in the communion. The same formulas are recited in their celebration; there is no innovation. If we could re-appear in a second-century church, we would hear quite a different sermon, but when we witnessed the baptismal service and the communion service, we would feel right at home. Our service of worship reflects each week these two sides of the word of God.

Some parts of the service are fixed and unchanged: certain prayers, the Psalter, the creed, the Lord's Prayer, the order. This weds us to the tradition of the church's life—the life that has been lived constantly and faithfully as a result of the living and abiding word of God. Yet other parts are fresh and new: the prayers of intercession and the hymns. These testify that the word of God is always preached anew; it comes to each new day with fresh power and grace. To slight either one of these is to slight the word of God. It is always the same, yet it is always new.

It is this word of God—the good news preached and the living and abiding word—that is behind our lives as the first cause. This is what got things going for us. "You have been born anew, not of perishable seed but of imperishable, through the living and abiding word of God" (1 Peter 1:23).

If we want to understand ourselves, then, we do not first of all discover the unmoved mover of Aristotle, the life-producing X factor of Darwin, or the psychological unconscious of Freud. If we really want to understand ourselves, we must listen to the word of God. God speaks his word in order to be understood, and to understand, we must listen.

In one of his most famous parables, Jesus spoke of the word of God as being like seed sown in the soil of human hearts, which then (depending on the quality of reception) produced a fruitful life. We find multiple cases of this principle throughout Scripture, but this is enough to make the broad truth clear: The word of God is the first cause of new life, of fruitful living. It is not surprising, then, that when Peter wrote of the first cause behind the new life he shared with the churches, he too designated it as the "word of God."

The adjectives Peter used to describe this word of God and the context in which he used them give us some valuable information to better understand what is at the bottom of the life we live in Christ. And inasmuch as we are so overwhelmed with Aristotelian, Darwinian, and Freudian views of how we live and move and have our being, it is all the more needful that we take a sharp look at this.

Peter explained that the word of God is the "good news which was preached to you" (verse 25). To put that in less theological language, he was saying that the word of God is the sermon. Does that surprise you? It surprises me. It seems like a massive claim to make for the sermons I am familiar with. In fact, it almost sounds like propaganda—an advertising campaign to inflate the value of the sermon by pretentious publicity.

Speaking personally, I would have it be almost anything else than the word of God. To the outsider it might seem like a great thing to be in such close and regular contact with something so exalted, but experience proves otherwise. I would much rather give you a series of lectures on Middle Eastern archaeology. There is so much fascinating information in that field, and I could make it interesting with a set of colored slides. And I would love to share with you the contents of a novel I read last week that superbly probed the dynamics of history upon the individual. It would be a real challenge for me to teach you the developments in contemporary philosophy, a subject in which I was once very much wrapped up. But none of these activities bear any claim of ultimacy or of cruciality. In all of them, it is possible to achieve a degree of competence and excellence that brings a sense of accomplishment or a job well done. But in the sermon, it is the other way. Because it is the word of God, it always has the claim of ultimacy and cruciality.

We need to practice an intense listening to the word of God—the word spoken in scripture, sermon, and sacrament—to find who we are and where we are going. When we hear that word of God, we discover that it is God's word about his work in us, for us, and with us. "His work is not mute; rather, it speaks with a loud voice . . . The Word of God is Gospel, that is, the good word, because it declares God's *good* work."* We hear that at the beginning of our existence God loved us, that in our rebellion and ignorance and confusion God loves us, and that the meaning of the future and eternity is that God will love us. Our lives are shaped

* Karl Barth, *Evangelical Theology: An Introduction* (New York: Holt, Rinehart and Winston, 1963), 19.

and purposed by the love of God. If we ask what that means exactly, we get a plain answer. The word of God is spoken in our language and in our presence by Jesus Christ. The work and words of Jesus Christ are the word of God—not the word of God as a general truth or an abstract idea but the word of God to us, with us, and for us.

One more thing we should consider is the public evidence of this first cause. If Aristotle was right about the first cause being a mechanical unmoved mover, the wisdom would be to resign yourself to the inevitable series of cause-effect relationships that would then work themselves out in a deterministic and mechanical way. You could not do much about any of it; everything that happened would result from something else, back and back. If Darwin was right and the first cause is chemical or biological and proceeds in evolutionary progression, the wisdom of living would be to work strenuously for the highest, give yourself to progress, and sacrifice lower forms of life whenever necessary. The unfortunate side effects of that mindset are that the sick, the handicapped, the ignorant, and the unskilled become drags on the process and need not be treated with dignity. If Freud was right and the first cause is personal experience, then the wisdom of living would demand that you be as well-adjusted as possible. The unfortunate thing about that perspective is that it leaves so much for others to do. If I want to be well-adjusted, I have to avoid all those people and situations that unsettle me, cause me anxiety, and cause me to suffer.

But if Peter was right—if the first cause is the word of God and that word of God is a good word about God's good work on our behalf, namely, that we are loved by God—then that frees us to love. Peter made the application himself, saying, "Love one another earnestly from the heart" (verse 22). This is possible because it proceeds out of the kind of creatures we are. It is the best counsel for living because it fulfills the nature in which we were conceived; it is realistic because it can be obeyed by everyone regardless of status or gifts.

The characteristic human action is not resignation, not ruthless actions, not self-oriented adjustment, but love. There is nothing trite about it. Just as the word of God expresses a love of God that is always old in the sacrament and ever new in the sermon, so our love for one another is always old in its meaning and ever new in its spontaneity and application.

So, "having purified your souls by your obedience to the truth for a sincere love of the brethren, love one another earnestly from the heart. You have been born anew, not of perishable seed but of imperishable, through the living and abiding word of God. . . . That word is the good news which was preached to you" (verses 22–23, 25).

Amen.

Put on the New Nature

You have put off the old nature with its practices and have put on the new nature, which is being renewed in knowledge after the image of its creator.

—Colossians 3:9–10

The perfect introduction to this sermon has already taken place in at least a dozen (probably a lot more) of the families represented here this morning. If we could just get some of you up here to reenact what went on about an hour ago, we would have it. I doubt that any of you are willing to do that, so let me guess at a typical conversation. You can tell me after the service whether I got it right.

The setting: any one of your homes that has children in it. The time: after breakfast. The situation: everyone leaves the breakfast table and goes to their rooms to dress for attending church on Easter Sunday. Maybe twenty minutes elapses. It is time to leave for church. As the family gathers at the front door to leave, the parents do a final check, and this dialogue ensues:

Parent: You are not going to wear that to church!
Child: Why not? What's wrong with it?
Parent: What's wrong with it? No child of mine is going to wear blue jeans to church on Sunday morning.
Child: I'm going to worship God, and I've never read anything

in the Bible about what I'm supposed to wear. God doesn't
care what I wear.

Parent: But I care what you wear. You might be worshipping
God, but you are sitting with me, and regardless of whether
God cares what you wear, I do. Go change your clothes.

Child: All you care about is what the neighbors think. You
just go to church to show off.

Parent: You have a closet full of clothes that I spent good
money on. Now go change.

A few minutes later the entire family gets in the car, minus the
blue jeans, and arrives at church. And now here we are all quite
properly clothed.

It is entirely appropriate that we should be concerned about
clothes on Easter Sunday. It makes good sense to purchase new
hats, dresses, ties, and suits to mark the day. Clothes are expressive. They display to the public what we are inside—or at least
what we would like to be inside. Easter is the day, above all other
days, when we proclaim among ourselves that God is alive in our
midst, that nothing can conquer his way of doing things, that
nothing can shut him up in a grave, that the world is helpless before his joyous love.

When Christ rose from the dead, he created the event that
stands at the center of existence, sending out waves of energy
across history, making the world vibrate with the reality of his
presence. That is something to be supremely happy about. Express
your joy every way you can. And if it means buying cheerful new
clothes, do it.

Well acquainted with the human habit of using clothes not just
to keep warm but to express character and personality, Paul used
the language of dressing and undressing to talk about the Resurrection: "You have put off the old nature with its practices and
have put on the new nature, which is being renewed in knowledge
after the image of its creator" (Colossians 3:9–10).

The words for "put off" and "put on" were the words used in Paul's day for "undress" and "dress."* So there seems to be some biblical basis for an Easter outfit. And since we are a people who give a fair amount of attention to clothes, we are in a good position to understand the Easter gospel that uses the metaphor of putting off and putting on clothing.

By connecting something very common, very everyday, like the wearing of clothes with something extraordinary and unusual like the Resurrection, we are transformed. The common is linked to the eternal, and the eternal is brought down into the everyday.

Some common characteristics that go along with wearing clothes provide suggestions in sharing the Resurrection. One of them is appropriateness. Dress that is appropriate is suited to the world in which we live. You don't wear thermal underwear, a fur-lined parka, and earmuffs in mid-August with both temperature and humidity in the nineties. And you don't wear a swimsuit when you are shoveling the snow off your driveway in January. The nature of the world in which we live makes some difference in what we put on and take off. When we get up in the morning and choose our garments, we pick appropriate things for the temperature of the day, the social setting in which we will move, and the kind of work we will be engaged in. We consider all those realities to make an appropriate choice. People who make inappropriate choices are deficient in either sensitivity or intelligence. We would wonder about the man who was digging a sewer in a tuxedo as much as about the man who went to a dance in mud-spattered overalls.

The objective reality of the world in which we live is resurrection. It is the overwhelming fact about the world we walk into each day: Christ is risen, God is alive, so dress appropriately. The world is dominated by God's truth and good news. So, said Paul, "put them all away: anger, wrath, malice, slander, and foul talk from your mouth. Do not lie to one another" (verses 8–9). These things have mostly to do with the way we talk, what we say. Lies

---

* Christopher Beetham, ed., *The Concise New International Dictionary of New Testament Theology and Exegesis* (Grand Rapids, Mich.: Zondervan Academic, 2021), 291.

and slander, gossip and anger are out of place. There is no reason for being angry with others, for trying to get an advantage through deceit. Why? Because God is for us. He is the great reality in our lives. If people are bad, that is almost incidental—God is good. We cannot shape our lives by the trivial evil that humans do. We must shape our lives by the magnificent good that God does. If the world were in fact evil, then it would be appropriate to learn the skills of deceit, slander, and malice. It would involve survival of the fittest in a world where the evilest person was the most fit. But the Resurrection is the dramatic demonstration that this is not how the world is. It is a world in which Christ is risen, a world where the conspiracies of evil humanity are defeated resoundingly. Appropriate dress in such a world is truth-telling and compassionate speech, cheerful announcements of God's love.

Another characteristic of the way we dress is expressiveness. Appropriateness means that what we wear makes sense in terms of the world we live in. Expressiveness means that what we wear expresses what we are and feel. Many cultural and social limitations dictate how far we can use our dress to give personal expression, but within those limitations there is much we can do. When you drive into the Amish countryside, you see people dressed very differently than we are. Their clothing gives expression to certain deeply held values about the world. At political conventions we may see people wearing hats that have no practical utility but that express personal political convictions. When we feel festive, we usually try to find an article of dress to express that festivity. When we feel solemn or sad, it is not unusual to find a way to express that in our dress.

Our inward reality is produced by the Resurrection. "If then you have been raised with Christ, seek the things that are above, where Christ is," said Paul (verse 1). The Resurrection is something that not only happened in the outer world but also is reproduced in the Christian who responds in faith to God's grace. The inner reality of every person's life is a response to God's love. The gospel response is a "yes" to that love. If that is in fact our inner reality, then we should dress like it, give some expression to this internal personal resurrection.

Paul continued, "Put to death therefore what is earthly in you: fornication, impurity, passion, evil desire, and covetousness, which is idolatry" (verse 5). Everything in that list has to do with intimate relationships between people—or rather the disruption of them. If in fact there is no inner life, no resurrection, there is little capacity for intimacy, for caring, for loving. If we have no life within us, we are quite right to grasp selfishly, to use and take advantage of people in whatever way we can, and to do anything possible to build up our lives at others' expense. But if we "have been raised with Christ," if God has created new life in us, we can dress very differently: "Put on then, as God's chosen ones, holy and beloved, compassion, kindness, lowliness, meekness, and patience, forbearing one another and, if one has a complaint against another, forgiving each other; as the Lord has forgiven you, so you also must forgive. And above all these put on love, which binds everything together in perfect harmony" (verses 12–14).

The Resurrection is an intensely personal experience through which we discover that God created new life in us that can then be shared. Expressive dress is cut along the lines of love, forgiveness, and kindness.

Another characteristic of dressing is that it is repetitive. It is a daily act. Every morning when I get out of bed, I get dressed. And every night when I retire, I undress. I put on clothes, and I put off clothes. The nearly habitual, routine nature of those acts obscures the fact that I am making constant, daily choices. When I put on shoes in the morning, I must choose from my four pairs: brown, black, scuffed cordovan, and canvas sneakers. There is not a lot of choosing to be done there, but I have to use my intelligence and, depending on what color suit I'm wearing and what my activity will be, make the right choice. And having made it on Tuesday, I have to make the decision again on Wednesday—it doesn't stay made.

The Resurrection participates in that everydayness. We do

make a choice for Christ and his resurrection that is basic to the direction of our lives. But that doesn't mean we are exempted from decisions along the way. There are a variety of ways in which the Resurrection can be "worn." It takes an alert, committed person to be decisive about the particular style to put on at the moment. This resurrection life is not static; it is not a garment that one puts on and that's it. Paul said that our new nature "is being renewed in knowledge after the image of its creator" (verse 10). There are developments, expansions, style changes. It is consistently resurrection, but decisions give it expression in the changing situations of the day.

I suggested earlier that this sermon's introduction had been acted out in a number of homes this morning. Imagine acting out the conclusion in a few minutes when you leave the church. What we would need are some magic mirrors out in the narthex. As you left the sanctuary and walked through this corridor of mirrors, they would pick up your image, but instead of reflecting your appearance, they would reflect the resurrection realities they detected in your personality, adding an article of dress for each one.

Men wearing narrow, dark ties might see reflections of broad cascades of sunlit silk on their chests. Women with cautious, demure hats might be surprised to see flamboyant turrets of flowers on their heads. The act of faith in Christ demands expression in a world where God is alive. On the other hand, it is possible that the magic mirrors might reduce the bright, colorful clothes of some here to olive drab. The clothes were a cover-up, claiming a reality that isn't actually there at all.

I am not really interested in what you decided to wear when you came to church this morning or in what you have on right now. I am intensely interested in what you wear as you leave. Like that family we started out with, let's do a last-minute check on what we are wearing. The great fact of the day is the resurrection of Jesus Christ. He lives, and he lives for us. The great decision we are faced with is this: Will we accept his act of love and victorious life as our own? Will we let him live in us? Are you wearing the right garments—the words, actions, values, and goals that express his reality?

There is still time to make the change if you find you have the wrong thing on. You can use this church as your dressing room so that you leave with the right Easter garments. "Put off the old nature with its practices and . . . put on the new nature, which is being renewed in knowledge after the image of its creator."

Amen.

What Is Not for Sale in Church

> Peter said to him, "Your silver perish with you, because you
> thought you could obtain the gift of God with money!"
>
> —Acts 8:20

The sin of Simon Magus—trying to purchase the power of God
so he could use it at his own discretion and benefit—reached
its most dramatic excesses in the late medieval church. Peter's suc-
cessors exchanged the indignation that Peter expressed so forcibly
to Simon Magus for an affable trade relationship with those who
sought after spiritual benefits, and ecclesiastical offices were sold
to the highest bidders.

In Dante's *Inferno*, the eighth circle of hell is filled with simoniacs, the men who engaged in such ecclesiastical mercantilism.
Dante addressed those he saw in the inferno with these words:

> O Simon Magus! O you wretched crew
>   who follow him, pandering for silver and gold
>   the things of God which should be wedded to
>
> love and righteousness! O thieves for hire,
>   now must the trump of judgment sound your doom
>   here in the third fosse of the rim of fire!*

---

* Dante Alighieri, *The Inferno,* trans. John Ciardi (New York: Signet Classics, 1954),
152–53.

Dante saw these men who corrupted the things of God placed in tubelike holes upside down, with their feet sticking out ablaze. The holes were debased equivalents of the baptismal fonts common in the cities of northern Italy. The sinners' confinement in these holes was temporary; as new sinners arrived, the souls dropped through the bottoms and disappeared eternally into the crevices of the rock. As always in Dante, the punishment was symbolic retribution. Just as the simoniacs made a mockery of holy office, so were they turned upside down in a mockery of the baptismal font. Just as they made a mockery of the holy water of baptism, so was their hellish baptism by fire, after which they are wholly immersed in the crevices below.

This buying and selling of church offices later moved into the area of buying and selling the forgiveness of sins, as the church became involved in the practice of indulgences—papers signed by the pope that assured the buyers that all penalty for their own sins or the sins of deceased loved ones had been remitted. The practice reached its worst stage in the sixteenth century when one particularly energetic papal huckster, Johann Tetzel, went through Germany reportedly shouting out his wares in good Madison Avenue rhyme:

As soon as the coin in the coffer rings,
The soul from purgatory springs.*

These are the practices of which Simon Magus was the father—practices that involved the church in treating its spiritual realities as barter. Such people thought, on the one hand, that they could corral God's grace and dispense it and, on the other hand, that there was something they could do (usually paying money to get it).

But our interest is not in bringing medieval sinners to trial

* Dan Graves, "Luther's Ninety-Five Theses Brought Huge Changes in the Church," Christian History Institute, https://christianhistoryinstitute.org/it-happened-today/10/31.

again, pointing daggers at them and exclaiming their horrible crimes. We read the Acts of the Apostles and the subsequent history of the church to familiarize ourselves with how God has worked in his church and how individuals have responded. God has not changed. And we have not changed. We easily see ourselves in the garb of people long dead.

The crassest expressions of simony are no longer around. No one attempts to buy the position of elder or deacon (at least no one has up to this point in this church!), and by and large, the abusive sale of indulgences has been reformed in the Roman Catholic church. Most of the practices that were so scandalous in the Middle Ages are no longer with us. Dante would have to look for other rogues to put into his blazing inferno if he were to write today. But is the sin of Simon Magus obsolete? Has it been eliminated as we have matured and grown? Is it simply a curiosity of church history, as so many diseases are in medical history?

I suspect not. Simon Magus lives today and might be living in us if we are not alert. The sin in which he had the infamous honor of being the first to engage subtly works itself into every society where there is spiritual power and grace from God. And here is how it works.

God is creator; we are creatures. He is beyond our comprehension, our manipulation, our control, and even our powers of definition. When the catechism attempts to answer the question "What is God?" it uses words like *infinite, eternal, unchangeable.** God is infinite, completely beyond all space categories. God is eternal, beyond and different than all our ideas about time. God is unchangeable, not recognizable or explicable in any historical process. God is beyond all this that we are, and we are his creatures. "We are his people, and the sheep of his pasture" (Psalm 100:3).

But somehow, we resist this doctrine of God. We make ingenious attempts to explain, define, and finally use God. Resistance to the idea of God in his freedom and as our creator and lord is

* Westminster Shorter Catechism, 1674, Christian Classics Ethereal Library, www.ccel. org/creeds/westminster-shorter-cat.html.

commonly known as the sin of pride. Its essence is that we modify the idea of God until we are in some sort of working relationship with him, have a share in the control of life, and are in a position to perform some of his acts ourselves. God diminishes; we grow. God decreases; we increase.

Most theologians think that this is the basic sin and the root of every other sin. Adam is the classic picture of it. He began to feel so at home in the garden that it didn't seem at all preposterous to substitute some doubts and a little enlightened reason ("hath God said?") for the command of the Creator and Lord of his life. He began to use the gift of God as if it belonged to him. It involved only a bite of fruit, to be sure, but the eating of that fruit revealed a deep spiritual defection from acknowledging the situation of Creator and creature. The minute that Adam supposed or assumed the gift of the garden to be his own to do with as he liked—that is, the moment he began to treat the garden and its contents as if he were the creator instead of simply a creature—was the moment disaster struck. And he ended up losing the whole thing.

Adam treated the gift of the fruit as something that could be used, traded, and purchased. Simon Magus is only a more recent instance of the same process. And the attempt to buy God's gifts is not beyond the range of possibilities for us. Our memory of the papish abuses of ecclesiastical power and the traffic in indulgences diverts our attention from the spiritual possibilities here for each one of us.

We are used to thinking in terms of privilege and obligation. It works in our everyday lives, and (we reason) it ought to work in eternity as well. If I do something for you, you ought to do something for me. In politics it gets very complex and occasionally unsavory. In business it is often the basic ingredient in public relations. And in church . . . well, if I am faithful, give of my time, am good to my neighbor, and support with my money, then it is not a bit unreasonable to expect some spiritual benefits. We are somewhat like the alumni who give large sums of money to the university's athletic department for scholarships. And if the team doesn't win, the donors feel they have a right to complain, which they often do in loud voices to the coaches.

That is why we may hear a person say that she doesn't go to church because she doesn't get anything out of it. The implication is that she has done her part, presumably by attending or contributing, and the church hasn't reciprocated in kind. There should be a quid pro quo situation, and there hasn't been. Now, I have a good deal of sympathy for this point of view. Often the complaint is legitimate. There are many expectations that should be fulfilled in church. Every person has a right to expect the church to be alert, informed, intelligent, disciplined, compassionate, hardworking, and faithful to the gospel. If the church and its ministry fall short, we have a right—and probably an obligation—to complain.

But when we do this (although we must), we are on dangerous ground. We cannot avoid the danger, but we must be doubly alert to the threat. The minute we begin evaluating or judging the church by what we get out of it, we are near to the sin of Simon. Many aspects in the church's life are subject to these evaluations and need them. But at the center, God is working freely and graciously, and any assertion of rights, any tendency to criticism or evaluation there, leads directly back to the sin of Adam and of Simon Magus.

The center of the church's life is the activity of the Holy Spirit. It is pure grace. God is the giver of life, the source of all goodness and mercy. We receive from him simply because he is concerned for and loves his creatures. The great mystery of redemption, restoration, and exchange is what takes place at the center of the church's life. The Holy Spirit of God is freely moving here in mercy and in grace, and every person can be only a humble supplicant. At the center we can do nothing but declare our need and receive unmerited grace.

In Paul's most complete and profound statement on what happens in church, the epistle to the Ephesians, he said, "By grace you have been saved through faith; and this is not your own doing, it is the gift of God—not because of works, lest any man should boast" (2:8–9).

The temptation to dispense God's grace, to usurp godlike authority in merchandising his love and in buying and selling his gifts is one we all fall prey to. Because our sense of obligation and expectation in the church is legitimate, it is easy to extend it into the center where God is at work and end up debasing the whole thing. Perhaps ministers are the most severely tempted in this regard. Parents are not far behind, for they know so well what would be good for their children. But the children are creatures of God primarily, and their deepest responses to life must be made within that vertical relationship, not along any horizontal one.

The Holy Spirit is not a power but a person. We do not wield the Spirit of God to do our commands, rather the Holy Spirit is our commander. More than a guide, the Spirit also demands our obedience. It is a basic fault of spirit, springing from the oldest sin in the book (pride), that enables us, however subtly, to get involved in the practice of simony. And as with all sins, the more civilized and hidden it becomes, the more corrosive and damnable. This one is certainly refined and gentle in its contemporary manifestations. But if Dante could observe its eternal ramifications, he would probably put it right back where he had it before: in the eighth circle of hell.

There are a number of things that you can buy in church. You can buy beauty; with thoughtful and informed architecture, you can give money to provide something that is an aesthetic delight. You can buy physical comfort; cushioned pews, heat in the winter, and air conditioning in the summer can all be bought with money. With interest and friendliness, you can purchase the goodwill of other people, the respect of your peers, and the admiration (much of it deserved) of those around you. And the church is often the center of all this. It should be, and there is nothing that smacks of the sin of simony up to this point. But when we get to the reason for having a church in the first place—that we may adore God, be instructed by him, and collectively serve him—at that point, all merit and all possibility of payment cease, for that comes as pure gift. It is God's gracious choice that we should live to his glory, and

he will move in our lives to accomplish it. We are already his creatures ("It is he that hath made us, and not we ourselves," Psalm
100:3, KJV), so there is no payment we can make.

And there are a number of things you can sell in church. You
can sell the need of adding an extra dimension to a person's life.
You can sell the importance of Christian education in the lives of
children. You can sell the personal benefits of religion. You can sell
the need for a new church in this community. But when you get to
the center of the church's life, you can sell nothing, for there it is
all given. "God so loved the world that he gave his only Son"
(John 3:16). If we persist in our salesmanship at that point, we will
participate in the sin of all those priests who have separated people
from God and have acted as such miserable substitute gods in individuals' lives.

Both buying and selling in the church exist on the periphery. In
the center it is all grace, God's giving himself freely to us and our
responding in our poverty to him. And that is not for sale in the
church.

An old hymn says, "Nothing in my hand I bring; simply to thy
cross I cling."* If Simon had sung that instead of flashing his money
roll, he would have entered into the rich treasury of God and
would have discovered in his hand the pearl of great price, of
which our Lord spoke.

Amen.

---

* Augustus M. Toplady, "Rock of Ages, Cleft for Me," 1776, public domain.

Love Lessons: Love Is of God

Beloved, let us love one another; for love is of God, and he who loves is born of God and knows God. He who does not love does not know God; for God is love.

—1 John 4:7–8

Love, like the weather, has so many different aspects: sometimes stormy, sometimes sunny, and always unpredictable. Unlike the weather, though, we are not stuck with just talking about it; we can do something about it.

I have never met anyone who was not interested in love. It is as important to our lives as the food we eat and the air we breathe. But even though we are all involved in it, we are not conspicuously good at it. There is confusion in the use of the word. There is awkwardness in expressing it. As a human race we have not shown ourselves natural experts in love.

Love is a subject on which the Christian gospel has something to say. Christians are persons who have access to the best counsel on love that has ever been given. Since we are all interested in the subject and none of us has yet demonstrated an expertise in or mastery of it, I am going to give some "Love Lessons" in this Eastertide season: instructions in the basics of love.

One of our children recently announced the desire to sign up for tennis lessons this summer. So, we are going to do that. The lessons will not make our child a championship tennis player. Yet it is realistic to think that our child will learn some basic strokes, avoid some common mistakes, and achieve a certain level of competence so that playing tennis will not be just one long uncoordinated mishmash of errors but will be fun.

That is my purpose in preaching these sermons under the heading "Love Lessons." I anticipate a certain basic motivation in the people who assemble each week here in worship—a motivation to become competent in love so that in your relationships with others you will not inadvertently or ignorantly break the basic rules and clumsily do the wrong thing. I don't expect any of you to become expert and flawless in your loving. But I do think it is possible to raise the level of competence in all of us, avoid some of the common mistakes, and find, beyond the frustrations and the failures, a definite pleasure in the love of God and neighbor.

For a textbook I will use the first letter of John, which is the best manual for this kind of thing that has ever been written. It has been used over and over again with impressive results. If a modern advertising agency were writing blurbs on 1 John for the mass media, trying to get people's attention and convince them to buy the little book, it would be easy to imagine statements like this: "I was the world's worst lover until I read 1 John." Or, "*Love* for me was just one more four-letter word, and then I read 1 John."

As an instructor in love, John has competitors but no serious rivals. Sigmund Freud's case studies and Hugh Hefner's bunnies may have received more publicity in the twentieth century than St. John's letter, but they couldn't even begin to catch up with him in matters of influence, in reputation for wisdom, or in results for the day-to-day lives of people like us.

John's authority as a counselor on love came from his association with Jesus Christ. He began this letter by establishing his credentials:

We are writing to you about something which has always existed yet which we ourselves actually saw and heard: something which we had an opportunity to observe closely and even to hold in our hands, and yet, as we know now, was something of the very Word of life himself! For it was life which appeared before us: we saw it, we are eye-witnesses of it, and are now writing to you about it. It was the very life of all ages, the life that has always existed with the Father, which actually became visible in person to us mortal men. We repeat, we really saw and heard what we are now writing to you about. We want you to be with us in this—in this fellowship with the Father, and Jesus Christ his Son. We must write and tell you about it, because the more that fellowship extends the greater the joy it brings to us who are already in it. (1 John 1:1–4, PHILLIPS)

Earlier John wrote a gospel, an account of Jesus Christ who revealed God's love to humankind. The theme of his gospel was that in Jesus we could see the very nature of God, and that nature was love. John then proceeded to show that love in action, so as we read the gospel, we find Jesus Christ speaking and acting in a variety of situations and showing how God's love works under every kind of condition, in every kind of need, with all kinds of people.

It is a story with which you are familiar, and you know how it ends. There was a trial of Jesus, a crucifixion, and, finally, a resurrection. The Resurrection shows two things: one, the unconquerable Christ, unstoppable by human sin, who carries on the work of God's love; and two, the inauguration of a new age in which men and women like you and me begin to live out the new life of love.

John's letter is an elaboration of the second point. In his gospel, John showed us that God is love and that Christ reveals that love. In this letter, he said, in my paraphrase,

This love is a love that you can receive, experience, and pass on. I wrote a gospel to show you the love of God in action in Christ Jesus—a love that was victorious in resurrection. Now I am writing you this letter to encourage you to let God repeat his loving actions in your lives. Let him put the love to work in you just as he put it to work in Christ, and let it operate victoriously in you, even as it did in Christ.

John was an expert on love. But he did not acquire his expertise by traveling all over the ancient world, interviewing people, and finding out what they thought about love and the ways in which they experienced it. And he did not become an expert on love by experimenting with every kind of relationship that could conceivably come under the heading of love and telling us the results. He was neither a Gallup pollster nor a Casanova. He was qualified to give lessons on love because he had been in on the revelation of love in Jesus Christ. First his gospel and then his letters are written from a realization that love originates in God, is revealed in Christ, and is practiced when we believe in God and have faith in Christ.

John included one sentence in his letters that is central to everything else he wrote: "We see real love, not in that fact that we loved God, but that he loved us and sent his Son to make personal atonement for our sins" (4:10, PHILLIPS).

Love originates in God. It is revealed in Jesus, especially on the Cross. If you want to get in on love at the beginning, you have to get in on God. Our problem is that we all want to love and we all want to be loveable, but we don't want to be bothered with God. So, we end up with a temporary form of love. Our love is a perishable commodity. The product is pleasing and attractive when we get it, but it doesn't last, and we have no way to replenish it.

One of the things I enjoy is biting into a crisp, mature apple. Occasionally I drive up into Pennsylvania toward Stewartstown and go to Shaw's great apple and peach orchards. I am very grateful to the owners for bothering to learn enough about apple trees and orchard cultivation so that I can enjoy an apple whenever I want it. It would be possible, I suppose, for me to put a couple of trees in my backyard and grow them on my own. But I don't. I am content to eat the fruit of what others are providing for me.

That is the situation with many people in relation to love. Everyone wants to eat the fruits of love, but not many are interested in growing the fruit. Many enjoy the product, yet only a few are involved in the cultivation and nurture that produces the product.

The Christian is a horticulturist in love. You don't have to be a Christian to experience or enjoy love. But you have to be a Christian to be in on the origins of love. And having gotten in on the origins of love, in God revealed in Christ, the Christian becomes the keeper of the orchards. We nurture those original relationships in which love is protected from disease, comes to blossom, is pollinated, and comes to maturity, exhibiting the mature joy and peace of the redeemed life in Christ.

I wonder if some of you are saying, "That sounds good enough, but it's all poetry and metaphors. I need some place to start." Okay, I will give you some direction and a starting point. I will give you a summary of what St. John gave. Here it is: Believe in Jesus Christ. Accept the love of God, which is revealed in his life. Let him forgive your sins. Nurture that acceptance, and grow in its meanings by being faithful in this place of worship each Sunday. Learn to sing the hymns of God's people. Become familiar with Scripture, God's Word, listening to it here and then reading it each day, thoughtfully and obediently. Attend to God in prayer, sharing your needs and your gratitude, and do it every day. Find a neighbor, someone in your family or your neighborhood, to be kind to. And find an enemy, someone whom you don't care about or who turns you off, and try to imagine what God wants for that person; then begin expressing it in your words and actions.

But you are saying, "I don't want a bunch of rules and suggestions. I want love. All you are giving me is a rule book." True. St. John has an answer, though: "His commandments are not burdensome" (1 John 5:3). They are guidelines for getting in touch with the originator of love and ways of copying the movements of love until they become second nature to us. We might complain that in order to get apples, we must do the rather unglamourous work of pruning trees, fertilizing roots, and spraying branches with insecticides. These operations seem far removed from the glorious apples that are invitingly red and coolly crisp in the autumn. But they are what makes the fruit possible.

If you avoid God, if you refuse to get in on the orchard operations, you will still have love, but you will always be dependent on what someone else is doing to get it. You will always be getting it in some secondhand form. The great calling of the Christian is not only to be in on the origins where you have the satisfaction of participating in a work that makes love available for others but also to be in on the victory that overcomes the world.

Amen.

Love Lessons: What Do I Do
When It Doesn't Work?

My little children, I am writing this to you so that you may not sin; but if anyone does sin, we have an advocate with the Father, Jesus Christ the righteous.

—1 John 2:1

This Eastertide sermon on Love Lessons begins with a question: What do I do when love doesn't work? When things go sour, how do I get them sweet again? When communication breaks down, how do I repair the equipment for sending and receiving love?

A description of what we are involved with is important: Love always has to do with a relationship. It is not a thing by itself. It is not an object or a feeling. It refers, always, to what takes place between two people. It is interpersonal.

The two kinds of people who have the most difficult time learning about love or understanding anything about it are the independent and the selfish.

Independent people have a difficult time comprehending the nature of love because they feel self-sufficient. They are not dependent on anyone or anything. Relationships are not primary to them; self-reliance is. They live in a world where they avoid entangling alliances. They like the feeling of not being obligated to anyone, not being in debt to anyone.

Selfish people have a difficult time comprehending the nature of love because they have gotten into the habit of treating everyone and everything as subservient to their own desires. They do look on people or things not as any good in themselves but as good only in relation to their own desires. They want to possess; they want to absorb the other into their own schemes. And in so doing, they of course eliminate the relationship. For in relationship there is difference; there is a separation between the two; there is a love.

Now love has to do with what goes on between me and another. It describes the content of the experience of interchange. If I say there is no relationship, denying or minimizing the activity that makes connections, or if I try to get rid of the distance by taking it into myself, then I am eliminating the necessary grounds on which love works. Love operates in the space between persons and things.

We learn the nature of that relationship as we look at the relationship between man and God. Both are separate beings, and though they are not necessarily equal, there is mutual honor and respect. The space between the two has lines of affection, help, shared idea, shared work, friendly exchange. Each gives to the other; each receives from the other. When this relationship works, we call it love. We see this modeled between God and man clearly in the opening pages of Genesis.

However, we know this relationship called love mostly in its unhealthy forms. We have a kind of innate knowledge of what we want—it is built into our created structure. But we experience it only in unsatisfactory ways. Our loves are always flawed. The Christian has a word to describe this flaw in relationship: *sin*. Sin means that something has gotten out of kilter in the relationship, that the love is not working right. There is miscommunication and error, and mistakes are being made.

The same two types of people who have the hardest time understanding love—the independent and the selfish—have an equally difficult time understanding sin. The successfully independent person has no good concept of sin because, as far as he can tell, he has no relationships that are important to him, so flaws in such relationships don't affect him much. And the successfully selfish person has no good concept of sin because she is so skilled at getting the people around her to fulfill her personal desires that she is not bothered by the possibility that the relationships are flawed.

It is the people in the middle who are conscious of sin. Relationships are important to them. They want to share their lives; they want to give, and they want to receive. Affection and trust are essential to them. And they frequently know that true relationship either doesn't happen at all or happens in a way that defeats their goals or doesn't satisfy them. For the person who wants to love and be loved, the first major task is to find out what to do about sin.

Anyway, that is what John thought. In this letter on love—again, the best counsel that has ever been given on the subject—the first thing he tackled was sin. John said two things: First, you must admit that you do sin, and second, you have to let God take care of it in his own way.

Of course, one way to deal with sin is to deny it. Many people in the first century did that, just as many people do today. But John said, "If we say we have no sin, we deceive ourselves, and the truth is not in us" (1 John 1:8).

Denial of sin is a misconception of the nature of love. It takes place usually in one of three ways. The first way is through accusation—something is wrong with the relationship because the other person did something wrong, You point your finger, and you blame. Now, the plausible thing is that the accusation is almost always correct. The other person has done something wrong. All of us do so many things wrong every day, whether in deed or in thought, that if we point our fingers at random at anyone around us, we have a pretty good chance of finding a correct target for some kind of blame. But accusations are a denial of sin, for they do not deal with the relationship; they address only the one point in the relationship.

Another way of denying sin is by taking all the blame yourself, or self-accusation—by saying, "I am no good; I never do anything right." If you take this to the extreme, you can form what psychologists call a negative identity, and you might live as a thief, liar, or embezzler. You then use your life in negative ways, becoming an outsider. You believe the evidence of other accusations and begin to live them out. You may say "I am a sinner," but you are not using the word correctly. Sin describes what you are in relation to another who loves you, not what you are all by yourself. It is not an identity you have; it is a relationship that doesn't work.

Another way of denying sin is covering it up—telling yourself that it isn't as bad as it seems and that all you need is to put on a smile, apologize and patch up the quarrel, and go on as if nothing ever happened. Very frequently this works, especially in the kind of society that we live in, and things do go on all right. But the unfortunate thing is that while the surface is smooth, the depths are still turbulent. The roots are not taken care of. Sin is what is wrong with our love, and if we don't deal with the sin, we cannot nurture our love. It is what I call the artificial-turf solution. Because grass is so much trouble and weeds often get into it and it has to be cut every week, our age has developed the marvelous expedient of artificial turf. It looks like grass, and it functions under certain conditions like grass (for instance, as a surface for playing baseball or football games), but it is not grass. It has no fragrance. Robins cannot pluck worms from it, and children cannot roll in it, enjoying its lush coolness.

As a boy, I took cornet lessons from Mr. Sothard, an eccentric man in my hometown. He lived in a small house surrounded by about ten or fifteen feet of grass. I was always afraid of him. He was gruff and precise and intolerant of mistakes. I visited him for a half hour each week for about a year and was always terrorized in his presence. I rode my bicycle over for my lessons and was told where I could park it. One day, the bike fell over while we were inside, and the handlebar dug into his lawn. He was furious. The children in the neighborhood told stories, as children do, about what a terrifying and ferocious person he was.

He grew more and more crotchety over the years. And one day

when I was home for a visit from college, I drove by his house and saw that he had removed all the grass and laid down concrete, which he had painted green. His little bungalow was on a pad of concrete. No more trouble with the grass. No more trouble with kids on his grass. No more weeds. No more relationships.

Well, that is one way to deal with sin. And you can't say it doesn't work, for it does. But it also eliminates the love.

When something goes wrong with love, as it does inevitably and frequently, the healing must start from within. The healing is what God does. And we learn how to deal with sin by first experiencing what God does with it. He looks to Jesus Christ, "the expiation for our sins, and not for ours only but also for the sins of the whole world" (1 John 2:2).

God loves us. But what if the love doesn't work? What does he do? Does he love all the harder, sending out messages saying, "I love you. Can't you see how much I love you? Let me show you how much I love you"? Do we start getting roses delivered at the door and cards through the mail—emissaries telling us what to do?

Or does God do the opposite? Does he retreat into a wounded sulk, retire from our presence, and go off into some other corner of the universe to try loving someone else with more success? Does he decide that being in love with such an unsatisfactory species as the descendants of Adam and Eve is a bad job and spend his time spinning stars, keeping the animals from tearing up Eden, and creating new species of zoological types?

God chooses not to do any of these things. You know what he does instead? He arranges for forgiveness. Jesus Christ becomes an advocate, the propitiation for our sins. He takes our sins seriously and does something about them. He sees our sin and its solution accurately. He sees that what is truly wrong with the love relationship between him and us is not that he hasn't loved hard enough or that we aren't capable of responding in love; it's that something has interrupted the relationship. And so, he concentrates on doing the one thing that can make a difference: dealing with the sin in such a way that the relationship is restored.

Forgiveness—for us, that entire transaction is focused on the cross of Jesus Christ. In Christ, God enters the pain of our separation. He bridges the loneliness of our rejection and offers himself. He convinces us that he is not aloof and that we are not incapable of love. No matter what others say about us, we are not so bad that we cannot experience love, and no matter how awful we feel about ourselves, God doesn't share that low opinion. The Cross is uniquely suited for demonstrating this new view of both God and us. But it is not only a demonstration; it is an expression of love that, when accepted, makes the love work again.

I am writing to you, little children, because your sins are forgiven for his sake. (1 John 2:12)

By this we shall know that we are of the truth, and reassure our hearts before him whenever our hearts condemn us; for God is greater than our hearts, and he knows everything. (3:19–20)

Amen.

Love Lessons: Love One Another, Just as He Has Commanded

This is his commandment, that we should believe in the name of his Son Jesus Christ and love one another, just as he has commanded us.

—1 John 3:23

I had entered the room on a pastoral visitation. I had not been to the home before and didn't know the young woman I had arranged to see. I introduced myself. There were a few moments of awkward small talk. Then she left the room to fix us coffee, an attempt to bridge the strangeness between us. While she was in the kitchen, I walked around the room admiring an impressive array of trophies won in athletic contests. She returned with the coffee cups, and I said, "Your husband must be a very good athlete and spend a lot of time at it."

"Oh yes," she said, "he is very good. Why, it's his second love."

"Second love?" I said. "What, then, is his first love?"

She didn't know me well enough to risk a direct look, but her shyness didn't prevent her confident answer: "Me."

It was a wonderful answer. Here was a person who knew where she stood in a highly competitive world. Surrounded by signs of her husband's love of sports, she was confident of her priority in his love. In a world in which others were constantly vying for his attention and his involvement, she was quietly sure of first place.

Do you know where you stand? You can know. God has made it clear that in fact you are first place. You are number one. He loves neither trophies nor games—he loves people. In a world filled with dazzling wonders (the trophies of creation) and made more complex with the excitement of games (the ways of the nations, the history of all people), God has a clear priority: to love you. You are his first love. The rest of it is his second love.

That reality is the basis for this Love Lesson from 1 John. In the first Love Lesson, we let John lay the groundwork of all love in God. We found that to discover what love is in its healthy state and to experience it at its best, we need to be in a relationship with God. In the second Love Lesson, we found out how practical John was about love. He knew that just being in love didn't solve all our problems, that it more often than not complicated them. All love is subject to discord and frustration. When love doesn't work, it is because of sin. There is no way to get better at love until we find a way to do something about sin. And we found John giving us good counsel for that. In this third Love Lesson, we will pay attention to the way John provided a basic orientation in the acts of love—he set us in the right direction, making clear two basic items that we have to get straight before we become skilled. Here is the passage that centers his teaching in this regard:

> We know and, to some extent realise, the love of God for us because Christ expressed it in laying down his life for us. We must in turn express our love by laying down our lives for those who are our brothers. But as for the well-to-do man who sees his brother in want but shuts his eyes—and his heart—how could anyone believe that the love of God lives in him? My children, let us love not merely in theory or in words—let us love in sincerity and in practice!
>
> If we live like this, we shall know that we are children of the truth and can reassure ourselves in the sight of God, even if our own hearts make us feel guilty. For God is infinitely greater than our hearts, and he knows everything.

And if, dear friends of mine, when we realise this our hearts no longer accuse us, we may have the utmost confidence in God's presence. We receive whatever we ask for, because we are obeying his orders and following his plans. His orders are that we should put our trust in the name of his Son, Jesus Christ, and love one another—as we used to hear him say in person. (1 John 3:16–23, PHILLIPS)

John knew that our feelings do not always express love and that we waver in our focus of love. When we are left to ourselves, love puts in a swamp of feelings and stirs in us a muddle of desires. We are bogged down in emotions or in dreams. Our feet get so stuck in the mud of emotions that we don't get going, or our heads get so high in the clouds of frustration that we fail to make contact with reality. John's instructions help us out of this. The RSV puts it this way: "This is his commandment, that we should believe in the name of his Son Jesus Christ and love one another, just as he has commanded us" (verse 23). Go back to the beginning, establish your base in Jesus Christ, and then do it the way he says: love one another. That sounds simple enough.

I am going to summarize the importance of this command in two sentences: First, love is something you do, not something you feel. Second, love is for persons, not for things.

Love is not what you feel but what you do. In other words, in the minister R. J. Campbell's phrase, it has to do with "deeds rather than disposition."* The observation leading to this statement is that in this brief letter of John, the word *commandment* occurs thirteen times. A common response to that observation is one of surprise: "How does a cold word like commandment get into a warm letter on love? Love is a feeling, a warm emotion, a passionate fire. Commandment is cold and austere. Love is sensitive and personal; commandment is businesslike and impersonal." We read the sentence "Love one another, just as he has commanded

* R. J. Campbell, *A Faith for Today* (London: James Clarke, 1902), 269.

us" and say, "But how can you command feelings? How can you order a person to be in love?" The answer, of course, is that you can't. But why, then, did John say it? Was he such an old man by the time he wrote this tract on love that his emotions were all dried up and all he had left in him were some withered old commandments?

But maybe we are the ones that have things turned around, not John. Maybe it is our idea of love that is out of whack, not his counsel. What if it is true that love is something you do and not something you feel? If that is the case, then you can command love—you can order love; you can speak of it in the imperative mood.

But we haven't grown up learning of love that way. Our greatest exposure and often only teaching has been through the commercial mass media that has always exploited love for its own ends. Frustrated poets with the aid of Metro-Goldwyn-Mayer and 20th Century Studios created romantic love for the world market. Their concept of love usually goes no deeper than boy meets girl, girl hassles boy (or vice versa), boy loses girl, girl and boy gain insight through some magical stroke of fate, boy gets girl (or vice versa), and they live happily ever after. All this with variation. Deodorant ads, romantic comedies, cosmetic companies play supportive roles in strengthening this insane notion of love. You are assured that love means running together through a meadow, walking along a moonlit beach, or applying a deodorant daily. You are given the idea that love just happens, usually at first sight. You don't have to work at love—love requires no teacher—you just fall into love, if you happen to be in the right place with the right person at the right time.

Nothing but mischief is done as a result of the idea that love is first of all a feeling, something we fall into. Love is something you do. It is a response to a command. It is following directions that God gives us. There are feelings, of course, an incredible array of emotions that develop out of such acts. But the feelings are not the love; the action is the love.

John's second basic item was that love is for persons, not for things. The only appropriate focus for love is another person. John's counsel was that we "love one another."

Some in John's congregations claimed to love God but actually hated the people around them. What they were doing was loving the idea of God. They had made an abstraction out of love and were directing their energy to that. That happens still. And it isn't a very satisfying love. Ideas and ideals, while very useful in their place, are not the proper target for love. They do not function in a relationship. No matter how fine the ideas—beauty, joy, peace, and even God—they are no worthy focus for love. We don't get connected with anything in a living way when we do that.

Of course, the motive is transparent. People are so vulgar and so difficult to love. People aren't nice. Why take a beautiful thing like love and direct it to such unsatisfactory creatures as persons, these lately evolved descendants of the ape, who make such noise and trouble? How much better to love the higher things of life.

Others in John's congregations had been diverted from loving persons to loving material things, what John calls "the things in the world": "the lust of the flesh and the lust of the eyes and the pride of life" (2:15–16). There is nothing wrong with what is in the world—it is God's creation; it is here to be enjoyed and appreciated and used. But it is not a proper focus for love. It cannot be a part of a love relationship. All materialism is love that has misfired. All greed and avarice are love gone wrong. All lust and all selfishness are directing the wonderful capacities of love to personalized sex or a dehumanized ego. The best energies that God has given us are used for unworthy ends. The glorious capacities of love are directed to mean and sordid occupations.

And it doesn't work. You cannot love without loving a person. The only relationship in which love works is a personal one. If we try to soar above the personal one into the ideal, love withers. If we avoid the personal and substitute the materials of the world, love dries up.

The gospel has made some things very clear to us.

As John's love lessons begin to take effect in us, one thing becomes increasingly clear: We know where we stand with God; we are number one, his first love. As we learn to love the way that he does—remembering that love is an act before it is a feeling and is for persons, not things—others will get that number one feeling too.

Amen.

PENTECOST

Suddenly a Sound

When the day of Pentecost had come, they were all together in one place. And suddenly a sound came from heaven like the rush of a mighty wind, and it filled all the house where they were sitting.

—Acts 2:1–2

"Suddenly a sound came from heaven like the rush of a mighty wind." That is the introduction to this great passage in the New Testament that tells us more about God the Holy Spirit than any other that we have.

G. K. Chesterton once wrote, "You cannot see a wind; you can only see that there is a wind. . . . The wind is up above the world before a twig on the tree has moved."* Neither can you see God. But you can see that there is a God. In the Bible, people account for that by talking of God the Holy Spirit.

Some men and women gathered together twenty centuries ago, "and suddenly a sound . . ." It broke upon them all at once and took root in their personal experience that God shared his very inner life with them. Things got started in God and moved toward them. Life originated in God and produced life in them. The reality of existence was God, and that reality moved among people and caused life and salvation.

* G. K. Chesterton, "Wind and the Trees," in *Tremendous Trifles* (New York: Dodd, Mead and Co., 1909), 91.

The meaning of the experience of Pentecost is that God personally and directly shares his life with you. It is the sudden discovery that God, unseen like the wind, causes this movement and action most directly associated with true life. The wind moves the trees; God moves us. The Greek word for "Spirit" means "wind."* When people have realized this primal movement of God upon humankind and experienced it personally, they have called God the "Holy Spirit"—the divine wind that moves us to love and joy and to a redeemed new life.

The Christian experience is rooted in the discovery that "the wind moves the trees." The great denial of it is that the trees move the wind.† All alternate religious programs figure out ways to produce a tree that will shake violently enough to produce a wind. The church is composed of those persons who believe in the invisible against the visible, who believe that things get started with God and then produce eternal effects among humanity.

We have daily decisions to make about whether we believe that or not. We must decide what kind of power we put our trust in. We see armies clash and nations stockpile weapons. We see police throw tear gas and students throw stones. As violence continues, we see both sides come more and more to resemble each other. We find that when we make a religion out of that kind of action, we become ultimately depressed and disheartened. There is simply no hope down that road for a life of gladness and meaning. It's a religion of trees trying to produce wind.

Then Zechariah's words are projected on the screen of our history: "Not by might, nor by power, but by my spirit, saith the LORD" (Zechariah 4:6, KJV). We hear, by some gospel miracle, that God is here: "suddenly a sound." God is at work in our time. His love is present, and his presence is power.

We read this passage in Acts 2 to find out what it means to experience this vast reorientation of life—to find out what it feels like to discover that existence is rooted in a living God and that a per-

---

* *Blue Letter Bible*, s.v. "*pneuma*," www.blueletterbible.org/lexicon/g4151/esv/mgnt/0-1.
† Chesterton, "Wind and the Trees," 92.

son's life is filled when lived openly in that direction. What is at issue here is the size of our individual lives: Will we live openly and responsibly to the huge reality of God and feel the wind moving vastly through all existence? Or will we try to produce our own power and create our own life force of love, joy, and peace by waving our arms or puffing air out of our lungs?

To get you started in your own understanding and meditation on this passage in Acts, let me tell you what emerges out of it for me.

The thing that stands out as I have read this again is the astonishing concentration of God on the individual. In the room where this Day of Pentecost action took place, a large number of persons were together, all doing the same thing—praying. But the experience of God that they entered into was not an absorption with groupthink; it was a sharpening of personal relationships. The imagery used to give us some insight into how they felt is this: "There appeared to them tongues as of fire, distributed and resting on each one of them" (verse 3). The fire is the symbol of the presence of God. What they experienced was not a great bonfire before which they could all gather and be warmed but a flame on each of them that God distributed. The human personality becomes the terminal goal of the divine movement and action. Each person is singled out for special attention and filling.

They discovered, you see, that God doesn't deal with mass humanity. God's power is not promulgated by governmental decrees announced through the newspapers or tacked on the post office bulletin board. He comes to each one. You are a unique individual. You have a history and an emotional life all your own. God operates in intimate relationship with you just as you are.

This intense concentration on the individual is highlighted in an unusual way in the sermon Peter preached right after the event. The Jerusalem crowd wanted to know what was going on, so Peter stood up and preached a sermon that interpreted what happened. His introduction is arresting. *Audacious* is perhaps the right word to describe it.

He began by quoting a prophecy from Joel that everyone in that crowd knew well. Here are some of the phrases:

In the last days . . . your sons and your daughters shall prophesy, and your young men shall see visions, and your old men shall dream dreams. . . . And I will show wonders in the heaven above and signs on the earth beneath, blood, and fire, and vapor of smoke; the sun shall be turned into darkness and the moon into blood. . . . And it shall be that whoever calls on the name of the Lord shall be saved. (Acts 2:17, 19–21)

The remarkable thing is not that he quoted the passage; Scripture was and is quoted often. The remarkable (audacious) thing was that he identified this prophecy of Joel with what was happening among those first Christians. He told the crowd, in my paraphrase, "You see these people receiving a personal experience of God? Well, this is what was spoken by the prophet Joel." Then he quoted from Joel these phrases filled with descriptions of extreme inner experience and violent cosmic imagery. "The most intense inner experiences (dreams, visions, prophecy) and the wildest outer experiences (heavenly disturbances, eclipses, volcanic eruptions)—these are all taking place before your eyes," said Peter, "among these persons who are experiencing the fullness of God."

Perhaps the worst form of infidelity to God is to always be looking someplace else for evidence of the fulfillment of his will and purpose and presence. We anxiously search through the newspapers for some shred of hope that God is working mightily somewhere. We hungrily read through inspirational books and magazines to get reassured that God does heal, he does comfort, and he does answer prayers. But our attention is always elsewhere. We are always looking for the mighty acts of God in someone else or someplace else.

Peter's sermon prevents that kind of spiritual tourism. The most brilliant works of God, the most fantastic exploits of the Almighty in the world, are taking place before your eyes. This is what God is doing in might and power. He is doing it in these persons who suddenly have become open and receptive to God.

Be careful not to misunderstand this. I am not saying, "If you believe, then these mighty works will take place." I am saying, "These mighty works are taking place. The word of God is being fulfilled in the inner and the outer world. If you do not see it, it is not because it is not there. It is there. Pentecost has happened. You must take seriously the declaration of Scripture and become open to the meaning of the nature of the presence of God."

This, of course, was not apparent to everyone, either then or now. If a newspaper reporter had been present at the meeting of Pentecost, I think there is no chance at all that he would have described things as Peter did—which ought to make us cautious about getting our interpretations of life and of history from journalists.

The crowd's two reactions tell us something about how people can respond to this presence of God. The first reaction was denunciation. They accused these men and women of being drunk on new wine. They were acting in a bizarre way. They were talking about things that were beyond the comprehension of the Jerusalem crowd's market mentality. And so the crowd invented a cause—these people were drunk.

It is a convenient way to deal with an experience that we don't understand or don't want to face. We indulge in disparagement of others—whether our children, parents, students, or government—because it is easier to avoid a responsible relationship with them if we denounce them as stupid, useless, and ineffective.

The crowd's second reaction was an open, interested curiosity: "What does this mean?" Here is something new. Great joy is being expressed. "We hear them telling in our own tongues the mighty works of God" (verse 11).

Something happened before their eyes that they were not accustomed to seeing. They were experts in the external world of commerce, ritual, and scholarship. But this was something else. Here was an expression of the mighty works of God. Human history, especially what has come to influence our modern American world, "has been distinguished, more than by anything else, by a drive to control the external world, and by an almost total forgetfulness of the internal world."* "We accumulate knowledge like the miser who interprets wealth as maniacal acquisition plus tenacious possession; but we bankrupt our capacity to be wonderstruck . . . perhaps even to survive."†

But here were some people who could let loose of the world where they were in control and ask with genuine curiosity and desire about what happened when God filled them with himself. When they saw the trees bend and the leaves flutter, these men and women asked about the wind, not the mechanics of the stress on the trees.

The story we have in Acts explores that experience with God that floods the ordinary details of life with meaning and glory. It centers on a realization that the wind moves the trees, not vice versa, and that God is the wind—the "Spirit." The mundane becomes a miracle. And it is the place where some ask the question "What does this mean?" and then pay attention to Peter's answer that this is the invasion of their lives with the power and presence of Jesus Christ. A great number of those persons responded to the answers; they believed and were baptized.

If you have never been suddenly, abruptly startled out of your earth orientation, your self-preoccupation, your thing-dominated routine by the sound of God—the wind that moves the trees of existence—listen today. May today you hear the sounds of God

---

* R. D. Laing, *The Politics of Experience and the Bird of Paradise* (Baltimore, Md.: Penguin, 1967), 115.
† Theodore Roszak, *The Making of a Counter Culture* (Berkeley: University of California, 1995), 251.

and ask the right question ("What does this mean?"). And may you make the right response, summarized in these words: "They devoted themselves to the apostles' teaching and fellowship, to the breaking of bread and the prayers" (Acts 2:42).

Amen.

What Does This Mean? . . .
What Shall We Do?

All were amazed and perplexed, saying to one another, "What does this mean?" . . . Now when they heard this they were cut to the heart, and said to Peter and the rest of the apostles, "Brethren, what shall we do?"

—Acts 2:12, 37

We got a telephone call this week from my family in Montana reporting on conditions there since the volcanic eruption that took place last Sunday morning. My family lives five hundred miles from the volcano, but the air is so thick with ash that they have to stay indoors. Everyone I know is awestruck by the explosion that has blanketed the earth with ashes. We are surprised by the suddenness in which a majestic, beautiful, placid mountain is changed into a roaring, smoke-belching furnace, disfiguring thousands of square miles of land, hurting and killing, and throwing an entire region into disheveled panic.

I have admired and enjoyed Mount St. Helens many times. A good friend once lived in a town not far from the mountain, and I often had occasion to look at it. I knew at the time that it was a volcanic formation. I knew that far beneath that lovely surface were fierce fires burning. But I didn't worry about it. It never occurred to me that the power down there would ever exhibit itself out here.

As I have been reading the stories of the volcanic explosion of Mount St. Helens, I have also been reading the story of the Day of Pentecost and have been struck by some similarities. That is not an uncommon experience for me—having the stories in the newspaper and the stories in the Bible illuminate and reinforce each other. Scripture and life corroborate each other.

Two thousand years ago in Jerusalem, a familiar scene that everyone was pleased and comfortable with was transformed into an extraordinary event that made it impossible for anyone to carry on as usual.

The familiar scene was the Feast of Pentecost, a major religious feast held every year in the spring in Jerusalem. It was a time when Jews returned to Jerusalem from far-scattered nations to remember God's blessing, to enjoy the great, centering, massive reality of God's word revealed among them. On Pentecost the people remembered Sinai, where God had spoken to Moses and revealed his law. Some believe that Sinai was a volcanic mountain since it was often engulfed in fire and smoke. It was a fittingly dramatic place for the people to receive God's word—the word that changed their lives, transforming them from a swarm of refugees out of Egypt into a pilgrim people of worship and witness, a word of God that changed a mob of slaves into a society of free persons. This is what happened at Sinai. And every year, the Day of Pentecost was the time to remember that event and to thank God for it. Pentecost was one of the striking landmarks in the landscape of Hebrew life.

It was immense, marvelous, awesome. But through the centuries of familiarity, it had also come to be taken for granted.

Then that day in Jerusalem, it erupted again. Not the mountain itself—Mount Sinai was a many miles to the south—but the people who in worship were remembering what had happened at Sinai, the community who had been formed by the word of God spoken from that mountain. An unexpected explosion of energy took place among these people. The event was described with metaphors that reflected the old Sinai accounts: "the rush of a mighty wind . . . tongues as of fire" (Acts 2:2–3).

Did you think that the old volcano of revelation was dormant? Did you assume that it was a vast mountain of snowcapped beauty, a majestic piece of scenery thrusting up from the horizon and inspiring us with feelings of strength and aspiration, of solid calm and quiet repose, but extinct in terms of energy? Well, it is not. It is active, alive, and terrifyingly powerful. God is not background to our lives, an eternal presence around which we gather occasionally to celebrate and then leave to go about our ordinary duties. God is an explosion of energy into our lives. He is here. He is active. He is not there. He is not dormant.

Newspaper and television reporters have been telling us of the people's reactions to the eruption of Mount St. Helens. St. Luke told us of the human reactions to the evidence of God's power on the Day of Pentecost. He reported two emotional responses, each of them followed by a question.

The first response is this: "All were amazed and perplexed" (Acts 2:12). And well they might be. People from all over the world were hearing "in our own tongues the mighty works of God." These perplexed people had never been perplexed before. They were devout Jews who thought they knew everything about God and about everything of importance he had ever done. The Hebrews were the best theologians in the ancient world. They were surrounded by superstitious, corrupt, and ignorant religions. In contrast, they held to a pure monotheism, taught by well-educated rabbis. These cosmopolitan, well-traveled, theologically sophisticated Hebrews had God in their pocket. They could point out to anyone the main features in the religious landscape. They had skillfully shaped stories to describe what it meant to live in relation to God: Abraham stories, Moses stories, David stories. They were excellent stories. And they were well told.

But on this day the tables were turned. They were no longer telling the stories to the tourists; the tourists—country-bumpkin Galileans who had just arrived in Jerusalem—were telling them, in their own languages, the mighty works of God. Not what God had done in the past but what he was doing in the present. Not what God said at Sinai but what the God of Sinai was saying right now.

Very understandably they were perplexed. For long centuries they had assumed the role of expert in matters that had to do with God. Now they were hearing fresh reports of new activity from people just arrived on the scene. The old mountain was active again. God was alive in their midst. The energy of the Spirit was moving powerfully through them. They had every right to be amazed and perplexed. One person wrote, "People put God so far away, in a sort of mist somewhere. I pull their coat-tails. God is *near*. He is no use unless he is near."*

These people had thought that God was far off but not near—a majestic mountain of revelation looming in the past, not a rushing wind blowing in the present. Amazed and perplexed, they asked, "What does this mean?" Peter answered with a sermon.

This, said Peter, is the Spirit of God poured out among us. God is sharing himself with us. It is what you always believed would happen. Remember what the prophet Joel wrote? Now it is happening. You are seeing it take place before your eyes. If you had meditated on the words of Scripture you say you revere, you would not be so surprised. The mountain has been a volcano all along, and you knew it. But for all practical purposes you forgot it. God is here among us—"whoever calls on the name of the Lord will be saved" (Acts 2:21).

And the pouring out of the Spirit of God, continued Peter, is not an accident. It is the result of a known cause. The cause is Jesus of Nazareth, whom you crucified and whom God raised up. Jesus was the divine in our history. He brought us to personal encounter with the acts and words of God. He brought us into unavoidable meeting with the purposes and love of God. The first thing that happened in that meeting was a violent, blasphemous, rejecting refusal to deal with God on a personal level; Jesus was crucified. Did you think that was the end of it? It was not. God raised him

* Gwendolen Greene, introduction to *Letters from Friedrich von Hügel to a Niece*, by Friedrich von Hügel (London: J. M. Dent & Sons, 1929), xxxi.

up—that was the second thing that happened. Crucifixion at the hands of humanity; resurrection by the will of God. Those two acts, the human and the divine, though seemingly minor incidents in a remote corner of the vast Roman Empire, caused this explosion of new energy in which the life of God is poured out into the lives of men and women, sons and daughters, young men and old men, you and me.

Do you know what set off the volcanic eruption of Mount St. Helens? Do you suppose that some mountaineers who had hiked to the peak carelessly left a campfire burning and that the live coals melted through the ice and fell through a crevasse and ignited the explosion? That is absurd. No, the mountain is on a fault line. At some point in the past few days, weeks, or months, geologists speculate, a deep underground shift of ground occurred: an earthquake. That caused the explosion.

If we want to understand the meaning of what we see around us as people receive power to love, bless, praise, heal, and give, we must trace it back to the crucifixion and resurrection of Jesus Christ. We will never understand it by measuring the temperature of the flames or analyzing the wind—those are only metaphors of the result. The cause is Jesus Christ revealing that God is among us and forgives our sins, that we cannot save ourselves but can live by faith. The cause is nothing on the surface of life, nothing we do or do not do, but what God does deeply at the center of things: Jesus Christ raised up. He is the cause of the power for new life experienced and shared among us.

Following the sermon answer, there is a second emotional response: "When they heard this they were cut to the heart." The first emotion was a kind of generalized confusion, a vast bewilderment; this second emotion is a focused pain, a dagger-point stab in the heart. "I am responsible. I am no disinterested spectator of God; I am no distant admirer of God; I am no impersonal expert on God. I am the one who rejects or ignores or accepts. I am in the presence of God. I am in personal encounter with him." The suddenness of this realization is a cut in the heart, a pain at the center of my being where decisions are made and actions are formed, where I am aware that who I am is significant and what I decide is important.

That is what the preaching of Jesus Christ does: It takes God out of the mist and fog and puts him in our company with a human face. We meet him. We encounter him. We are in a place of response.

It is painful, but it is the best thing that ever happens to us. We try to run our lives and the lives of those around us. We want to be in charge. We want to be the center. We want to be our own gods. Certain small pleasures come from doing this, but they are essentially trivial.

Faced with Jesus Christ—God personally and powerfully before us—we are challenged to new life. We try to get rid of him, but we can't. God raised him up. We are cut to the heart. But it is not a pain to be avoided; it is the pain signaling new birth. "When what we hoped for came to nothing, we revived."*

The pain provokes the second question: "Brethren, what shall we do?" Peter answered, "Repent, and be baptized every one of you in the name of Jesus Christ for the forgiveness of your sins; and you shall receive the gift of the Holy Spirit. For the promise is to you and to your children and to all that are far off, every one whom the Lord our God calls to him" (verses 37–39). "Repent . . . be baptized . . . receive." Quit keeping God at a distance; throw your lot in with those who will live by faith in Christ; receive the poured-out life of God into yourselves.

Repent means that we quit trying to be our own gods. All of us have schemes for getting our own way, managing our lives, being good, and doing the best we can. None of these things is terribly bad in itself, but the accumulation of detail excludes God from the center of our lives—the only place where he belongs. *Repent* means that we must turn our backs on ideas or practices that trivialize us into the mediocrities of merely feeling good, getting more, making others like us, or manipulating others to get our own way. Repent.

Be baptized means that we let God do what needs to be done in

---

* Marianne Moore, "Elephants," in *The Complete Poems of Marianne Moore* (New York: Macmillan, 1967), 129.

us—accomplish our salvation and restore his lordship over us. We are passive in baptism. We let someone else immerse us in the river or pour the water over us. We permit it. We let God be God.

Baptism is the acted-out symbol of that. It is terribly difficult to do this. We were programmed for action the moment we crawled out of the nursery. We must return repeatedly to this condition of which baptism is the sacramental sign so that we understand ourselves as persons acted upon before we act; saved by grace, not by works; saved by Christ, not by ourselves; and worshipping God, not ordering him around.

Receive means that in one way or another, in one degree or another, in our lives we can experience everything that God is. The Holy Spirit is God's life in your life. Christian living is, or can be, a continuous exploratory, celebrating advance in experiencing God's life in us. Each Christian becomes a field of energy—a personal instance of God active, doing his work of saving and blessing. It is far from merely a nice picture of a beautiful moment on a calendar. Receive.

What does this mean? God is here, powerfully active in this place among these people. What shall we do? Get in on it. Participate in the action. Receive the power.

I've used up the illustration of the volcanic action at Mount St. Helens. At this point it is of no more use, for though it was a great display of energy and power, it was a power of destruction. People were killed; curiosity seekers died; millions of people are inconvenienced in a difficult cleanup. Pentecost is not like that—here all the energy and the power are redemptive. Those who respond to it are more alive than ever. You don't find these people huddled in their houses afraid to breathe the air outside. God's power, accepted in the gift of the Holy Spirit, sets us on a way in which we work and love, believe and hope, with a sense of augmentation, of enhancement, of blessing, and of centeredness and wholeness. We become people, as St. Luke describes them, with glad and generous hearts, "praising God and having favor with all the people" (verse 47).

Amen.

Filled with the Holy Spirit

They were all filled with the Holy Spirit and began to speak in other tongues, as the Spirit gave them utterance.

—Acts 2:4

What are your first memories or first impressions of the church? Here are some of mine: My aunt Hazel playing the piano (magnificently, I thought) with flourishes and runs at every pause in the stanzas but always out of rhythm with the congregation. They seemed to have an understanding that each would do their own thing, the congregation singing the hymns and my aunt embellishing them with whatever she could think up in her fingers, and for the most part they ignored each other. I remember Oleg and Lenora Storm, a large and morose Norwegian couple who were farmers of supposedly considerable wealth. Each Sunday, they came to church pushing their son, who had muscular dystrophy, in a wheelchair. At an early age I learned that they came to church so that their son could be healed—every week, they hoped that the miracle of that healing would take place. Their repeatedly disappointed expectations accumulated in their slow melancholy.

My father, receiving the offering and then going out of the church to count it, sometimes let me accompany him and sort the pennies, nickels, and dimes. It was always exciting to know that everyone else was inside doing the routine Sunday things and I was outside doing the money counting. I have suspected in my adult years that my father had a particular dislike for our pastor and used this as a dodge to avoid hearing his sermons. But I didn't have that idea then; it was simply a matter of priorities: Counting money with my father took precedence over anything else.

I spent a lot of time in church and have a lot of memories. Put them all together and what do you have? A true picture of the church? Hardly. Simply some reminiscences of my experiences that happened to take place in the vicinity of the church. The same is true of all of our memories.

It is better to go to Scripture to find out about the church. And there is no better place to go than Acts chapter two. This is the model memory of the church's origin. This is the church remembering itself, its first impressions of what it means to be a church. By reading it and meditating on it, we know what we can expect from being a part of the church.

That doesn't mean that whatever we find here will be reproduced in our congregation in just the same way. There are many times when the church has failed to be what our Lord the Spirit created it to be. Many details get added, and too many get left out. So, we don't have a prediction here or a kind of computerized program that keeps getting run through congregations over and over in whatever time and place for twenty centuries.

Rather, we should look at this as a model. This story tells us what is significant and possible about the church. This is the model story for understanding our church experience. It will clarify our past memories and shape our expectations.

The first thing I note in the story is the strong emphasis on "Spirit." Spirit is the energy of God, his acting in human affairs. It is not the collective minds and hearts of devout people put into operation. It is God putting his people into operation with his own motive power.

Jacques Ellul, the French writer, notes that there are two different ways of looking at a religious person: as a watch and as a compass.* The workings of a religious "watch" are all within the

---

* Jacques Ellul, *The Presence of the Kingdom,* trans. Olive Wyon (New York: Seabury Press, 1967), 111.

person; it is a matter of arranging the parts correctly and making the proper adjustments. Once it is set up correctly, it works and produces its effects (like telling the correct time) out of itself. The major workings of a religious "compass" are outside the person— the magnetic fields, so to speak. The compass, a much simpler mechanism, merely responds to what is already outside. The outside energies are what make it work, and it produces its effects by responding to them.

A great many religious organizations are conceived on the watch model—putting things together correctly so that we can do a great job, getting the best people together so that we can do something significant. The church has a different origin. It is more like the compass. Its job is simply to respond to what is outside, to God.

You can find many similarities to the watch in any church you look at. But when you look at the church's earliest memory of itself, you see something much more like the compass. The believers are together because God has called them and is working among them. What is outside them is more important than what is within. The theological dimension is more important than the sociological.

We have tried to symbolize that in the architecture of this church. We spent a lot of time trying to get the right shape and arrangement of space and furniture. But by far, the greatest amount of space in this church is empty. In other words, as a church we gather together for worship and we need pews to do that; we need to be obedient and responsive to the Lord and word and sacrament, and the font, table, and pulpit center those attentions. But beyond that, we don't know what will happen. The presence of God—the active grace of Christ—is the biggest thing here, and we will symbolize that by creating as much emptiness as we can. It is not a vacuum but an emptiness that is charged with expectation. We know that God is going to do something, so we provide a holy emptiness, a waiting, an expectation.

Another thing apparent in this early memory of the church is the experience of unity in diversity. There were a lot of different people, speaking different languages, with different personality profiles, from different countries, and with different ideas about religion. And they were together, and they had the same things happen to them. They heard the sound; they saw the fire distributed on each head; they spoke the glories of God.

That sets up an expectation in us. When we come to church, we are not looking for a group of like-minded people who will support us in all that we already think and feel. We are not looking for homogeneity. Rather, we are looking for the experience of being with others who have different backgrounds, different feelings, and different goals but whose differences are respected and brought into control by our Lord the Spirit. And we find ourselves brothers and sisters in the faith.

The church has often become defined by its sociology rather than its Lord the Spirit. That can be done. But the Acts model is something different. It is not a guarantee that sociology won't predominate, but it provides the data to guide and lead us to something else.

Another thing that is part of this model is the element of communication. We note that they "began to speak in other tongues, as the Spirit gave them utterance" (Acts 2:4). And later, "we hear them telling in our own tongues the mighty works of God" (verse 11). The whole matter of "speaking in tongues" is of heightened interest in the church today, and many are experiencing this in small groups and sects. What this model emphasizes is that the tongues are first an instance of misunderstanding that then produces understanding. People speak a lot of different languages—we have communication problems in the world. And here, in this room on this day, the communication problems are solved. Everyone hears the same message: the mighty works of God.

Amen.

Church Burning

When the day of Pentecost had come, they were all together in one place. And suddenly a sound came from heaven like the rush of a mighty wind, and it filled all the house where they were sitting. And there appeared to them tongues as of fire, distributed and resting on each one of them. And they were all filled with the Holy Spirit and began to speak in other tongues, as the Spirit gave them utterance.

—Acts 2:1–4

This church is a big disappointment. If you aren't disappointed yet, you will be. Or at least you will be if you hang around long enough. A church, any church, is one of the more unsatisfactory experiences that human beings have. Some of us deny our disappointment; some of us mask it. But sooner or later, if we are honest, we have to admit and face it. The sooner the better.

I hate it that this church is a disappointment to you. I really do. I am pastor of this church and feel a responsibility for its excellence; I don't want anyone who enters here to be disappointed.

I know some things it would take to have a church where you would not be disappointed. If when you entered this place God were absolutely clear here and all doubts about the meaning of life and the purposes of God in your life were wiped out, you would not be disappointed. If you walked in here on a Sunday morning and immediately realized that you were in fact a most loved and thoroughly saved creature by God's grace, I would have a hard time getting you to leave after an hour. When you gathered here in worship, if everything happening in the world were fully submitted to the rule and the salvation of God in Christ—I mean everything and everyone, the most recent tragedy, the latest political debacle, your misunderstanding spouse and your disobedient child, the death that leaves a gaping abyss in your life and the accident that disrupts your comfortable routines—if all those things were perceived as integrated into something grand and eternal, you would not be disappointed.

But as it turns out, you are disappointed. We get glimpses of those things I just mentioned, partial clearings in the skies in which God comes into greater focus. But then it gets all cloudy again.

And if when you came to this church you realized that people really loved you just the way you are, you would not be disappointed. If you found yourself in a community where no one was being used, slighted, or criticized, you would not be disappointed. We all have so many disappointing experiences in relationships—with our children, parents, spouses, chance acquaintances, and long-term friends. If there were a place where the love was guaranteed, the love was simply there unconditionally, you would be dragging not only neighbors but also absolute strangers into this wonderful place where people knew how to live in mature, healthy loving relationships with one another.

But as it turns out, you are disappointed. We get hints of this love—genuine experiences of compassion, of affection, of acceptance—but then someone forgets our name or is insensitive to a need or leaves us out, and we feel hurt and rejected again.

We come to this church expecting the reality of God to be wonderfully clear. It isn't, and we are disappointed. We come to this church hoping for human friendships that are satisfyingly deep and dependable. They aren't, and we are disappointed.

So why are you still here? Why do you keep coming back to this disappointing place?

I think I know why. St. Luke told the story that accounts for our being here this morning.

The story began in this bi-level disappointment that we know so well ourselves: disappointment with God and disappointment with people. The people in this story had been attracted to Jesus because they thought they saw God being revealed in him. There were times when they were sure of it. The evidence accumulated. They listened to him teach, watched him heal, and met with him in prayer. Then he was killed and buried—a catastrophic disappointment. They recovered partially when he was raised from the dead and appeared to them as the risen, living Jesus. But even then, they were not wholly convinced. There was room for doubt, and they doubted. And then he disappeared completely. No more evidence of his real presence.

They were also disappointed with one of their companions. They were a close company, having gone through so much together. They thought they could trust one another. And then one became a traitor. Judas Iscariot betrayed Jesus and all the rest as well. They had been thrilled to be in a new community in the presence of God with companions who were committed to honest acts of love. And just at the moment when everyone was enjoying it and thinking it was too good to be true, they were knifed in the back by Judas and abandoned by Peter, who they thought was a dependable friend.

Yet they were still together, as we are still together. Things hadn't turned out the way they expected and hoped, but they hadn't quit. They were together in a building in Jerusalem and becoming a church. What happened there is happening here. St. Luke's story of what happened helps us understand what is happening here.

The experience of church is composed of two sets of action. The first is listening/answering, and the second is receiving/giving. Listening/answering is where we start. Jesus spoke to these men and women. As he spoke, they heard God speak. They listened and they answered.

In Jesus's last meeting with his disciples, he opened the Scriptures to them and showed them how he had fulfilled everything that had been written. He promised that they would experience for themselves everything that he had spoken. He told them to stay in the place of prayer until this happened. And they did. They took it all in; they made the connection between the Scriptures, this Word of God that they accepted as authoritative for their lives, and Jesus, this living person whom they had come to know and trust. They listened to the message of God in a personal way.

That is what we do in church—listen to God's word personally. In that way, the church is very different from a lecture hall or a schoolroom. In those places we study books or listen to lectures to acquire knowledge and information that we can use. In this place we listen to God speak to us so that we can become our true selves.

In the act of listening, the disciples began answering. They were, St. Luke told us, in the temple praising God. Prayer is answering speech. God is a conversationalist. He speaks personally to us to get us to speak personally to him, to answer. When we answer, we pray. That is what we do in church—personally answer God's personal word. We sing and speak our answers. In song and silence, in confessing our faith in the creed, and in reciting the Lord's Prayer, we answer.

And then receiving/giving. In the midst of the church's listening/answering, the Holy Spirit was poured out into their lives, and it resulted in an overflow of energy into others' lives.

This is what Jesus had promised. This is what the Hebrew prophets had promised: that the very energy of God, the being of God, would become internal to them. They would find themselves participants in the action of God, not just admirers of it.

Fire is one way of understanding that. Fire is participatory. In the biblical stories it is sometimes set in contrast to water. If I throw a piece of wood in water, the wood floats; if I throw a piece of wood in a fire, the fire consumes the wood. Water is an exterior experience; fire is an interior experience. When water is poured over us, it stays on the outside; if fire envelops us, it gets inside us and we are consumed.

And it keeps going. Water doesn't make more water, but fire

makes more fire. It spreads. If you receive fire into yourself, you give fire to others.

That is what is going on in this story. They are experiencing God within themselves, and it is spilling over to others. They speak quite miraculously, not their ideas about God, but God's working in them. Bystanders see and hear the mighty works of God being enacted and proclaimed before their very eyes, in their very ears.

That is what we do here: We receive God, and we give God. We do it most explicitly in the Eucharist, the Holy Communion. "This is my body," says Jesus. "This is my blood" (Mark 14:22, 24). Our Lord Jesus gives himself to us, and we take him in. We receive God.

But we also do this implicitly all the time, or we can. *Faith* is the word we use to mark that reception. When we use a word a lot, it sometimes loses sharpness of meaning. Faith gets dulled that way for us. Let's put a sharp edge on it again: Faith is the opening we make in our lives to receive God. Just the smallest of openings is enough for a start. God is constantly active, pouring himself out. Often we close ourselves up tight as a clam, and he pours off our lives like rainwater. But then we relax toward the mystery of God; we quiet down and wait and sit here in worship. We loosen our anxious grip on our lives and open upward, and the God-life enters and penetrates our insides like fire. We sense that we are in on something large or, rather, that something is in us that is more than us—some love, some hope, some energy that is more than we came here with. This is the Holy Spirit, God's gracious entering into our lives and becoming himself in us.

And without really deciding to do it, we find that we are giving what we have been receiving. We do not hold on to this life; we release it in words and acts among the people with whom we live. The fire spreads. A church burning.

Amen.

The Trinity Mystery

Frankly, I stand amazed at the unfathomable complexity of God's wisdom and God's knowledge. How could man ever understand his reasons for action, or explain his methods of working?

—Romans 11:33, PHILLIPS

One of the answers you get when you ask why a person comes to church is "to learn about God." It seems like a good answer. We reinforce it with hymns that say, "More about Jesus would I know."* Yet church is about more than just passing out information—it is also about worship. The common worship of the people of God is not an exercise in pious education. It is a response to and an engagement with God. This God is unseen and sometimes not at all obvious. The spectacle of a group of people devoutly doing things to and for and because of an invisible being might seem more than a little mysterious to an unsympathetic outsider.

Some express their lack of sympathy with the elements of mystery in the church in sharp terms. If the church would stick to its business of teaching morals and explaining existence rationally, it would be all well and good. But the prayers, hymns, adoration, sacrifice, and discipleship based on invisible relationship smack of superstition and mystery. These people see nothing but confusion

---

* Eliza E. Hewitt, "More About Jesus," 1887, public domain.

in the church. It is the last place they would go to learn anything. They think the church is more interested in mystifying people than in enlightening them.

This is Trinity Sunday. More than any other word in the church's vocabulary, with the possible exception of *predestination,* the word *Trinity* brings sighs of incomprehensibility to the lips of Christians and resigned comments that it is "all a mystery." If anyone were asked to explain the meaning of the Trinity, there would likely be only a sputtered refusal. The word has come to be associated with a tangle of theological double-talk and a bewildering potpourri of metaphysics, mysticism, and mystification.

That is surely the final irony, for the concept of the Trinity was formulated to combat just such a situation. It was the church's attempt to organize the truth of God in a comprehensible, orderly way so that Christians of even an average intelligence could grasp the meaning of the word God. It cut through all the ideas and speculations, the myths and guesses, the ignorance that posed as wisdom, and the lies that pretended to be truth. It was a powerful and victorious intellectual penetration by Christian thinkers into the disorderly and contradictory religious atmosphere of the Roman times. The history of the thinking out and formulation of the Trinity doctrine is one of the most enduring monuments to the brilliance of the human intellect.

What we have in religion, in the Bible, and in the experience of the church is the raw, unorganized contact of humanity with God. God creates, provides, orders, and redeems—and humans are involved in all this action. But it doesn't happen in a tidy, systematic way. The function of theology is to give a "methodical interpretation" of this divine activity and this human response.*

Moses looking at a burning bush heard God speak to him. Isaiah praying in the temple was commanded by God to be a prophet. Jeremiah felt the fire of God's word burn within him. God spoke to David through the mediation of the prophet Nathan. St. Paul

---

* Paul Tillich, *Systematic Theology,* vol. 1 (Chicago: University of Chicago Press, 1951), 15.

was met by God in a blaze of light on a country road. St. Peter (along with many others) looked at a Palestinian rabbi named Jesus and saw God. Early Christians experienced a common bond of living love in their worship and knew that it was God. Is God the voice, the man, or the feeling? In the midst of all this experience and description, how does one speak plainly of God? How can one account for the diversity and variety of God's activity in the Bible and in our experience? Theologians work on this material. They see the common threads woven through it. And then they make statements to assist the rest of us in understanding with our minds what the church has experienced in its heart. In the case of God, the theologians have seen a unity and a variety that they have described as a *trinity*.

This doctrine of the Trinity attempts to speak in an organized and plain, yet accurate and complete way about God. It is intended to clarify, not confuse; to enlighten the mind, not darken it; to make sense, not to create mystery.

The Trinity begins on the sure and firm foundation of one God. Monotheism is central in the development of the Trinity. But this one God cannot be described as you would describe an object. God is not a cosmic thing that you can examine or make a picture of. God is the active, willing, creating Lord of all things visible and invisible, who has revealed himself to us. No single experience can contain all that God has shown of himself. No single statement can say all that God has spoken about himself. But the Trinity doctrine has proven useful in the church in giving form to the contents of the God who reveals himself to us as our Lord.

The usual terminology is God the Father, God the Son, and God the Holy Spirit. God the Father refers to the God who is over us, is Lord of all things, yet in his rule loves us as a Father. There is kinship and relationship between God and us, and that kinship is characterized by a Father's love. God has made himself known to us as our Father—the one who created us, cares for us, and has a purpose for us. We are children who have a heavenly Father.

God the Son refers to the way in which God has revealed himself to us. In Jesus Christ, people saw God operating among them—acting and speaking. The invisible God revealed himself in his creation visibly in the life of Jesus of Nazareth. In his love, humility, service, and compassion, the shared life took visible form. God the Son refers to God in our history. God makes himself known in a human life. God is not, in other words, an abstract idea to be talked about, nor is he a spiritual power we grope after. He is the God who meets us and speaks to us in Jesus.

God the Holy Spirit refers to the results of God coming to us and revealing himself. Something happens in the world and in people when God acts among us and speaks to us. We are judged, converted, and redeemed. We are restored to health. We are united in love. We become alive to the fact that every person is a neighbor to every other. We are moved upon and charged by God. This result of God's activity, speech, and presence is God the Holy Spirit.

Thus, a denial of the Trinity becomes a rejection of this ruling, invading, active God. It is a refusal to admit God into history, to accept the declaration that God acts in such a way that brings results in human existence. A rejection of the Trinity is an attempt to keep God far off in the heavens, to consign him to outer space where we can look at him through a telescope but need not account for him in the flesh-and-blood world of family relations, politics, business, school, and recreation.

The question of faith put forth by the Trinity is "Will we have God with us?" A rejection of the Trinity is then a rejection of "God with us." The Jews' rejection of Jesus made it shatteringly clear that one can affirm the God of the Old Testament, apparently with the deepest reverence and most zealous faith, yet deny him to the point that his tangible form becomes an offense to such a pious soul. Israel denied the presence and action of God in Jesus, exactly as

the fathers in the desert had murmured against Moses and later stoned the prophets, not from irreligion but in the protest of the most refined, most ponderable religion against revelation, which definitely does not leave the pious man to himself but confronts him literally with God. Therefore, the Jesus revelation ends with his crucifixion by these most pious folk of their time, who, with Immanuel daily on their lips and in their heart, refused this particular Immanuel.*

The doctrine of the Trinity, then, is the church's way of describing the God who speaks to us in the love of the Father, shares his love with us as the Son, and brings forth living results in us through the Spirit. It is a statement about the living, acting, creating, redeeming God who fills the pages of Holy Scripture.

But the Trinity doctrine not only brings clarification and plain knowledge; it really does carry mystery as well. When we speak about God, we quickly exhaust our vocabulary. When finite humanity dares to talk about infinite Deity, we very soon use up all the ideas we ever had without making much of a dent in the subject matter.

In Scripture, a perfect instance of this process of logical analysis and rational understanding ends up in a declaration of mystery. It is found in St. Paul's letter to the Romans. In chapters nine through eleven, St. Paul engaged in one of the most complex, intellectual arguments in the New Testament. He used all his powers of intellect (with which he was amply endowed) to clarify the activity of God among the Jews. He wove arguments, explained the Old Testament, analyzed the historical situation, and meticulously traced the ways of God's grace in what looked, from the outside, to be a very confused situation. It is not easy reading, and it is not a simple argument. But it is an honest, sustained, skillful, and brilliantly successful application of human brain power in the service of understanding God.

But take special note of how Paul concluded that passage. After such a glittering display of intellectual prowess, you might expect a concluding summary statement that wrapped the argument up in

---

* Karl Barth, *Church Dogmatics*, 1.1 (London: T&T Clark, 1975), 366.

an unforgettable way. You might expect an admonition to the readers that, having had the subject put before them so plainly and undebatably, they had no excuses to misinterpret or forget it. But that is not what we find. St. Paul, who had been using his intellect, concluded with an awed expression of wonder and praise: "O the depth of the riches and wisdom and knowledge of God! How unsearchable are his judgements and how inscrutable his ways!" (Romans 11:33). Or as J. B. Phillips translated it, "Frankly, I stand amazed at the unfathomable complexity of God's wisdom and God's knowledge. How could man ever understand his reasons for action, or explain his methods of working?"

The first several hundred years of the church's history were marked by thinking on the Trinity. The church was under attack from all sides—it needed to think through its position so it would be strong in debate and solid in its instruction. But the thinking led directly to worship. It still does. The mind extends itself to its limit and moves into wonder, awe, and praise. God is (as we find out when we think about him for long) beyond all the calculations of the human mind. After all our thinking, we still find ourselves lost in God, so it comes about that *worship* "is the important word. The Trinity is continually spoken of in churches, not to provide a stimulation for our minds, but as an invocation to worship."*

Our life in the church is more than a mental activity, though it is that. It is more than an intellectualization of experience, though it contains that. It is more than a moralistic understanding of existence, though there are places for that. It is the confrontation with the living God, who meets us in love, serves us with grace, and powerfully works out his purposes in our lives. We can trace with our small minds only the "outskirts of his ways" (Job 26:14). The little bit of knowledge that we garner creates a hunger for more than knowledge, for deeper and more extensive experience with God. And if our knowledge of the Trinity does not lead us to that experience of the Trinity, we will have wasted our time.

* David H. C. Read, *The Christian Faith* (New York: Charles Scribner's Sons, 1956), 130.

The Imitation of Christ wisely says, "Talk as learnedly as you will about the doctrine of the Holy Trinity, it will get you no thanks from the Holy Trinity if you aren't humble about it. After all, it isn't learned talk that serves a man or makes a saint of him; only a life well lived can claim God's friendship."*

Let us pray.

Keep us, O Lord, from the vain strife of words, and grant to us a constant profession of the truth. Preserve us in the faith, true and undefiled, so that we may ever hold fast that which we professed when we were baptized into the name of the Father, and of the Son, and of the Holy Spirit; that we may have thee for our Father; that we abide in thy Son and may know the gracious efforts of the Holy Spirit. We pray this in the strong name of the Trinity.†

Amen.

---

* Thomas à Kempis, *The Imitation of Christ*, trans. Robert Knox (San Francisco: Ignatius Press, 2005).
† Paraphrase of St. Hilary of Poitiers, "For Perseverance in Faith," Catholic Doors Ministry, www.catholicdoors.com/prayers/english/p00384.htm.

Angels Long to Look

The prophets who prophesied of the grace that was to be yours searched and inquired about this salvation . . . things into which angels long to look.

—1 Peter 1:10, 12

Sometimes a single detail can illuminate an entire landscape. A painting attributed to Rembrandt called *Old Woman Cutting Her Nails* shows little else in the revealing light besides the gnarled hand of the old woman and the knife she is using on her ancient hands. But the detail is more than enough—the burdens of years and the futility of a life spent in small pursuits, or perhaps imprisoned by small-minded masters, come flowing out of that detail.

Here is another illustration: Pascal once remarked wittily that history would have been radically changed if Cleopatra's nose had been a quarter of an inch longer:* a very small detail, but what a difference it would have made.

St. Peter included a detail like that in this portion of his letter. He referred to "salvation" twice but then stepped aside to consider it in a kind of parenthesis. This salvation, which is a result of conversion, of being "born anew," received a few remarks of its own. And at the conclusion of those remarks is this fascinating detail that tells more than volumes of theological exposition could do.

---

* Blaise Pascal, *Pensées*, no. 162.

But before we look at this detail, let's examine what St. Peter said about salvation.

Salvation has an elaborate history: "The prophets who prophesied of the grace that was to be yours searched and inquired about this salvation" (1 Peter 1:10).

At the mention of these searching and inquiring prophets, our minds run back through the centuries in which they lived. Salvation did not appear suddenly with no precedents. It did not explode without preparation on the world. It was rooted in the millennia of Israel's history, especially in the lives of the men called "prophets."

Abraham was the first and the father of salvation history. It was in him that the whole movement of salvation history was initiated. The faith with which he responded to that call of God in Ur—that brought him across strange deserts to a foreign land, that revealed a moral and unified God in the midst of the divine brutality and immorality that then existed—was the first building stone in the massive structure to which Christ was the capstone.

Moses was another. In quite a different way he searched and inquired. It was out of Egyptian wealth and affluence that he threaded his way to the salvation center of history. Where gods were worshipped with monumental pyramids and the entire focus of the religious life was on life after death, Moses was led by God to forge a community in the desert. The entire purpose of this was the fulfilling of a new law in the everyday actions of social life and ritual worship.

Isaiah lived in a time where the meaning of salvation was becoming clearer and more specific. His search and inquiry led him to one of the most beautiful and accurate anticipations of the meaning of salvation in the entire history of Israel. In Isaiah 53, he wrote:

Surely he has borne our griefs
   and carried our sorrows;

yet we esteemed him stricken,
    smitten by God, and afflicted.
But he was wounded for our transgressions,
    he was bruised for our iniquities;
upon him was the chastisement that made us whole,
    and with his stripes we are healed. (verses 4–5)

For hundreds of years, in countries ranging from Ur of the Chaldeans to the villages of Palestine, to the tremendous Nile River civilization in Egypt, between the Tigris and Euphrates Rivers in Mesopotamia, and finally spread out all the way from Persia to Spain, the Hebrew people were caught up in an elaborate history of salvation. There were outstanding leaders, but more importantly, there was a continuous people who carried the memory and growing experience of search and inquiry to the point of climax in Jesus Christ.

The history of Israel is not learned by memorizing dates or mastering geography or even by assimilating the ideas that their fertile minds produced. It is learned only by discovering it as a salvation history—a history experienced and expressed as the story of a people called, delivered, and governed by God.

And Peter's word "salvation" can be understood in its completeness only by seeing it as the product of this elaborate and intricately wrought history.

Salvation has a personal directness: "the grace that was to be yours."

But lest we think salvation is defined only by the grand movements of grace in and out of succeeding centuries, Peter directed it all to people. The personal pronoun your or you occurs in this paragraph four times.

That personal pronoun is as equally important as the prophets. Salvation is not the general description of the past; it is the focus of the present on our lives. We stand at the end of the history. It impinges on us; we are the ones to whom salvation comes.

That is made most plain in the person of Jesus Christ. The revelation of salvation was made fully known in him. In our Lord's encounters with Palestinian people in the first century, salvation became a wonderfully personal, absolutely direct restoration of humanity's health in mind, body, and soul by the act of God.

The man who was carried by four men and let down through the roof so that Jesus might minister to him was saved by having his sins forgiven and his body healed. And recall the great individual attention Jesus gave him.

The woman who suffered for so many years with a hemorrhage timidly approached Jesus through a crowd and touched the edge of his coat. He turned to her and quickly established an intimate, personal communication with her, declaring her wholeness.

Peter himself was called by name and treated with profound respect and consideration. A blustering man by nature, he was treated by Jesus with great gentleness and care. And through this direct, personal application, he was saved.

Salvation is the most individual thing that can happen to a person. It is the most personal and intimate and private of all the activities of grace. Here God meets with humankind in redeeming power and wholeness, and health is shared.

Salvation includes both history and individualism, the prophets and the pronouns. It would be a mistake to think that we could favor one of these sides over the other. Peter mixed them up in the same exposition. Neither can be slighted; both must be embraced.

Separation of the two gives way not only to grave theological errors but to gross human tragedy too. To concentrate only on the historical aspects of salvation to the neglect of the personal develops a colorless, dull religion that gives no inspiration to daily living. As a result, people seek other inspirations—some of which destroy rather than save. The large-scale inability to enjoy leisure that we observe in America today—precipitating many to overindulgence in drinking or narcotics, to experimentation in marriage, and to meaninglessness in acquiring material possessions—can be traced, theologically, to a failure to deal with personal aspects of salvation. Those who so exist are often members of churches and have participated in the historical aspects of salvation history, but it has never reached them.

On the other hand, to concentrate solely on the personal with no regard for the historical is to encourage that souring, visionary pursuit after the righteousness of God with callous disregard for the rights of others. The Crusaders in the eleventh and twelfth centuries were fired with a tremendous love for Christ and demonstrated a supernatural courage and determination in their task. But as they marched to their holy wars, they killed every Jew they could lay their hands on, saying, "Why should we leave Jews here to get rich while we risk our lives in the Holy Land?" Their lives ware narrowed down to a personal salvation. The elaborate history by which their lives were inextricably bound to every living human being was somehow, unaccountably, forgotten.

Both parts of the truth must make up the whole truth: Salvation is a grand and elaborate history; salvation is the grace of God announced to you. It is a glorious combination of prophets and pronouns.

And now to pick up that detail—Peter concluded this brief excursus with the phrase "things into which angels long to look."

It is difficult to form any consistent image of angels from the biblical data. They sometimes appear in human form, indistinguishable from any other human. Twice in the Psalms, they appear to have wings (Psalm 18:10; 104:3), but these isolated references scarcely permit the widespread generalization in pictures where we never see angels without wings. More commonly, angelic beings seem to not fit with a certain image at all but to be specific applications of spiritual energy in carrying out God's will—emissaries of the Godhead.

But a purely spiritual principle is difficult to handle if you can't make some kind of picture out of it. Our imaginations are incorrigibly pictorial. And so here with this reference to angels, we are bound, I suppose, to construct winged creatures.

It looks, though, as if Peter was doing the same thing. When he said that the angels "long to look," the word he used (*parakyptō*) literally means to "lean over to look into."* That little detail builds a whole landscape for me. You have to imagine heaven as a kind of circular balcony stretched out over the earth, and behind the balustrades the angels are lined up, leaning over, trying to get a look at what is going on. Salvation is what is going on—an intricate salvation history culminating in personal encounters with God.

It provides the same kind of spectator pleasure for the angels as an athletic event or a parade does for us. The elaborate intricacy of the history of salvation provides a never-ending plot and endlessly unfolding pageant. And the personal directness provides the continuous surprise of new response, the refreshing individuality of salvation as it becomes an event in a unique person. It is the passion of angels to lean over the balcony rails of heaven and watch such salvation drama.

But for you it is no spectator sport. You are right in the middle of it.

Amen.

---

* *Blue Letter Bible,* s.v. *"parakyptō,"* www.blueletterbible.org/lexicon/g3879/esv/mgnt/0-1.

Follow in His Steps

To this you have been called, because Christ also suffered for you, leaving you an example, that you should follow in his steps.

—1 Peter 2:21

This portion of St. Peter's letter is addressed to "servants." These servants were slaves, but not in the exact sense that we think of slavery today. In the Roman Empire at this time, slave laborers constituted a majority of the workforce. There was a great deal of unrest among them, and frequent strikes were called and rebellions ignited. The "servant" problem was a critical one in the first century.

Not only that, but a great many of these "servant-slaves" found their way into the early church. There is no way to tell for sure, but it appears that a large percentage of the church's membership in the first couple of centuries came from this social class. Part of the evidence for this is that in many of St. Paul's letters, and in this letter of St. Peter, special paragraphs of admonition were written directly to the servant or slave class.

Here, Peter told them (which is also essentially what Paul preached) that they should be obedient to their masters, even to the bad ones. And if they did suffer under an evil and arrogant master, they should find a special meaning in this suffering by looking at the life of Jesus Christ. He also suffered, and he plainly did not deserve to suffer. He was the most innocent, most guiltless of

all who have ever suffered, and his life is an example for us. We are
to follow in his steps.

Peter quoted four times from Isaiah 53 to show what he meant.
This great passage in Isaiah paints the Messiah in the unusual style
of a despised man who suffers innocently. This is in contrast to all
the hopes and expectations of an international-hero Messiah who
would openly conquer all wrong and rebellion triumphantly. The
insight in this passage is profound—it pinpoints the essential
wrong in the human existence as sin and the deepest need as forgiveness. If the Messiah had come as a world hero and a triumphant champion of the right, the essential problems of life would
have been unaffected. As a matter of fact, several messiahs have
come that way, and the world has been the worse, not the better,
for their coming.

But God entered into human life in Jesus and attacked what's
wrong with the world at its center, overcoming the power of sin
and forgiving the guilt of sin. Our Lord met this need on both an
individual level and a social level. And a very important part of his
achievement involved suffering—innocent suffering.

There is no explanation for this in Scripture. We are given the
facts of the case and the faith that developed out of it. The innocent suffering of Christ came to crisis proportions on the Cross.
His total suffering was the result of complete innocence. All the
ignorance, evil, hate, pride, and selfishness of the world poured
out and found a culprit. Those are the facts of the case: the facts of
the Cross.

The faith that developed out of it is that, contrary to appearances, evil was conquered and forgiveness of sin was made real. A
deep spiritual transaction took place on the cross—the sin of humankind was dealt a death blow, and the age-old problem of dealing with guilt was met. Sin was no longer the unconquerable
anti-hero, and guilt was no longer tragedy.

This is what they experienced in the early church. This was the
basis for their new life. This is what St. Peter discovered. And it is

what made them joyful (for sin was no longer unbeatable) and free (for guilt no longer chained them). So, marked by this joy and exuberance and this freedom and energy, they plunged into society with the example of their Lord to shape their way. And they turned the world upside down.

But make careful note of these often-overlooked facts. These people were, for the most part, the working class—the servants and slaves of that society. That is, they were on the bottom rung of the power structure. As yet, Christianity had no historical proofs of superiority. It was only a few decades old; many had not heard about it, and there was no way of knowing that it would one day be a worldwide religion. In other words, they had nothing but their own experience and faith to support them in whatever action they took.

They really did suffer. Life was not easy for them. Even when they were not martyred (which was not very often, statistically), they were given a hard time. The standards for slave masters were not what we would call humane or enlightened. So, the people really did follow in Christ's steps and suffer innocently and submissively, with the confidence that their suffering was a part of Christ's work of conquering and forgiving sin. They did this without any better explanations for innocent suffering than we have—which is to say, without understanding it at all but quite sure that it did have meaning—and saw the results of their victory and forgiveness in the lives around them, made joyful and free by Christ.

Peter's letter was a successful sermon, then. He may have had doubts when he wrote such unpopular advice to those early Christians. Suppose you were chafing under the brutal treatment of an unjust master in a pagan environment and had a chance to break away, to escape and find a new freedom. But then you received a letter from your pastor, and all it said was "To this you have been called, because Christ also suffered for you, leaving you an example, that you should follow in his steps" (1 Peter 2:21). It held no attempt to philosophize about the suffering, no explanation to show that there was good cause for it—just the command to be submissive and to imitate Christ in his suffering. What would you do?

Would you not have a real tendency to say something like this? "He doesn't know what I'm suffering. He is all caught up in his beautiful ideas of theology and writing us letters from his ivory tower—he has nothing to offer us and no advice worth taking seriously. We want help; we want deliverance; we are hurting enough; we want rescue."

There were probably some who said that, even as some say it today. But the more important thing to note is that many did not say it. A great majority listened and obeyed. This message to a suffering people became truth in their lives. It was not "just a lot of talk." It was the entrance of the Spirit of God in their lives, whereby their sins were forgiven and by which they overcame the world. Their suffering became a part of God's work of redemption. The sermon was listened to, and it worked.

But now we have a problem. This was written to slaves. There is no slave here this morning. And what's more, none of us even own slaves! A church full of slaves is something we have not even the remotest connection with. So, how does what Peter wrote to slaves twenty centuries ago have anything to do with us?

We have to do two things when we read Scripture. First, we must find out what the text says. We do this by studying the language, searching through the history, examining archeological evidence, and analyzing the grammar. This is called *exegesis*. Second, we must find out what it says to us. And this is always the more difficult task, for it involves a human willingness to be spoken to.

There is a very illuminating stage in a child's growth where we can see this dual understanding. All children have to eat. In the first stage of their lives, we could say to them "Eat your dinner," but knowing full well that they can't understand what we say, we usually don't bother to say it. As our children grow and develop, we are never quite certain when they are capable of understanding what we mean. But a time does come when they understand it. So,

we say "Eat your dinner" with more force and expect obedience.
But we are not always obeyed. Around the age of two years, we
are faced with a new problem—not in their understanding language but in their responding to it. The words have meaning to the
child, but he does not always apply them to himself.

I can call into the next room where two of my children are playing and say, "Pick up your toys," and come in a few minutes later
to find no toys picked up.

So, I say to the older, "Karen, didn't you hear me?"

And she says, "Yes."

"Didn't you understand me?"

"Yes, but I thought you were talking to Eric."

The evasions of children are simple compared to the evasions
we make, the rationalizations we construct, and the excuses we
give in confrontation with the Word of God. After we have solved
the first problem of understanding Scripture, we still have the
larger problem of obediently listening to it. The first task is one of
the mind; the second involves the will or, in biblical language, the
heart. It requires a whole personal response, a life involvement, a
dedication of self.

We understand what Peter said. Now what do we do? We can
say, "Oh, I thought he was talking to slaves." Or "That applied to
the first century." Or "Our modern world is so revolutionary, our
times are so complex, that simple word will no longer suffice. It's
probably true enough, but it doesn't speak to me."

But the church has held a firm conviction that all of Scripture is
for us. No matter to whom it was first addressed, it has a message
for us. We must use our minds to understand what it is saying to
us, but when we understand it, we then have to obey.

St. Peter wrote, "To this you have been called, because Christ
also suffered for you, leaving you an example, that you should follow in his steps." We understand what it meant when he said it to
the slaves. What does it mean to us?

It means that suffering for the Christian is not a catastrophe but
a vocation. "To this you have been called." In Latin, "called" is

vocare, from which comes *vocation.*[*] This is our profession—to be at the point of suffering. This is not what we are to avoid at all costs but what we are to embrace in the name of Christ.

The reason is that in suffering, the contest between God and Satan is at its critical point. Suffering is sometimes the conflict between right and wrong, between doubt and faith, between love and hate, or between health and disease. Because this is where the battle is thickest, it is where the best individuals must be deployed, and those men and women are the Christians.

It is not among the lilies of the field where Christ is seen in power but on the Cross. The Cross is the point of suffering, and the point of suffering is where the Christian is called to be, for this is the place of victory.

At this crucial point, sin is overcome and guilt is forgiven. Suffering people often look for guilt: "What did I do to deserve this?" they say. But the Christian can proclaim forgiveness to them. For suffering is not the place where we try to determine the responsibility for sin; it is the place where we proclaim the forgiveness of its guilt.

This is the theology behind the Christian's involvement in the suffering that comes from ignorance, poverty, racial injustice, or disease. It is not our task to denounce evil, to deplore violence, or to castigate the sinner. We are called to the place of suffering— and there, with Christ living in us, to overcome sin and proclaim forgiveness.

This week, a man told me that his son wanted to go into the ministry but that he was doing everything possible to prevent him. The reason? A minister has to deal with the worst kind of people: the hypocrite, the self-centered, the inconsiderate, the weaklings. He explained that a former pastor of his had a nervous breakdown under the stress of living and dealing with such people. He didn't want his son to get involved in that kind of life, with those kinds of people. I suggested that if his son felt deeply called to such a life,

---

[*] *Merriam-Webster,* s.v. "vocation," www.merriam-webster.com/dictionary/vocation#word -history.

there was no place where he could work more meaningfully or do more to change the downward course of people's lives. But this man would have none of it. The people he described were all suffering people. And suffering people need to have Christ enter their suffering to overcome sin and forgive guilt. It is not only ministers who are called to do that but also each one of us who has heard Christ's call.

Many people today think of walking with Jesus only in terms of improving our lives, as if walking in the steps of Jesus was an afternoon stroll with the sun shining. And too often the church and the Christian have imagined that to be the truth.

Notice how differently the gospel writers described Jesus steps—his steps went to the hopelessly sick, to those racked with doubt, to the bereaved in their anguish, to the outcast and despised, and finally into the turbulent politics of Jerusalem that took him to the Cross. He left us an example, Peter said, that we "should follow in his steps." We cannot follow in his steps without walking to suffering people. The central symbol of the church is not a lily of the field but a cross. And that cross was once drenched with the blood of the One who chose to voluntarily and innocently suffer on our behalf. We are called to do the same.

A final word about Peter. St. Matthew recounted that it was only Peter who attempted to imitate his Master in walking on the sea. As he walked toward Jesus, Peter saw the wind and was frightened and began to sink. He called out, "Lord, save me," and our Lord did. And then Jesus said, "O man of little faith, why did you doubt?" (Matthew 14:28–31). Peter was rebuked not for the daring venture of walking on the water but for his lack of faith. And that's a parable for us. If we follow in our Lord's steps, we will make mistakes, and we will sink sometimes, but he will save us from our mistakes and from our sins. The danger is that we will never get out of the boat of our comfort, security, and safety. "To this you have been called, because Christ also suffered for you, leaving you an example, that you should follow in his steps."

Amen.

ORDINARY TIME

✳

The Most Dangerous

First of all, then, I urge that supplications, prayers, interces-
sions, and thanksgivings be made for all men, for kings and all
who are in high positions, that we may lead a quiet and peace-
able life, godly and respectful in every way.

—1 Timothy 2:1–2

Do you know that the most dangerous thing you can do is go
to church? I mean as a Christian, as a person who is searching
for God's will for your life. I don't mean that you are likely to be
physically endangered while attending a church. We have a substantial building that is well constructed and safely maintained. I
mean it is dangerous to you as a person to be here—because this is
the place where you are tempted and most liable to the sins that
can most easily damn you.

The temptations that take place inside church are much more
severe and have much bigger consequences than those outside.
You would be incensed if someone came into this church and
slipped pornographic literature into the hymnbooks, so that as
you were searching for a hymn, you were suddenly exposed to
words and pictures that might draw your soul away from God.
You wouldn't be very happy if while you were worshipping, you
suddenly saw off in some corner or underneath some pew a group
of our children gambling with money stolen from the offering
plate. You would say this can't be. Yet I tell you quite seriously—
and this is not hyperbole—it is more dangerous for you to be here

under the present circumstances than either of those things I mentioned.

Just think back to what our Lord talked about when he was on this earth. Who did he become angry with? Who were the people that gave him the most trouble? Who were the people that seemed to be most in danger of damnation? It was the scribes and the Pharisees, which can very easily be translated into our language as the Methodists and the Presbyterians. What about the others—the prostitutes and the tax collectors? Jesus didn't say they were okay, but he went to them and ministered to them and seemed to get a good response with them. And we never find him expressing frustration with or anger at them. However, with the ones who were in church every Sunday, he seemed to have a very difficult time.

The lesson is clear to us that the spiritual sins are much more dangerous than the physical. When people steal, they know that they are stealing and that if they get caught, they will be punished. But when someone feels proud, that's harder to gauge. She doesn't have everybody watching her to catch her. In fact, our society is more likely to admire her and give her a medal or a promotion. So, we become envious, proud, jealous, smug, and callous to our neighbors. We get by with the kinds of things that take place inside our spirits without anybody seeing them, and we can very easily perpetuate them in the church. It is very easy to sit here and think, *Because I am here and all those other people are outside, I am better than they are. Lord, aren't you pleased to have me here?*

The most dangerous place you can be is in church. So, if you are going to come to church, you have to be on guard. You have to take special precautions against slipping into those most dangerous of sins that can silently erode your inner life, separating you from the mercy and grace of God with no one even knowing it and being hardly aware of it yourself.

And when you enter a church, the most dangerous thing you can do is pray. In this most dangerous place, there is a most dangerous activity: prayer. Because in prayer, we have decided to engage in that most intimate of acts—to open ourselves personally to

God. It is very easy to fool others and ourselves by deciding inwardly, *I really don't want to do that,* yet going through the forms of prayer anyhow, so that other people think we are praying. We do this often enough that we think we are praying, but in fact we are not. While engaging in forms that look like the most intense, personal, and honest kind of religion, we are doing the opposite. We are separating ourselves from the very personal word that God brings to us.

Jesus once told a story about a Pharisee and a tax collector (Luke 18:9–14). In this story we find a Pharisee praying a beautiful prayer and a tax collector hardly praying at all. He was just yelling, telling God how bad he was. And Jesus used the story to show us how dangerous prayer is. Jesus's point was not to go and pray better. He was saying, "Be careful if you pray; it is very dangerous. And you might get yourself involved in something that will ruin your life eternally."

I am tempted to repeat everything I have said because I want you to know it. And I want you to be persuaded that being here is dangerous and engaging in prayer is dangerous. It is as if our text says, "First of all, pray, and if I am going to pass on his counsel to you, I want you to know all the ways it can go wrong."

It is almost like those who work in a nuclear power plant where there is an intensely high danger of radiation. It is very important work. Somebody must be there, but the workers take extraordinary precautions so that the radiation does not touch them. They have lead shields, special clothing, and special procedures to observe because it is dangerous work. Well, prayer is that way. It must be done. It is at the heart of the Christian's life, yet we must take extraordinary precautions so that we do not end up like the Pharisee or involve ourselves in a perpetuating, snowballing type of self-righteousness and smugness.

Paul knew how dangerous prayer can be. He knew all the things that could go wrong, but he still said *pray.* He wanted the people to pray so they would not get involved in a religion that simply talked and did empty things. In the early part of his letter to Timothy, Paul reminded the young pastor that some people in his church were "swerving" away from love and sincere faith and thereby wandering "into vain discussion, desiring to be teachers of the law, without understanding either what they are saying or the things about which they make assertions" (1 Timothy 1:6–7). If religion is mostly a matter of talk—of teaching, telling, discussion, arguing, or debates—it goes off into an unproductive, sterile, kind of life where people make shipwrecks of their faith. Paul said this is why we must pray. The conversation at the center of the gospel is not with one another but with God.

We have to do something when we come to church. We can't just come here and sit. What do we do? First, pray. Now, throughout this letter Paul said a lot of other things. He instructed Timothy how to conduct a church, covering many different topics: women, bishops, deacons, older men, younger men, older women, younger women, widows, beggars, slaves, and the rich. But first of all, prayer. Prayer is the first thing that you do. Emphasizing this first-of-all-ness of prayer, Paul said we should pray "for all men" and then mentioned kings and authorities in particular (2:1–2).

I have wondered why he said that. If you say "all men," isn't that enough? If you say pray for everybody, can't you just stop there? Why would he go on to say pray for the kings and the authorities? Well, I think he did that because when you're giving somebody instructions, the one thing you will probably enumerate for them is the one thing they are most likely to leave out. I can't think of anyone more likely to be left out of prayers by first-century Christians than the kings and the authorities, because they were the bad guys at the time. They were men like Nero, who persecuted Christians. They were judges and governors in local places, like Pontius Pilate. They were persons who made life difficult for Christians, calling themselves gods and setting themselves up as spiritual rulers while the Christians huddled together, sometimes in secret. When the believers prayed for "all men," it would have been very easy to leave out kings, emperors, and other authorities.

So, to make the "all men" phrase stick, Paul named a couple of them just so his readers knew that he really meant "all."

As you assimilate this message into your own life, make some notations under "all men," listing the people you are most likely to forget. As I pray, I'm not likely to forget my family, my friends, the hurting, and others I am concerned for, but there are some people that could easily get left out of my prayers. I have to make my own notations for that, and so do you. We are urged to pray, firstly, for all people. We begin our lives as Christians by talking to God, by addressing God, by opening ourselves to God. And we let that first address develop into something that is inclusive for everything in our lives.

Sometimes I hear people say, "We've done all that we can. I guess all we can do now is pray." I have said it myself, but I hope I never say it again. On reading this passage and trying to find out what it means for my own life, I have been struck with the truth that prayer is in the wrong place if it is put last. To be effective, prayer must be first. It is the first thing we do, not the last. It is what we begin with so that all our other actions may be directed rightly. Prayer does not solve all problems. It orients us to God so that God, through us, can solve our problems. When you have prayed, then you'll be in the right place, you'll have the orientation, and you'll have the sensitivity. You will be in touch with the energy that will then equip you to begin to add, to move, and to minister.

First of all, pray, and then let that prayer spread out. Let it move into everything that goes out into your lives, reaching all people—touching even kings, the people you don't like, the people you think are against you, and those you think are hostile to the love you are trying to share in Jesus Christ.

I know I am preaching about something that you don't think you are very good at. Don't brush me off. It is amazing how sparse the Bible is in instructing us in prayer. Jesus doesn't come saying, "You don't pray enough. Let me show you how to pray. I'll give you the techniques of prayer so that you will be good at it." Jesus never did that. Once and only once did he give us a model for prayer. The rest of the time, you know what he did? He told stories and made statements that said God answers prayer. The important thing about prayer is not that we do it but that God answers it. The great task before us is not learning how to pray but simply believing that God answers prayer from people like us—however halting, sporadic, casual, or infrequent our prayers may be.

God is good at dealing with people like us, people who don't pray very well. He knows how to listen to us. He knows how to respond to us. He knows how to help us, and since that's true, start there. That's where God wants us to begin so he can begin with us. First of all, pray.

Amen.

The Camel's Nose
and the Needle's Eye

"It is easier for a camel to go through the eye of a needle than for a rich man to enter the kingdom of God." And they . . . said to him, "Then who can be saved?" Jesus looked at them and said, "With men it is impossible, but not with God; for all things are possible with God."

—Mark 10:25–27

It is a mark of our sin that we can read the entire Scriptures without once breaking out in laughter. One of Solomon's proverbs prescribes the medicine of "a cheerful heart" (17:22), but we instead settle back in a pious gloom and take aspirin. There are humorous stories, sayings, and figures of speech in the Bible, but we persistently misread them because we cannot imagine any mixture of religion and humor. As a result, we have a picture of Jesus that deliberately excludes lightness, laughter, joke making, and merriment. Despite the extensive evidence in the Gospels that Jesus was frequently at parties, entered into the merrymaking, and was adept at coining a humorous phrase, we consistently picture him as a man of a sober, solemn mood. If some daring artist painted a portrait of our Lord laughing with great gusto, we might instinctively label it a sacrilege. But our instincts would be wrong.

In the lesson for today, we hear Jesus saying, "It is easier for a camel to go through the eye of a needle than for a rich man to enter the kingdom of God" (Mark 10:25). Now that is a very funny statement. A camel is a large, ungainly, clumsy animal. His awkward ways are the butt of many jokes in Eastern lands. The eye of a needle is a very tiny opening, and threading a needle requires sharp eyes, a steady hand, and a small thread. Deliberately throwing the huge, misshapen camel and the minute, carefully wrought needle into the same figure of speech should have brought at least a smile from the disciples, if not outright guffaws.

Some of the story's first interpreters in the second century missed its humor. In Greek, the word for camel (*kamēlos*) is nearly the same as the word for rope (*kamilos*). They suggested that Jesus said, "It is easier for a rope to go through the eye of a needle than for a rich man to enter the kingdom of God." The point remains the same—it is still impossible—but it is no longer funny. In the fifteenth century, another humorless variant appeared. This time the theory was that Palestinian cities had two gates side by side (which they did): one large for regular, daytime traffic, and another very small one, which was easy to protect and guard, for nighttime access. This second gate was barely large enough for a man to squeeze through so, of course, a camel could never make it. This gate was sometimes called the "needle's eye." These scholars would then read the passage this way: "It is easier for a camel to go through that little gate called the needle's eye than for a rich man to enter the kingdom of God." Again, the point is the same: It can't be done. And again, it's no longer funny.

All this humorless scholasticism doesn't eliminate the truth of Jesus's words, but it does lose the spirit in which he said them. The atmosphere that Jesus created by his presence and manner—full of life, merriment, and zest—is traded for a dusty seminar in rabbinic lore. To get the real feeling of Jesus's ministry, we have to capture some of the wild incongruity in his speech, the boisterous humor in his images, and his sheer delight in reversing a centuries-old line of thought with an irreverent joke.

The incident we are dealing with today begins with Jesus setting out on a journey. He had no sooner gotten out on the road when a man ran up breathlessly, knelt before him, and asked him a question. There was an urgency in this man's encounter with Jesus. It was no casual meeting in the street. There was nothing in this man of the easy procrastination with which so many treat religious matters.

The man not only had an impressive energy in his approach but showed intelligence too. He asked the right question: "Good Teacher, what must I do to inherit eternal life?" (verse 17). Whatever else we conclude about this man later on, we must remember that "he at least asks the question that really matters."* There are no curious questions about the "furniture of heaven or the temperature of hell"† ; his query goes to the heart of the meaning of life. For the Jew, "eternal life" meant the lasting life, the worthwhile life, the life in which God was involved even on this earth, a life that wouldn't be swept away like chaff by the winds of death. Put another way, it was the good life—life with God in his good world, not a life filled with goods.

One couldn't ask for a better setting for the exposition of the gospel. The stage was set for Jesus to preach the good news. Everything was right. The man was eager to know, and he had the intelligence to understand. He was motivated and bright, and he had come to the right place. Our anticipation rises as we wait to hear what Jesus would say to this ideal candidate.

But before Jesus answered, he made a correction. The man addressed him as "Good Teacher," and Jesus said, "Why do you call me good? No one is good but God alone" (verse 18). Jesus made an issue of the man's use of the word *good* not to disclaim goodness from himself but to call into question the man's conception of his own goodness. The man could call Jesus "good" so glibly and easily because he thought of himself as good. He used the word to describe an expert ethical and religious performance (at which, as

---

* C. E. B. Cranfield, *The Gospel According to St. Mark: An Introduction and Commentary* (Cambridge, U.K.: Cambridge University Press, 1977), 327.

† Reinhold Niebuhr, *The Nature and Destiny of Man: A Christian Interpretation*, vol. 2, *Human Destiny* (London: Nisbet and Company, 1943), 304.

we discover later, he himself had been a great success) and never thought of God. You notice how he put the question: "What must I do?" In this man's world, he was the chief performer. He did things well; therefore, he was good. He was a religious man whose religion consisted in what he did. There was no active God in his religion—God was a spectator watching him perform. He was at the center.

He must have been an impressive person. The other gospels add details to Mark's account, telling us that he was not only rich but also young and a ruler in the high Jewish councils. He had riches, youth, and power—yet he wasn't satisfied. He sensed something missing. And that brought him to Jesus. But in assuming that Jesus was like himself (a "good man"), he was mistaken. Jesus said, in essence, "Let's stop talking about being good and start talking about God. The trouble with you is that there is no room for God in your life."

Jesus followed this up by saying, "You know the commandments" (verse 19). Of course he knew the commandments. The Ten Commandments that we hold as the foundation of the Christian life were even more highly held then. The man would know them meticulously. They would be as much a part of him as his name and address.

Knowing that, what follows is a surprise. Jesus recited the commandments to the man, but as he did so, he made three curious mistakes. He said, "Do not kill, Do not commit adultery, Do not steal, Do not bear false witness, Do not defraud, Honor your father and mother" (verse 19).

If you were asked to recite the commandments and they came out that way, I would put it down to your bad memory. But we must assume that Jesus did it deliberately. The mistakes were not slight slips of the tongue—they were glaring and obvious and undoubtedly intentional.

The first mistake is that he didn't begin at the beginning. He omitted the first four commandments completely, the ones that kept a person in constant remembrance and in vital relationship with God. By omitting them in his recital, Jesus indicated that the man had omitted them in his life. By saying "You know the commandments" and then skipping the first four, he implied that the man didn't even know the first four, that he had left God out of his life. He knew only those commandments that had to do with performance. The depth of life, the meaning of existence, and the creativity of spirit that spring from a living relationship to a living God—that was all a vacuum. The "one thing lacking is the all-important thing, a single-hearted devotion to God, obedience to the first of the Ten Commandments."*

The second mistake is a misquotation. The tenth commandment is "Do not covet," but Jesus said, "Do not defraud." It was a deliberate change to emphasize its meaning. Covetousness is a secret, inward sin. No one would know if someone was doing that or not. You can try a person in a court for murder, adultery, stealing, and perjury, but no one has ever been on trial for covetousness. Jesus saw in this rich man a deep and pervasive covetousness, a greed for possessions, an insatiable thirst for things. Covetousness created a pattern of acquisition in his life by which he accumulated wealth at the expense of less-fortunate persons. It was all very legal, but it was still very wrong. He got richer, his neighbors got poorer, and he broke not a single law to do it—except, of course, the tenth commandment "Do not covet." But Jesus saw through the man's moral pretense, penetrated the screen of ethical goodness, saw entrenched covetousness, and laid it bare to the light of day by deliberately substituting "defraud" for "covet." The man could not have failed to notice the paraphrase.

The third mistake Jesus made with the commandments was in getting them out of order. He began with number six, "Do not kill," then went to seven, eight, nine, ten, and concluded with five, "Honor your father and mother." Why take the fifth commandment out of its normal sequence and put it at the conclusion? Presumably to emphasize it. It was a common practice among the

* Cranfield, *The Gospel According to St. Mark*, 330.

Pharisees (as Jesus pointed out in Mark 7:10–13) to take what was due parents and make a special gift of it to God, and because God was higher than parents, you were free of parental obligations. It was all very legal and was defended by some rabbis, but it clearly denied the spirit of the commandment. It is a reasonable assumption that this man had been doing that. Maybe that was how he had become so rich at such a young age.

But despite the skill and deftness of Jesus's exposé and the courtesy and kindness of his manner, the man did not respond. He brashly maintained, "Teacher, all these I have observed from my youth" (10:20). Of course he had, but didn't he see that the reason he could say that was because Jesus had left out half of what he ought to have been doing, and that before all the rest? He was so impressed with his own goodness that he was blind to the whole universe of God's grace and his neighbor's need. He had excluded a living God from his life for so long that he no longer noticed the omission. This man has mastered the letter of the law, meaning he fully understood it, but the author of the law—God himself—had not mastered him. But how to get the man to understand this?

Up to this point, Jesus had been the Great Physician prescribing a pill. Now he proceeded to something more like surgery, saying, "You lack one thing; go, sell what you have, and give to the poor, and you will have treasure in heaven; and come, follow me" (verse 21). Riches had so narrowed this man's life that all reference to what was not visible and of material value was lost on him. He was a big man by all the standards by which society determined bigness, but he had become "like Gulliver; he wakes up on the beach . . . bound to the earth by a multitude of little strings."* He was awake and aware that something was wrong—his coming to Jesus showed that—but he little realized the source of his trouble. In two sentences, Jesus discovered how tightly the man was bound and ordered the only remedy: "Cut the strings—sell the riches, give them to the poor, and come and follow me."

* George Buttrick, *The Interpreter's Bible: General Articles on the New Testament, Matthew, Mark* (Nashville: Abingdon, 1951), 806.

Many people in Jesus's day thought that riches were a special sign of God's favor. Some passages in the Old Testament appear to teach this, and it was a firmly held doctrine among some people. The richer you were, the better you were. God blessed you with money because you were good. Money was a sign of goodness. A very rich man was on the brink of heaven's gates. Imagine this man's stunned disbelief in hearing Jesus's command. He was supposed to give up the very signs of God's blessing, to throw away the very things that proved he was a good man. His riches had become identified with his goodness to such an extent that he couldn't conceive of giving up one without losing the other. So, the man refused and went away. George Buttrick's words capture the sadness. "Perhaps no man ever made a poorer bargain: great possessions are tinsel compared with apostleship and a gospel."*

The man left Jesus to spend the rest of his life keeping his favorite six commandments and amassing riches in a compulsive attempt to demonstrate that he had already inherited eternal life and had no need of God. He would be his own God.

A mood of melancholy and depression must have settled on the disciples as they watched the man walk away. There was something heroic and tragic in his rejection of Jesus. They may have hoped that the man would join their band—his riches would have relieved their perpetual poverty, and his youth and reputation would have bolstered their own self-esteem. They had lost a potential disciple, one who would have been a great asset.

It was at this point that Jesus made his famous remark: "It is easier for a camel to go through the eye of a needle than for a rich man to enter the kingdom of God." Humor is an excellent device for deflating a pompous ego or exposing a pretentious pose. The disciples were in danger of seeing in the man's rejection a noble tragedy. So, Jesus poked a little fun at him: He was just like a camel trying to get its enormous nose through the eye of a needle, with as little chance of success. A ridiculous picture, really—a man

* George Buttrick, *The Interpreter's Bible: Luke, John* (Nashville: Abingdon Press, 1951), 313.

trying to develop eternal life on six commandments and a thriving bank account.

But the disciples didn't think it was funny, for they too had thought riches to be a sign of God's blessing. They were "exceedingly astonished" at Jesus' levity (verse 26) and asked the obvious question: "If the rich man cannot be saved, who can? If a man who is that good and successful, who obeys the rules and is conspicuously blessed by God, cannot be saved, how are we going to make it?"

Jesus responded, "With men it is impossible, but not with God; for all things are possible with God" (verse 27). Christian living does not mean the achievement of every human potential but the breaking open of our lives to the activity of God. Eternal life is not the culmination of our possibilities but the invasion of God's grace. By our actions we can be moral and ethical and rich, but we cannot become gods. But God can become human—he did it in Jesus, and he continues to do so in the life of grace in the Christian. He invades our lives in word and sacrament and brings a genuine love, a rational meaning, and an eternal destiny.

One situation in our home that never fails to bring a laugh is when the children dress up in adult clothes. With a hat three sizes too big and shoes nearly as long as they are, they provoke instantaneous fun. That is how Jesus saw the rich man—walking around pretentiously in the clothes of a god. And he didn't look like a god at all! He looked more like a camel, trying to nose its way through the eye of a needle.

If we could cultivate the ability to laugh at ourselves every time we make the ridiculous venture of acting as our own deity, it might do more good than a prayer of confession to restore our sense of dependence on God and our expectation of divine grace. With our perspective restored, the things that were great to Christ will be great to us, the things that were small to Christ will be small to us, and our impossibilities will become the everyday possibilities as Christ lives in us.

Amen.

You Are the Christ

He asked them, "But who do you say that I am?" Peter answered him, "You are the Christ."

—Mark 8:29

"Who do you say that I am?" "You are the Christ." That question and that answer center life. With that question and that answer, we are at the core of things. A seven-word question, a four-word answer: eleven words that are the root system of life.

Jesus asked the question. Peter gave the answer. Jesus was a person who lived in the first century. Through a process that they couldn't understand but on sufficient grounds for a reasonable decision, certain individuals became convinced that Jesus was God in human flesh. When Jesus spoke and acted, they heard God speak and saw God act. When Jesus was crucified and rose again, they witnessed God dealing with sin and death, making forgiveness and eternal life out of it.

Peter was a person who also lived in the first century. He was the leader of a small group of people closely associated with Jesus. These people listened most carefully, observed most accurately, and tested most thoroughly—through denial, doubt, argument, faith, obedience, and discipleship—every word and every act of Jesus, up to and including his crucifixion and resurrection. Peter was spokesman for this group.

In Jesus, then, we find God speaking to us. In Peter, we find a person speaking for us. A conversation between Jesus and Peter is a historical instance of conversation between God and a human being: God and you. This conversation, brief as it was—eleven words—is the root of the tree celebrated by the psalmist that is

> planted by streams of water,
> that yields its fruit in its season,
>   and its leaf does not wither.
> In all that he does, he prospers. (Psalm 1:3)

"Who do you say that I am?" "You are the Christ." God asks. We respond. When we get to the center of things, we find that it is God who asks the questions and we who make the responses. God questions, and we answer.

Every gospel writer, all masters in the Christian faith, and every instance of healthy discipleship insist on this. God is in charge. God takes the initiative. God rules. This proposition is established and maintained in all details of life.

Yet how many times have you heard the statement "Christ is the answer"? That is wrong. Christ is the questioner. To say that Christ is the answer may seem like a harmless inaccuracy, but it is a massive mistake. It leads people to supposing that the main thing in life is getting answers to their questions and that if they get them, everything will be fine. They treat Christ like the information desk at an airport terminal; they run up breathlessly to ask a question and then run on to their next flight or appointment.

God knows all this about us. And he is patient with us. He lets us ask our questions, lets us chatter, lets us run around trying out this and then that answer. He waits us out. And then, one day when we have gotten all our questions asked and exhausted the subject, on some road away from the noise of the crowds and the clamor in our own hearts, we hear not an answer but a question: "Who do you say that I am?" Long silence. Slowly dawning comprehension. Adoration. "*You* are the Christ."

Now we are at the center of life. God is questioning me, and I am answering him. God is probing my heart, and I am opening up to him. God's question brings out the best in me. He does not question me to show me up, expose my ignorance, or make me squirm in guilt. His question penetrates my thick, insensitive, pride-calloused skin, and I realize that, yes, God speaks the first word and I the second. God is creator; I am creature. I perceive his majesty and, kneeling before him, experience my own dignity.

God speaks. We answer.

Our answer is an act of adoration. We wait before God, are still before God, respond to the word of God, and sink ourselves into the immensity of God. "*You* are the Christ." We don't know what questions to ask God—we don't have enough knowledge or an adequate grasp of reality. But God knows us. God grasps every detail of our personalities: our hungers and our satisfactions, our weaknesses and our strengths. He knows what to ask. His question draws the truth out of us; our deepest instincts for wholeness are called up by his question and brought into relationship to him.

Once we hear that question and make that answer, we will no longer run helter-skelter, picking up items of information that might perchance tell us how things work or how we can be happy or how we can get ahead. Life is not a matter of explaining or labeling. Life is being in the presence of God—a living personal God is the single great reality of our existence. We are most alive, most ourselves, when we are personally responsive to him. We cannot manipulate him. We cannot order him about. We cannot ignore him. He is there: massive, majestic, eternal, unchangeable, glorious in holiness, full of love and compassion, abundant in grace and truth. He is the Christ.

I don't expect you to know that all at once. And I don't expect you to retain it uninterruptedly. Peter didn't. Peter had spent months and months with Jesus before he quit asking and started answering, before he quit trying to run God and let God run him, before he quit enviously trying to put God at his disposal and simply knelt in adoration: "*You* are the Christ"—his life now an answer to God's searching, loving, centering question.

"Who do you say that I am?" "You *are* the Christ." God reveals. We recognize. God in Christ was in Peter's company for
months, even for years. Christ spoke and acted. He healed and
taught. He helped Peter with his fishing, calmed the storm, fed the
hungry, and saved the demoniac. All that time, Peter was looking
for God. Then he recognized what was right before his eyes all the
time: "You *are* the Christ."

The BBC once brilliantly produced a television series on the
world's religions. It was excellent in every way—except for the
title. It was called *The Long Search*. That is wrong. We don't hunt
all over the universe for God. We don't stay up late in libraries,
pouring through books to find God. We don't look intently through
telescopes into the skies to find God. There is a scene in one of
Peter De Vries's novels that goes something like this: A man came
up to another on the street corner and said, "Have you found
Jesus?"

And the man replied, "I didn't know he was lost."

God reveals himself. We recognize him. You *are* the Christ.
God does not play hide-and-seek with us; he reveals himself. He
patiently, continuously, convincingly presents himself. And then
one day we see it: not by searching, not by reasoning, not by luck—
but by faith. We see what is there. He *is*. We think that God is far
away, remote, hidden. One person wrote, "People put God so far
away, in a sort of mist somewhere. I pull their coat-tails. God is
near. He is no use unless he is near."*

Mark helps us see this by preceding the question-and-answer
exchange between Jesus and Peter with the story of the healing of a
blind man in Bethsaida. Jesus put spit on his eyes and said, "Do you
see anything?" The man answered, "I see men; but they look like
trees, walking." Fuzzy. Out of focus. He could see vague forms but
not details, movement but not identity. Jesus touched his eyes a
second time, and the man saw everything clearly (Mark 8:23–25).

Then follows the question-and-answer story, also in two parts.

---

* Gwendolen Greene, introduction to *Letters from Friedrich von Hügel to a Niece*, by
Friedrich von Hügel (London: J. M. Dent & Sons, 1929), xxxi.

The first part is "Who do men say that I am?" The disciples reply vaguely, "John the Baptist, Elijah, one of the prophets." They had the general idea: Jesus was set apart by God for bringing people to God. But it was fuzzy, like trees walking. Then the second part. "But who do you say that I am?" And the clear, precise answer: "You are the Christ" (verses 27–29). The first answer told what others said; the second answer was a personal recognition. There is a first stage when we are generally aware that God is active in the world. Then there is a second stage—the second touch, the second question—and we respond personally in the immediate, focused present, recognizing clearly what he has revealed. You *are* the Christ.

"Who do you say that I am?" "You are the *Christ*." God saves. We receive. God rescues us from whatever hopeless, helpless, hapless conditions we find ourselves in. He finds us. And we receive his salvation.

Christ is not a personal name but a title, a description of the assigned task of salvation. In Hebrew, the word is *Messiah*; in Greek, *Christos*; in English, *Christ*. Christ designates God entering this history, this humanity, this trouble and doing something about it. God saves; I receive.

And don't we get that turned around? We take charge of our lives. We want to put them together ourselves. We think if we can get the right combination of information and motivation, we will be able to pull it off, and when we do, God will say, "Well done." He will reward us with heaven. He will give us health and wealth. Or—if we can't manage to get on top of our lives, troubles, sins, inadequacies, problems, and doubts, then God will have nothing to do with us. He will walk off, thoroughly disgusted with such a sorry excuse for a human being.

Either way, we have it backward. God does for me what I cannot do for myself. He gives me life and breath, forgives my sins mercifully, and deals with me graciously. I am acted upon by God, savingly; I receive, gratefully. I am able to function, singing, willing, creating, working, and playing.

How clear Mark made this, yet how stubborn and unresponsive we are. What do we read in this story of God among us? From the way we act, one would suppose that it is the story of Jesus going from village to village holding auditions for righteousness. People who have been practicing righteousness come and perform for Jesus. One man who has been practicing humility for years comes and strikes a humble pose. He holds it for a convincingly long time, the spotlights playing over his face and the snare drums rolling a crescendo of climax, and then everyone breaks into applause.

A woman who has been practicing chastity for sixty years is next. She parades across the open square modeling spotless gowns, the white glorious fashions of her purity—beautiful skirts and scarves and finery. Each dress has been designed exclusively to show off her virtue, and she wears it gracefully and elegantly. Everyone is caught up in envy.

Then there is a virtuoso in compassion. He sings his heartwrenching songs and goes through his dazzling dances of kindness. Absolutely stunning. The crowd catches its breath, moved and delighted. This goes on in village after village, with Jesus selecting the best of these performers and bringing them to Jerusalem for a grand saint show.

You've never seen anyone do anything quite like this. Jesus, God among us, goes from village to village, person to person, and touches everyday speech and action among everyday people. Jesus saves, and they receive. He comes among people who are convinced that they have no worth, that they cannot please God—the discards and rejects. But by his word and act or look, he invades their sin with salvation. Many of them receive him. Others are convinced that they can make it to God without any help. Jesus exposes the emptiness of their pretenses, the hopeless inadequacy of their vaunted virtues. And many of them see it and receive what he gives, and they are saved. Always, it is God who saves and people who receive. God acts and speaks in ways that restore us to wholeness.

"Who do you say that I am?" "*You* are the Christ": God asks. You respond.

"Who do you say that I am?" "You *are* the Christ": God reveals. You recognize.

"Who do you say that I am?" "You are the *Christ*": God saves. You receive. Those who hear that question and make that answer call it good news. It is better news than anything you have ever heard. It is the very best news.

Amen.

You Should Turn from
These Vain Things

We also are men, of like nature with you, and bring you good news, that you should turn from these vain things to a living God who made the heaven and the earth and the sea and all that is in them.

—Acts 14:15

The gospel of Jesus Christ joins together two worlds that our sin has split apart. It restores an original unity and makes them look radically different than they ever did before.

Imagine a hunting knife broken at the point where the handle and blade meet. The two parts are in the possession of two men who are widely separated, neither of whom knows that the other exists, let alone what the other possesses. The man with the handle has something that, while comfortable to hold in the hand, is quite useless. Suppose he has had this handle for a number of years, wondering what it is for. Sometimes he holds it, pleased with the easy way it fits into his grip. But he doesn't do anything with it—what is there to do? It is a common object without use.

The other man has the sharp, dazzling blade. It quite obviously is a sensational piece of workmanship and could be a very wicked weapon. But it is useless because there is no handle. It is all blade and sharp at that. He can pick it up gingerly with his fingertips, but he cannot use it—for in cutting another, he would cut himself.

He admires his blade, perhaps showing it off, but it is only something to be looked at, talked about, and admired. He has seen handles, of course, but has no idea that they are supposed to be attached to blades.

Now further imagine these two men becoming the leaders of communities. One group of people has handles, and the other group has blades. The handle people carry the handles around in their pockets. They can tell you that the handle is one of the most common objects in their society and, further, it is perfectly safe. It feels good in your grip. It gives you a comfortable, secure feeling.

The blade people, on the other hand, manufacture their sharp pieces of steel, but not to carry them around. It wouldn't be safe. They have to set the blades as objects on mantles or mount them as decorations. They boast of the sharpness of their blades, talk learnedly of the tempering of the steel, and display their skill in sharpening them to a razor's edge.

Now, suppose a man wanders through the earth and spends some time with first the handle group and then the blade group, learning about each object. And one day, he suddenly realizes that they belong together and that until they come together, the two parts are of no use. He would be something of an evangelist running first to one group, saying, "I know where you can get a handle for that blade and start using it for some practical work around town" and then to the other group, saying, "Let me tell you where I can get a blade for that handle so you can do some of the things that you can't easily do by yourselves."

You can imagine some of the reactions. Some of the handle people are sure to say, "We've gotten along with these handles all our lives. Don't go trying to put blades on our handles; there's no telling what it might upset." And some blade people would object to getting their blades dirty in the common events of the day, taking them off their shelves and dulling their edges in actually cutting.

Yet others on both sides would be delighted—there is some sense to handles and blades after all! The safe world of the handle can be joined to the sensational, dangerous world of the blade to produce action that is neither fully safe nor dangerously sensational but is simply responsible and useful.

Throughout history, humans have found themselves in one of these two kinds of communities. Some have seen God as part of the common life: a handle—comfortable, secure, and part of the ongoing natural processes. The sun rises and sets; rains water the crops; birth and death occur with regularity. And God is behind all that, built into the way things have always been. Nothing to get excited about, really. He is there, and if you ask the question "What for?" they shrug. He's just there, that's all. One of those things you assume and take for granted.

And then you cross the street and find that God is on dazzling display: a glittering, sharp blade. Looked at with awe, he is exalted above everything else. He is set apart from everything common and ordinary. Some have set up museums on his behalf, and crowds of people pay admission to get a look at some representation of his power.

Others use him for spectacular displays, for miracles and wonders. But if you ask these people the point of it all, they impatiently tell you that it has nothing to do with their lives. God is different; he is to be reverenced, feared—and life wouldn't be worth living if there wasn't this occasional demonstration of the power of God.

There is little love or respect lost between these two groups of people. The natural-God people look across the street at the miracle-God people and shake their heads at their immaturity and irresponsibility. They accuse them of wanting only entertainment from their religion. They suspect that what they really want is just another excuse for a party when they go to church. They see all the sensationalism and the invocation of the supernatural as a diversion from more serious work. And they claim to see little connection between what these individuals do in relation to this miraculous religion and the routines of their lives—work, marriage, family, and society.

The miracle-God people look across at the natural-God people and comment that they have quit believing. They say they have settled into the routines of the world and have given up the effort to believe in anything beyond themselves. They see dullness, regularity, and an assimilation to the conventions of the culture. Pretty boring stuff, all in all. If you can't have a God who does something you can't do yourself, why bother with one at all? They comment that the competitors have confined themselves to a narrow world of routine and then have tried to give some color and romance to it by saying that God is in it somehow.

Paul and Barnabas preached the gospel to people who fell into these two camps. A fascinating story of their skill in putting these two segments of religion together is found in Acts 14. One day, around the year A.D. 48, Paul and Barnabas were traveling in a southeasterly direction across a high plateau region in southern Turkey. They came upon a little rural village, quite out of the centers of politics and commerce, named Lystra. As they entered the city, there was a lame man sitting along the road. Paul looked at him and saw the possibility of healing. He said, "Stand upright on your feet" (Acts 14:10). The man, miraculously, sprang up and walked.

That, of course, created a sensation in the village. The word spread excitedly. The people of the village were bilingual; they could speak Greek (the language of Paul and Barnabas) for business purposes, but their own language was Lycaonian. In the flush of enthusiasm that swept through the town, the message traveled by Lycaonian, which naturally Paul and Barnabas couldn't understand. What they were saying (and what Paul and Barnabas weren't understanding) was "The gods have come down to us in human form." That part of the world was thick with stories of gods who did such things: Zeus, Hera, Apollo, Athena, Poseidon, Hermes— scores of them, with enough stories of their exploits in human disguise to fill a library of books.

The villagers determined that Barnabas was really Zeus and that Paul behind his disguise was Hermes. The distinction was probably based on what they observed: Barnabas was perhaps a large, heavily bearded man who didn't say much. That would be Zeus, king of the gods, inscrutably and silently in control. Paul would have been smaller, quick in his movements, alert, and the spokesman for the two. That would be Hermes, the messenger and spokesman of the gods.

There just happened to be a temple of Zeus in that city, so they knew what to do. The priest organized a processional. They draped oxen with bright garlands and ushered in a great celebrative parade in honor of the two gods among them, to be climaxed in the sacrifice of the oxen followed by a great banquet. All of this had been happening in a language Paul and Barnabas didn't know. But suddenly they saw what was going on and rushed before the people to try to stop the whole thing.

The way Paul stopped them—but only barely—was by giving them a strong dose of "natural religion." He talked about the God who "did good and gave you from heaven rains and fruitful seasons, satisfying your hearts with food and gladness" (verse 17). He pulled them into the world where there were seasons, weather, crops, and blessings, the world of regularity and providence that God created and sustains.

I don't imagine that was very appealing after the healing of the lame man. The people had been attracted to these men by the miracle, but now they found them talking about the God who sends rains—and robbing them of their party. The town was in a joyful uproar, and Paul and Barnabas were now saying nothing.

Paul was engaged in putting two worlds together. His few days in Lystra, the healing of the lame man, and the refusal to accept the roles of Zeus and Hermes—all this constituted an attempt to join together two worlds that had been split apart. I imagine the message that came through as gospel must have been something like this:

You are all excited because a man has been healed; a miracle has taken place before your eyes. Well, don't be. That is routine. God is among us in healing and salvation. There is nothing exceptional about that; it is part of the normal everyday existence of the Christian. The other side of this is that all the things that have fallen into a dull routine for you—the rain, the crops, and the seasonal blessings—come from God. The same God who healed the lame man sends the rain. You don' t sacrifice oxen when you have a thundershower do you? Well, don't do it when you have a healing either. But look at both of them as lively proofs that God is present among you in Jesus Christ. God has come among you so that his presence is realizable in your lives in ways you never thought of, miraculous ways, if you will. It is realizable in ways you never thought of in the other direction too, in natural commonplaces of the week.

What the gospel does is make the miracle routine and the routine a miracle. Christians don't get overly impressed by the miraculous; after all, God can do what he wills. But neither do they get complacent over the routine, when all the engines of God are spilling out of their creation. The gospel of Jesus Christ takes the commonplace handle, joins it to the spectacular blade, and makes a knife—a whole life that is both ordinary and sensational, natural and supernatural.

That means that in your life, miracles are always a possibility. God is not limited to your imagination, confined to your routines, or reduced to the commonplaces of your life. He can and does break through into your life in surprising, unexpected ways. At the same time, he is never excluded from the commonplace. He is never absent, even when things seem most humdrum. He is there to be praised, obeyed, and celebrated in the ordinary universe. The Christian gospel is a total life, refusing compartmentalization and avoiding fragmentation. What Paul said to the people at Lystra, he says to you: "Turn from these vain things to a living God."

Amen.

But You Have Come . . . to Jesus

But you have come . . . to Jesus, the mediator of a new covenant, and to the sprinkled blood that speaks more graciously
than the blood of Abel.

—Hebrews 12:22, 24

I have a friend who really ought to have been born two hundred
years ago. He is a misfit in the twentieth century. He neither ap-
proves of nor enjoys the so-called improvements that modern
progress has brought to humankind. Every once in a while, he
does something deliberate to demonstrate his preindustrial-age
loyalties.

Several years ago, he discarded his electric razor and purchased
a straight razor (since a safety razor smacked too much of compro-
mise). He began each day lathering his beard with a badger brush
and shaving it with his elegant straight razor. In the course of time,
the razor's edge dulled. My friend tried to sharpen it but only made
it worse. Shaving each day became more and more reminiscent of
the ancient ritual of the morning bloody sacrifice. Finally, he gave
up and took his razor to a barber, who honed it and stropped it
until it had a fine edge again. The barber pulled a hair from his
head and demonstrated—the razor was so sharp it could split a
hair.

Now my friend returns periodically to the barber to get his
razor sharpened. The sharpness that can split hairs is functionally
important to him. Hairsplitting is no idle diversion; it is the proof

of a sharpness that has personal consequences every day as he shaves.

The letter to the Hebrews has a lot of hairsplitting arguments and analogies in it. And every one of them has practical consequences in ordinary Christian living.

By definition, Christians are those who make their primary identification with the life, death, and resurrection of Jesus Christ, which was expressed historically twenty centuries ago. However modern we may be in our language, tastes, technology, clothes, and culture, still our essential link with reality is an event that is quite outside our century.

We outdo my friend by several centuries. He retreats for his ideals and models a mere two hundred years; the Christian goes back two thousand. To find out what it means to be a person, to find out what it means to love and be forgiven, to find out what it means to be created by and redeemed by God—for all this the Christian returns to the history of the first century. In basic orientation, the Christian is a first-century person.

But we have to do our living in the twentieth century. We take Christ as our Savior. We believe in him as the revelation of God to us. But our discipleship is carried out in the present in a world of work and play, neighborhoods, streets, and cities. In our daily living, the edge of our faith gets dull. The blade of the spirit is blunted. We try to sharpen it ourselves and only make it worse. And finally we decide to go and get some help.

The place we go for help is Holy Scripture. We read it again and meditate on its meaning and significance. Our faith is honed and stropped on the leather of the Bible. Every Christian who is using his faith daily finds he needs regular, periodic returns for this sharpening.

That is the function of the sentence "But you have come . . . to Jesus" (Hebrews 12:22, 24). It is a reminder of history. A refresher course in what we commit ourselves to when we believe in Christ. A taking out of the old photographs of the faith, dusting them off, and tracing their exact features again.

It appears that in the years following their original conversion, trials, persecutions, and controversies washed over the community of Christians to whom this letter was first written, eroding the sharp features of the gospel. The gospel as originally defined in Jesus Christ was blurred. Everything "religious" was melted into the same mold. The vocabulary and ritual of all religion were assimilated into a common exchange. People were saying such things as "All religions are basically alike, you know" and "It doesn't make much difference what you believe; it's how you live that counts."

Ten or fifteen years of this made it terribly difficult to tell the difference between Mount Sinai and Mount Zion, the Hebrews in the wilderness and the Christians in the desert, the old covenant and the new covenant, the blood of Abel and the blood of Jesus.

After a while it sounded like people were making a great deal of fuss about what was basically the same thing after all. The street-corner theologians set out a position that would maintain itself for centuries: "It is all religion, and religion is about God. There is only one God, so there must be only one religion. And people are really talking about the same thing. Let's quit the hair-splitting. Let's quit the arguments and controversies. We found out there was not so much difference between Methodists and Presbyterians; there is probably no more difference between Buddhists and Muslims and Hindus and Christians. It is all so very vague anyhow; let's get on with the business of being religious." The result is a generation like our own, which can entertain the foolishness of *Jonathan Livingston Seagull* along with the hysterics of *The Late Great Planet Earth* without embarrassment.

One set of ideas that is paired in Hebrews 12:24 illuminates the situation: the blood of Abel and the blood of Jesus. The two concepts are superficially similar. Abel was killed, and so was Jesus. Abel was killed because he was good; he had done the right thing before God. Jesus was killed because he was good; he had fulfilled God's will obediently in the world. The murder of Abel was deliberate; Cain did it. The murder of Jesus was deliberate; Judas betrayed him, the high priests were accomplices, and the Romans were executors. The blood of Abel had spiritual consequences: "The voice of your brother's blood is crying to me from the ground" (Genesis 4:10). The blood of Jesus had spiritual consequences: "This is my blood of the covenant, which is poured out for many" (Mark 14:24). The imagination picks up parallels and assimilates them to all blood sacrifices in all religions until the distinctions are thoroughly obscured.

At least some first-century Christians seem to have been muddling the mind of the church in this way. The consequence was that all the old superstitions, taboos, fears, and uncertainties of the mysterious supernatural crept back into their lives. Religion, instead of freeing them from their sins and equipping them to live strongly and confidently in the world, released all the threatening mysteries of a world of demons and angels and priest-ridden ritual.

If religion is everything anybody says about God, how do you know that all the threatening things people feel and say about God are not true? If there is no definition of what God is, how do you know that he might not be cruel, unpredictable, and mean?

One thing we frequently forget is that outside the Christian gospel, religion is largely a matter of fear and mystery. The coming of Jesus Christ chased away the shadows of obscurity, vagueness, and mystery that are breeding grounds for fear and replaced them with a definite hope, a clear love, and a confident joy in relation to God.

But once you slip back into a religious atmosphere where Christ is just one item among many, all the old half-gods sneak back to do their evil work. Religion is all flattened out into mythology and superstition where one person's opinion is as good as another's. Fear is inflated into dogma, and guilt is mistaken for the voice of a god.

The phrase "the blood of Abel" represents all that. It is the blood of a murdered man. Its consequence is alienation, and its world is fear. The blood of Abel represents all those human efforts to get back to God by the laborious effort of appeasing him, making sacrifices to alleviate his anger. It is the summary of the basic religious experience of terror before the known reaction of God to our sin.

Three results of a religion based on the blood of Abel are referred to in the verses that surround the text. They are fear, negativity, and vacillation. An example exposes the fear. Moses said, "I tremble with fear" (Hebrews 12:21). Opposite to Moses who was fearful because he didn't know what might happen at Mount Sinai, Christians are not fearful because they know what has already happened at Mount Zion. Jesus Christ has demonstrated God's love for us in "the sprinkled blood that speaks more graciously than the blood of Abel."

A warning pins the naysayer: "See that you do not refuse him who is speaking" (verse 25). Religion without Christ is marked by negatives. Prohibitions and warnings and taboos are characteristic. This carries into daily living. If life at its root is a refusal, this rejection comes to mark everything in relationships between God and humankind. But Christ is different. He is accepting and acceptable.

An invitation counteracts the vacillation: "Therefore let us be grateful for receiving a kingdom that cannot be shaken." (verse 28). When we are not sure of what God is like or what he will do, we are on slippery ground. When God is a mystery, then anything unexpected that happens shakes us up. But that is not the case for the Christian. The entire book of Hebrews traces the exact outlines, the lineaments, of the God who comes to us in Jesus Christ. When there is a shaking of life, of history, of mind and body, there is something beneath it all that cannot be shaken: "Therefore let us be grateful."

"You have come . . . to Jesus." You have not come to a blazing mountain full of frightening sounds and sights. You have not come to a place of vengeance or retribution. You have not come to a dark universe where vague threats lurk behind unexpected turns. You have come to Jesus Christ. You have not come to the blood of

Abel, the representation of religion that is connected with hate and hopelessness. You have come to Jesus whose blood speaks more graciously than the blood of Abel. There is a great deal we do not know about ourselves and about God and about the world. But we know some things definitely. And we know them because we have come to Jesus. Jesus is the demonstration that God loves, that he heals, that he forgives, that his intention for every individual is redemption, that he actively seeks to make us whole persons. We know that no time or circumstance is inaccessible to his grace. We know that no disaster (even crucifixion) can limit his power. We know that his characteristic action is resurrection—the bringing to life of that which for us is beyond hope.

Amen.

What You Therefore Worship
as Unknown

What therefore you worship as unknown, this I proclaim to you.

—Acts 17:23

Imagine yourself going to the mailbox and finding a letter addressed to you. You open it to find a plain piece of paper with the written words "I love you." No signature. No letterhead. No return address. Not a hint of the person who wrote it, or why. Just the words "I love you."

The experience is repeated. Several days later, it happens again. And then a week or so later, another letter comes, bearing the same message. Sometimes a week goes by without a new letter; sometimes several weeks. But despite the irregularity, the letters continue to come.

How would you feel? There would perhaps be a good feeling. It is nice to know that you are loved. To know that somewhere in the world is a person who loves you likely makes you feel good.

The good feeling develops into a curiosity about the source of this love message. Who exactly is saying it? You run through your acquaintances—can it possibly be any of them? You begin to act very nice to everybody you meet. No telling who is sending the message. Everyone you meet is a possible source of personal love.

Then the thought crosses your mind, *Why the anonymity? Is*

the person trying to drive me mad? Maybe there is a malicious in-
tent behind the message—the I love you *is a sinister disguise for*
something to take me off my guard, setting me up for a trick.

So you begin to suspect the people you meet, as any one of
them might be behind this. You get edgy and snippy.

One day you think, *Maybe it isn't a person at all; maybe it's an*
organization. It would be just like some computer-run bureau-
cracy to make a mistake somewhere along the line and get my ad-
dress on some advertising list. I'll bet nobody knows who I am at
all. I'm just a series of clicks on a computer, and I'm being softened
up for a hard sell later on. The insistent message of love that I was
gullible enough to think was personal will be used to sell me a new
deodorant. And gradually you develop a thick skin of cynicism to
the love messages.

That is precisely the mental climate that Paul walked into when
he arrived in the old Greek city of Athens in his first visit there
around A.D. 50. Except that it was gods, not love, that had people
in that combination state of curiosity and frustration.

The Athenians were intensely aware of the existence of gods.
The air was saturated with dissuasion, stories, and a vocabulary
that made continual reference to them. But this awareness was
combined with a great deal of baffled ignorance about the gods,
which then progressed to speculation and fantasy. And all the
moods that became associated with those things began to prevail.
The simple joy of knowing that there were gods transitioned to
other moods of angry fear (since the gods might be up to some
mysterious evil) or sullen cynicism (as the whole business began to
have all the marks of an elaborate hoax).

One story that comes out of old Athens illustrates the mood
perfectly. A plague had hit the city. Terrible and ravaging it was,
with many dying and nearly everybody sick. Nothing they did
seemed to improve matters. They did the normal things: sacrificing
on the altars of the gods that had jurisdiction over the city. The
assumption, of course, was that some god was behind this, was
probably angry, and needed to be appeased. The question was

which god? And what was he angry about? They sent for advice to an outsider, who provided them with wise and ingenious counsel. He said, "Take a flock of sheep to the hill in the middle of the city and let them go. Whenever a sheep lies down, kill the sheep and make a sacrifice there. Mark the spot, build an altar to an unknown god, and sacrifice the sheep to the unknown god."* Because of that incident, altars to unknown gods were scattered all over the city of Athens. Several ancient travelers mention seeing them, and inscriptions are known of altars dedicated to "unknown gods" (plural), the reasoning was that one or other of the gods might show anger at having been overlooked."†

The story captures the Athenian mood: widespread awareness of the presence of gods combined with an ignorant and anxious, uncertain curiosity about their character and nature.

That all seems very contemporary to me. The Athenians and the American mood share deep roots of identity. Only the vocabulary and the art have changed. The religious mood is the same. If you substitute the American words "peace and love" for the Greek gods, you will hardly be able to distinguish the two places.

Peace and *love* are biblical words. They have been developed in their meaning for four thousand years of intense experience between God and humanity, particularly visible and accessible to us in the history of the Hebrew people and the Christian church. These two words dynamically represent the deepest energies that the human person is capable of expressing. They are creative words, bringing scattered fragments of lives into unexpected combination and making sense out of them. They are happy words, joyously exalting the nature of human existence into something that expressively gives meaning and satisfaction.

And you see and hear the words everywhere. They are on posters and bumper stickers. Artists have made them look like the best

---

* This is my paraphrase of content from a story Don Richardson tells. Don Richardson, *Eternity in Their Hearts* (Minneapolis: Bethany, 1981), 9–25.
† Oxford Reference, s.v. "unknown God", www.oxfordreference.com/display/10.1093/oi/authority.20110803114806732.

words that have ever been used (which they are). They are decked out in colors that expand their meanings and impact. They range over every sector of human history. No one supposes any longer that peace is what happens when you successfully escape the horrors of the world or that love is some mysterious chemical reaction between two adolescents. Both words have recovered the aggressive, energetic qualities that the Bible gave them so long ago, and they represent the best that can take place in human history. They are not only a goal but also a strategy; not just an end but a means. Love and peace are not just words that describe the state we would like to be in; they characterize the specific actions that will get us there. Peace and love.

Yet with all their prevalence and attractiveness, with all the attention given them, a strange anonymity surrounds them. They float, unattached, through our culture. They have neither subject nor object. And I begin to ask questions: Who loves whom? Who gets this love going? Who gets this peace started?

In 1831, Alexis de Tocqueville arrived in America from France and was not here long before he concluded that "the Americans are a very religious people." He went on to say that Americans "do no rely on religion alone. . . . and they do not call in the aid of religion until they have reached the utmost limits of human strength."*

Paul walked into a city where he saw an altar to an unknown god.

I walk through a culture where I see posters to an unknown love and unknown peace.

Having discovered the common identity between our two worlds, the Athenian and the American, I begin to think, *Would Paul's sermon work as well here as it did in Athens?* And I rather think it might.

The first thing Paul did was commend the Athenians for their religious awareness. "I perceive that in every way you are very re-

* Alexis de Tocqueville, *Democracy in America,* trans. Henry Reeve (London: Oxford University Press, 1946), 464.

ligious" (Acts 17:22). He did not lampoon them for their idolatry or ridicule them for their nervous altar building. He recognized that their concern about gods was rooted deeply in the human awareness that there is a God to be worshipped and served. No matter how the altar is constructed and no matter what the name of the god to whom sacrifices are made, the impulse that gets the whole thing started is a good one. Humanity is made for God and reaches out for him instinctively.

I think Paul would have been equally accepting of the religious enthusiasm in America over love and peace. He would see in these words the insight that they represent the best action of which humankind is capable, the finest goal toward which human history can move. He would see them rooted in an ancient history of God-man relations and would commend them. I share what I suppose his attitude would be. An unbelievable number of persons are affirming the best things that can be affirmed in life. There is a zestful proclamation of the qualities that raise men and women to their saintly best.

But while Paul was happy about the fact that there was a religious life in Athens, he was very unhappy about the ignorance that surrounded it. That there should be gods is good; that they should be unknown gods is bad. So, Paul set out to improve the situation: "What therefore you worship as unknown, this I proclaim to you" (verse 23).

He said that God is living—the creator of everything that is— and that his being is not dependent on what humans do or think. This God is present to everyone and has decisively entered into human history in the humanity of Jesus Christ, who was raised from the dead.

Paul gave God a name (Jesus Christ) and provided a history (the observable creation) and named his characteristic action (resurrection). No more is there an excuse for ignorance about God. We know his identity, his history, and his way of working. Unknown gods are a thing of the past; now God is known by name and action.

I can hear Paul doing the same thing with our American equivalents to the Athenian altars to the unknown god. He would put a subject to the words *love* and *peace*. "God so loved the world that he gave his only Son, that whoever believes in him should not perish but have eternal life" (John 3:16).

Love can become an event in Jesus Christ. It is specifically refined in what God did for me. We hear the gospel preached and find that love is always the center of an action—God does something to humankind in a great way. And humans participate by doing something back for their neighbors.

Love is never abstract. It is never unconnected with the God who loves or the person that he loves. There is a name at both ends of love. Love gets a history, an identity, and a character. And so does peace.

We live in a time that is intensely spiritual, religious in many ways. And a major part of what we call religion is expressed in the word *love*. The messages of love are all over the place. The mailbox keeps providing a reminder: *You are loved.*

But many are confused about it and experiment throughout their lives to find out what love means. Others are afraid, as the powers of love seem dangerous and obscure. And others are cynical; their hope for love is dissipated in the disappointments and soiled experiences of actual living.

In such a time, the gospel is proclaimed. What you therefore worship as unknown, this I proclaim to you: God loves you. He has demonstrated and proven this love in Jesus Christ, and he calls you to share this love.

Amen.

This Prior Love

We love, because he first loved us.

—1 John 4:19

"God is love," said St. John (1 John 4:8), and the statement sounds a trifle innocuous in our ears. We have been bombarded with the truth since nursery days, and it has taken on the tones of a tired bromide—to the point where it seems futile to protest that when first stated and written, the words sounded strange and, if true, wildly revolutionary in the ancient world.

Every god known to humankind had been a tyrant—capricious, willful, and terrifying. At their best they were benevolent despots, and at their worst bloodthirsty beasts. The Greek and Roman gods were for the most part deified adolescents; their counterparts were lustful, vengeful Semitic kings. The one nation that didn't quite fit into the picture, Israel (which did have knowledge of the just and righteous God), was so preoccupied with popular religion that the original revelation to Moses was obscured into a far-off dream.

The atmosphere was so bad in those days that the best course for a person of sensitivity and insight was to renounce all gods and proclaim an atheistic morality. Thus Socrates, while he never explicitly denounced the gods, poked fun at them so effectively that he was condemned and killed for his influence. If you wanted to live the good life, ignore the gods—know yourself. And later, in another part of the world, Buddha reformed the religious culture by explicitly denying the existence of all gods. There simply was no god or gods. They were all so bad that none could be taken seriously by a sensitive soul. And he went on from there to build his own religious and ethical system. It may seem far away and remote to us, but the simple facts of the ancient world were that no person put forward as a serious idea the proposition that God loved. There were a few hints in the background, but no declaration.

And then Christ came and not only demonstrated that God loved but also exhibited a new kind of love. It was a new event in human life, and the early church saw it as the crucial event in their lives. They dated everything from the time when God first loved them. God loved, and history progressed from there. Philosophers used to play the game of first causes. The early church was not so interested in philosophy, at least not at first, but they had a first cause: God loved. When pressed to find some reason or explanation for the phenomenon of which they found themselves a part, they said, "God first loved us, so we love."

We can perhaps better understand its initial thrill if we try to recapture a little of the mood of the day. The ancient Greeks told a story that might help.

Minos, king of the island of Crete, off the southern coast of Greece, sent his son to the Greek mainland for a visit, and the son was killed. As a penalty, the angered Minos established that every year, seven young men and seven maidens were to be sent to him. He had constructed a complex and intricate labyrinth out of which no one could possibly find his way and in which was a brutal Minotaur, half bull and half man. The seven youths and seven maidens were placed in the labyrinth to be discovered by the Minotaur and to meet their doomed end. You can imagine the frantic flight of the victims racing down passage after passage, any turn of which might lead to safety, only to find a dead end and the awaiting savage Minotaur. This went on year after year until the son of the king of Greece, Theseus, volunteered to be one of the victims in the hope of ending the cursed annual massacre. Theseus arrived on Crete on the fated day and was seen by Ariadne, daughter of

King Minos, who, of course, promptly fell in love with him and devised a way to save him. She took him aside secretly and gave him a ball of thread that he was to let unwind as he was taken into the labyrinth, thus providing a way of escape. Accepting her aid, he went in and in heroic fashion slew the Minotaur with his bare hands, then found his way out of the labyrinth with the thread of Ariadne.

Biblical statements about humankind anticipate these insights. Humanity is in a labyrinth. And who has pronounced the anguish better or more poignantly than the Hebrew psalmists?

> Thou hast put me in the depths of the Pit,
>> in the regions dark and deep.
> Thy wrath lies heavy upon me,
>> and thou dost overwhelm me with all thy waves. (Psalm 88:6–7)

> I sink in deep mire,
>> where there is no foothold;
> I have come into deep waters,
>> and the flood sweeps over me.
> I am weary with my crying;
>> my throat is parched.
> My eyes grow dim
>> with waiting for my God. (69:2–3)

> I am weary with my moaning;
>> every night I flood my bed with tears;
>> I drench my couch with my weeping.
> My eye wastes away because of grief,
>> it grows weak because of all my foes. (6:6–7)

The biblical writers knew about the labyrinth, and they lived its horrors. But they also knew the hope of deliverance. There is hardly a page of Scripture on which the hope of deliverance isn't written in a bold hand. The scarlet thread of salvation, an Ariadne's thread, weaves its way through the tapestry of the Scriptures with compelling regularity. Ancient people, both Greek and Hebrew, knew the labyrinth.

But at this point where the Greeks began their careful search for Ariadne's thread (and none have searched quite so thoroughly as they), the biblical witnesses took a surprisingly different stance. They announced that they had been discovered by a rescuer. They, the seekers, had been found. Positions had been reversed. Instead of laboriously seeking out salvation, an exit from the labyrinth, they testified that the initiative went the other way. Hardly had they realized that they were lost than the seeking God searched them out on his initiative and found them. They were not the seekers but the sought, not the finders but the found, not the saviors but the saved. They were not Greek heroes like Theseus, triumphant with a tragic sense of life. Rather, they were human sinners with a gladness—the act of God finding and saving lost, baffled men and women. We more commonly translate the word as "gospel," but it is much better translated as "the gladness."

This gladness gives us, I believe, a clear clue to the meaning of our text. What had happened? Quite briefly, God had first loved. Or, as our text puts it, "He first loved us." The word used here, *prōtos*, could legitimately be translated as "first of all" or "before anything else" he loved us.* And however commonplace this seems to us, it was completely unexpected to those who first experienced it. They were surprised by God's love seeking them out and saving them.

And in a sense, it is always unexpected. We become so obsessed with our troubles and with our plight, so intent on discerning a way out of the labyrinth and ferreting out Ariadne's thread, that the sudden presence of the Savior always comes as a surprise. But it is such a glad surprise. Love in a god was not entirely unheard of, though it was rare enough. But that God should take the initia-

---

* *Blue Letter Bible*, s.v. "*prōtos*," www.blueletterbible.org/lexicon/g4413/esv/mgnt/0-1.

tive through Jesus Christ and seek out a person—that God should first love—was a flat contradiction of everything known about protocol.

For years, there has been a lot of talk about all religions being the same and holding the same beliefs and adding up to pretty much the same thing. But here is a place where they radically contrast. People are used to climbing toward where they think God is. They are not used to having God suddenly coming to them. They are used to constructing elaborate and ingenious towers to heaven; they simply are not used to the descent of the dove. Babel is commonplace, while Pentecost is a surprise.

And thus the gladness. Anticipated by good news, we are glad. Before we had a chance to cry out, he saved us. There are many ways of making a person glad, but one of the sure ways is to anticipate her needs and to unexpectedly fulfill them. The characteristic mark of the early Christian community was that they were jubilantly happy. They rejoiced in the Lord. The gladness, you see, was evidence that God first loved them. They were surprised by this prior love.

To that same sudden experience of God's prior love, St. Augustine, the great classical theologian, had a more intellectual reaction. Augustine was an intense and ardent seeker after God. He was part of one of the great religious movements of his day that promised a person direction to heaven, the thread of Ariadne then in vogue. The thread was exceedingly complex, being a mixture of occult astrology, ritual purifications, over-intellectualized philosophy, and magic. It was a full-time job understanding it, let alone living it. Yet Augustine was serious about his religion, and his frustration and disappointment were compounded when the machinations of the new religion never led him out of the labyrinth. In his confessions one can read all the anxieties and frustrations of a modern soul. After about fifteen years of struggle and experiment, he was sitting in a garden in Milan, Italy, tired and dissipated, when he felt compelled to pick up the Scriptures and read them.

His gaze fell on the passage in Romans, "Put ye on the Lord Jesus Christ, and make not provision for the flesh, to fulfill the lusts thereof" (13:14, KJV). And he said, "Instantly at the end of this sentence, by a light as it were of serenity infused into my heart, all the darkness of doubt vanished away."[*]

Augustine was surprised by an infusion of new life, confronted by God working in him, and overwhelmed by God's grace. God's love redeemed and rescued him from the abyss that he had grown to hate so much. When he explained it to others, he talked of God acting previously to him. Before he was righteous, God loved him, planned his salvation, and poured grace into his life. God was previous to him. And this led to the doctrine for which Augustine is most celebrated: predestination.

This doctrine has fallen on evil days. It conjures up in our minds babies in hell and an arbitrary despot in heaven damning and electing according to whim. But that is surely a vicious parody of the happy announcement that first flowed from the great doctor's pen. He who had tried so hard—who had given the best of his mind and youth to the current bootstrap religion and found only the taste of ashes—was suddenly surprised by God, who was already working to save him. Anticipating his desires, predestining his rescue, God became known to him. It was first the experience and then the doctrine. And it was because so many had the experience that the doctrine became so universal.

That is why we baptize our infants: to witness before the world the fact that God works in and for us before we are able to know him or respond to him. He first loved us, so we love him. The baptism of an infant (among other things) is the testimony of the church that God's grace, his love, is operative previous to our love for him.

The evidence for this prior love is weighty. The sudden gladness of the early Christians, the persistent though much maligned doc-

---

[*] Augustine, *The Confessions of Saint Augustine* (New York: Crown, 1960), 165.

trine of predestination, the sacrament of baptism to infants, and the gospel that John wrote of are a vast compendium of corroborative material for the point.

And so, we love. Without this experience and this knowledge, said John, we would never have been able to love. For it is a special, new, never-before-heard-of love that is here talked about. We know well enough how to be affectionate, how to be friendly, how to love our family and friends and those who love us. But this is a redemptive love for the one who awakens no natural love in our hearts. It is love for the unworthy and the unlovely—as one old gospel hymn puts it, for "a poor, lost sinner."* It is a love that seeks out, searches out, is the aggressor with a goal of saving and redeeming. And all of this is what God, first of all, did. God first loved. This is the gladness.

Amen.

* Johnson Oatman, "Jesus Took My Burden," public domain.

Christ in the Church

Let Christ's peace be arbiter in your hearts; to this peace you were called as members of a single body. And be filled with gratitude.

—Colossians 3:15, NEB

If someone were to stand up here and make the flat statement that everyone present was in church, that would appear to be a safe and undebatable assertion. You might even think it a kind of crude truism, for this is a church, and we are all obviously in it. But St. Paul liked nothing better than a good argument, and if he were living, being the skilled dialectician that he was, might well offer us argument. He would be unimpressed with our building. And the fact of physical proximity to one another would seem irrelevant to him. He would not be interested in whether we were in this building or not and would certainly question the validity of equating that with being in church. What Paul was interested in talking about was Christ in the church.

The church, by definition, was where Christ was and where there were Christians—that is, men and women who were incorporated into Christ. All the people who are in Christ are formed into a new created entity, which is the church. The church, Paul said, is Christ's body (Colossians 1:24), and Christ is the head of this body. The church is the incorporation of Christians (that is, Christians made into a single, organically functioning body) with Christ as the head.

Paul saw the church only as it exists in Christ and as Christ is present in it. Apart from being in Christ, it has no existence. Buildings, people, programs, goals, reputation, tradition—none of these have anything to do with the church. Only as Christ is in it and its members are incorporated in Christ can we talk of anything that has spiritual reality.

But that isn't the way the church is being talked about nowadays. On the contemporary scene, there is an incredible amount of talking and writing about the church that sounds a good deal different from Paul's. There are new studies, final pronouncements, but most of all criticisms from without and within.

Everyone seems to have an opinion on either what is right or what is wrong with the church, and most of the opinions eventually find their way into print. Just by way of contrast with Paul, notice how many of these outside critics are looking at the church. I imagine some of their conversations like this:

A Social Worker: I spend my week trying to change society. And do you know who furnishes the biggest obstacle to my work? The churches and the "good solid church people." Ever try to get a church board interested in a slum-clearance project? I did, last week. I found that half of the members owned property in the slum and would have no part of any project that might lower the income they were getting from it.

A Person of Integrity: I want to be honest. And I simply can't be in church. Christians get up Sunday after Sunday with straight "religious" faces and sing, "We are not divided, all one body." Not divided? They're divided into so many fragments you can hardly count them. They repeat pious phrases about being "one in Christ Jesus" and at the very moment they are saying these things—eleven o'clock Sunday morning—America is at its segregated worst.

A Person Disturbed About the State of the World: What do I hear in church? Either a lot of irrelevant nonsense about loving our enemies or else a lot more nonsense about pearly gates or a last judgment. I'm concerned about the next ten years. Will we blow ourselves to pieces before then? Are we going to have a war? Why doesn't the church do something about these things?

An Intellectual: I'm willing to bet that not 10 percent of the people who recite the creeds, sing hymns, and read the Bible have the foggiest notion what's going on. "He descended into hell . . . He ascended into heaven." What kind of mumbo jumbo is this? "God in Three Persons, blessed Trinity." What kind of mathematics is that? And the Bible. I simply can't believe in the "credibility of Genesis and the edibility of Jonah." I've read too much science.*

Now, Christians who hear these criticisms and evaluations cannot deny the truth of many of them or avoid the plain fact that they have been party to most of the sins mentioned. Yet they suspect that these critics are failing to put their fingers on what is really essential in the church. They miss seeing what Paul said—Christ in the church (or, in their case maybe, the absence of Christ in the church). Paul was not blind about the church, and some of his criticisms of it are much more devastating than those we have just read. Yet he still loved the church. No matter how bad it might look, it was still the place where Christ dwelt. In an old medieval manuscript these words were found: "The Church is something like Noah's ark. If it weren't for the storm outside, you couldn't stand the smell inside."

Paul often talked about the church in his letters. In his letter to the Ephesians, he worked out the meaning of the church in great

* Paraphrased from Robert McAfee Brown, *Theology in a New Key: Responding to Liberation Themes* (Philadelphia: Westminster, 1978).

detail; in the letters to the Corinthians, he dealt with several practical problems of discipline in illuminating and definitive form; and in the greatest letter of them all, Romans, he put the church into a long-range perspective in the purposes of God.

But in reading Colossians, we have found that Paul was primarily interested in an exposition of Christ. If we were to summarize briefly the thrust of his exposition, it would be that "Christ is all and in all," that he is the completion of all things. Christ is both the center and circumference, and without him everything falls apart and becomes meaningless. The reason that we see so much falling apart and so much meaninglessness today is precisely because Christ is not known.

But even in this letter, which is devoted primarily to other things, the church receives some of the light shed in the exposition of Christ. Paul mentions the collective body of men and women in Christ, formed into a new unity by the work of the Holy Spirit, and the context of the reference is relevant and instructive.

Paul had been talking about our individual conduct as men and women in Christ, and then he moved to our collective conduct—how we live as "members of a single body," that is, as a church. And he offered two commands that in retrospect seem almost as if they were the marks of the true church. They sound plain and unpretentious, but out of all the verbiage, advice, and criticism, their simplicity and authenticity have the power to reach into our collective lives and reform us around the principle of Christ in the church. The two commands are "Let Christ's peace be arbiter in your hearts . . . And be filled with gratitude" (3:15, NEB).

"Let Christ's peace be arbiter in your hearts." Let us get the picture clearly in our minds. Paul was speaking to us. We are a fairly large group of people, sharing a common life in Christ, given to a single goal, separated from the world, and dedicated to a particular kind of life. Yet we are still all individuals, have conflicting opinions, contradictory feelings, various backgrounds, and different emotional responses. Just as sure as anything else in this world, it is certain that we will get out of harmony. So, we need an external authority. Something or someone must orient us in the same direction. We need an "arbiter."

The word *arbiter* here is one of Paul's athletic words. A more idiomatic translation would be "umpire" or "referee." An arbiter is the one who kept order in the Greek athletic contests, who enforced the rules, who made decisions when differences of opinion arose among the athletes themselves, and who handed out the prizes. Anytime there is a group of athletes, competitive and determined, there has got to be a referee to sort out the right from the wrong and objectively discern the true state of affairs. Paul knew that believers are very much like a group of athletes in hard-fought competition, and he named a referee: Christ's peace.

Strange that he didn't simply say Christ, isn't it? But Christ's peace is a more descriptive designation and exactly appropriate to the situation. Peace is not just that individual quietness of soul that we experience when everything is going well. Christ's peace is the working together in harmony of the whole universe of creation. God has cosmic purposes in operation, and our individual peace is only a shared part of the whole. It is this overall peace that is to be the rule in settling our differences, not just how you or I might feel about the matter.

During the fall and winter months, one of my responsibilities is to coach the youth fellowship basketball team. Every Saturday morning, we get together along with some of the men of the church and have a practice scrimmage in a nearby gymnasium. Now, normally when you have a basketball game, one of the essentials is to have a referee to keep order in the game, enforce the rules, and keep the opposing players from each other's throats. But it would be expensive to hire a referee every Saturday morning, and nobody wants to give up the privilege of playing to act as one, so we have a system by which we call our own fouls. We all know the rules of the game, and each player is entrusted to calling those rules on himself. If a defensive player fouls another as he is shooting for the basket, the offender calls the foul on himself. If the ball goes out of bounds, the last person who touched it admits to it. All of us, playing the same game under known rules, let those rules operate by common consent. You might almost say that we let the rules of basketball be the arbiter, the referee, in our hearts. (It works pretty well too. The boys are consistently honest, but it's only natural that the men, not having read the rule book for some time, are a little insensitive occasionally.)

It is in a similar vein that Paul is urging us as a church in whom Christ dwells to "let Christ's peace be arbiter in our hearts." Knowing the purposes of God, the eternal harmony of God's will, we call our own fouls and take individual responsibility for conforming our lives to his rule so that all can work together smoothly and uninterruptedly.

The second command is "be filled with gratitude." Again, remember we are a lot of members but joined into a single body of which Christ is the head. We have a single source of life but many ways of expressing it. It would destroy our individuality to dictate exactly how we had to express this new life in specified words and regimented acts. But Paul did suggest a way in which whatever we do may be consistent and give a unity of witness: "Be filled with gratitude." Obedience to that command ensures a true and healthy expression of Christ's centrality without censorship or regimentation.

Earlier in this letter, Paul said, "As therefore you received Christ Jesus the Lord, so live in him, rooted and built up in him and established in the faith, just as you were taught, abounding in thanksgiving" (2:6–7). Notice that he began with rooted and ended with thanksgiving. The gratitude with which we are to be filled comes directly from being in Christ and from Christ being in us.

In *The Rock,* his pageant play about the church, T. S. Eliot wrote, "The Church must be forever building, for it is forever decaying within and attacked from without."* Those criticisms we voiced at the outset mirrored some of that decay and revealed some of the attack. What Paul wrote to us in these two commands

---

* T. S. Eliot, *The Rock* (New York: Harcourt, 1934), 21.

is a strong defense against the attack and a sure prevention against the decay.

"Let Christ's peace be arbiter in your hearts"—that is the strong defense against outside attack. Christ's peace is the only rule, the only referee we recognize. No alien voice, no strange authority, no outside subversive's leadership, no bullying demands, and no private individual selfishness will influence our actions.

"And be filled with gratitude"—that is the sure prevention against decay. Rooted in Christ, we are radiant with his love and grace. Anchored in the redemptive work of Jesus, we can abound with thanksgiving. We live gladly because we live in Christ, and with this gladness at both root and crown of our lives, no decay can get started.

Christ is all and in all. And Christ is in the church. The conclusion to that is refreshing and brief: "Let Christ's peace be arbiter in your hearts; to this peace you were called as members of a single body. And be filled with gratitude."

Amen.

God's Splendor—
His Righteousness

Now the righteousness of God has been manifested apart from
the law, although the law and the prophets bear witness to it.
—Romans 3:21

There is a long, morose, tedious play in the avant-garde circles
of the theater that some in the church see as an almost clinically accurate portrayal of humankind's stance before God. It was
written by Samuel Beckett and is called *Waiting for Godot*. Two
tramps are waiting, passing the time in desultory conversation.
The stage is bleak—a tree, a log for sitting, and a path along which
someone may walk. The action is unrelieved by variation or
change: It is one long, unbroken exposure to the two men and
their conversation. They have nowhere to go; they suspect that life
must hold something better for them, but they have no clue about
what it might be. So, they wait for Godot to come, to break into
the monotony and senselessness of their lives. They are further
troubled that when he does come, they won't recognize him. Their
minds fumble at everything; they are all thumbs when they try to
think and converse about what is beyond them. They are disturbed
about the absence of Godot but no less disturbed about his anticipated presence for they might not recognize him.

The play is a parable about ourselves and the absence of God.
We are tramps baffled by his absence and disturbed that if he

comes, we will miss him. Whether he shows himself or not, we are troubled. But the possibility that he will show himself further threatens us with anxiety and confusion. Both God's presence and his absence are difficulties in the deep parts of our lives.

But we are in Romans, not on Broadway, and conveniently for us, Paul was interested in identical matters as he treated the subject—God—and our relation to him. We have the advantage of Paul's thinking and understanding, so we continue to follow the maxim "When in Rome, do as the Romans do" and think with Paul as he guides us on these matters concerning the things that matter most.

Paul had an aptitude for epigrammatic speech; he had the facility for putting the whole truth in a sentence. And he did it here: "Now the righteousness of God has been manifested apart from the law, although the law and the prophets bear witness to it" (Romans 3:21).

Speaking to our sense of and our speculation about the absence of God is the single word *manifested*. From the same Greek root, we get our word *phenomenon*. When a manifestation takes place, when a phenomenon occurs, it means that there has been a showing, a revealing, a display. In other words, God has shown us something of himself. He is not absent; he is here, and we can see the evidence, the phenomenon.

The Scriptures have a word for these showings, these phenomena of God's display of himself, but the word is particularly hard to translate. In Greek it is *doxa*, familiar to us when we sing the doxology. It is usually translated as "glory," and recent scholars have been using the word "splendor." A sense of brilliance, effulgence, spreading light, rare worth, and dazzling purity is what needs to be conveyed. *Splendor* probably does better than any other, but we should footnote it by saying that it is not as big a word as *doxa*; it does not carry the wide range of suggestion, the kaleidoscopic brilliance, and the flashing lights.

Now the reason for making a point of this word is to understand the force of Paul's individual words in this carefully and concisely written letter. We must feel something of the force of the stream of tradition that he was standing in—a stream full of instances of God manifesting himself. *Splendor* was a stock word in his vocabulary; it was woven into everything he knew about God.

There is a spectacular instance of it in the early part of the Bible. Moses was on Mount Sinai for the second time, getting a new edition of the Ten Commandments. He asked God whether God was pleased with his recent leadership (he had just had reason to doubt its effectiveness) and, if so, to show him his ways (Exodus 33:13). He continued by saying, "I pray thee, show me thy glory" (verse 18). God agreed and said, "While my glory passes by I will put you in a cleft of the rock" (verse 22). And then, with Moses adequately protected in the rock, God showed himself, manifesting his glory in a stunning and dazzling brilliance, a display of splendor.

Further testimony is in Psalm 80. This psalm is a powerful, stirring prayer that three times calls out, with steadily increasing intensity:

> Restore us, O God;
> let thy face shine, that we may be saved! (verse 3)

The prayer shows that the psalmist knew enough about God to realize that it was characteristic of God to manifest himself, to shine, to show his splendor—and that the most realistic prayer when you feel in need of him is to simply and directly ask for a manifestation of that glory.

As a Jew, Paul looked at the history of Israel and saw God's revealing, or unveiling, acts all the way from Abraham to Ezra, deliverances and judgments on every side. History was conspicuous with the activity of God, which invariably served to tell about God—to manifest him, to reveal him. "He plants his footsteps in the sea and rides upon the storm."*

---

* William Cowper, "God Moves in a Mysterious Way," 1774, public domain.

God, you see, was no hidden manager of the universe, no enigmatic universal force, no mysterious secret occult. He was a God known among his people. God's splendor was that he showed himself.

But just because Paul was heir to a tradition that was full of God's splendor is not to say (as we often do) that the world in which he lived was. In fact, the Roman world in which Paul lived was very much like our world. There were gods aplenty, but they were not gods that showed themselves or told their purposes. The gods were conspicuous for their absence, and the most eloquent religious monument of the ancient world was the Athenian altar to the unknown god. Like the two tramps talking incessantly about Godot, the ancient world talked about the gods, passed around rumors about them, and engaged in endless theological gossip. But the gods neither acted nor talked plainly. It was an age, as is ours, of the absence.

As we read Romans, there are these two things to keep in perspective: The Roman world was full of the rumors, legends, and secrets of the gods; and it was a world of religious darkness, superstition, and mystery. There was cheerfulness to be sure, and there was clever thinking and profound philosophy, but these played out against a backdrop of veiled shadows and murky darkness. And in the midst of this, the Christian world stood at the end of a long shaft of light—the light of the splendor, the showing of God. In this light there was clarity and knowledge. God was dependable and knowable. He revealed what he was by mighty, observable acts of salvation; he spoke his promises and his judgments through the lips of people.

So when Paul said that the righteousness of God was manifested, was shown, we must keep in mind the world to which he spoke: the dark world of rumor, omen, and bewilderment. (And we cannot omit the two tramps.) And we must keep in mind the world from which Paul spoke: the bright world of God's splendor, where he manifests himself, called by John Calvin "a dazzling theatre."*

* John Calvin, *Institutes*, Book 1.

But, we ask, if God so clearly shows himself, why are there so many who do not see him? For it is undeniable that many brilliant, intelligent, honest, and sensitive people profess not to see him. Bertrand Russell, whose erudition no man can doubt, published a collection of essays titled *Why I Am Not a Christian.*

We come back to Paul for help. Paul said that the righteousness of God is manifested apart from the law, although the law and the prophets bear witness to it. And he meant of course, as he explicitly stated in other places, Jesus Christ. In other words, Paul indicated, seeing God is not first of all a matter of intelligence, sincerity, honesty, or sensitivity but quite simply a matter of looking in the right place—namely, at Jesus Christ.

It was the French mystic Simone Weil who said, "Absolutely unmixed attention is prayer."* And the American poet John Ciardi is believed to have once said, "A man is finally defined by what he does with his attention." And Paul the apostle said, in effect, that those who fix their attention on Christ will see the great act of God showing himself, and by faith, that will make them new creatures. The Christian church ever since has held it to be the central truth of the Christian faith.

To the non-Christian, the person who does not believe this idea that God has definitively and conclusively shown himself in Christ, this appears to be monumental arrogance. To the Christian, the person who has actually fixed his attention on Christ and seen God's splendor there, it seems to be a commonsense truth arising out of ordinary logic. It would be a digression to try at this point to understand the reasons for the disbelief on the one hand and the belief on the other. What is germane is to try to understand that Paul's belief in, expectation of, and experience of God showing and manifesting himself reached a conclusion, a climax, a final definition in the appearance of Jesus Christ. "In Him dwells all the fullness of the Godhead bodily" (Colossians 2:9, NKJV).

In our text, Paul's phrase "the righteousness of God" defined

---

* Siân Miles, ed., *Simone Weil: An Anthology* (New York: Grove Press, 1986), 212.

exactly what is shown, what is manifested. *Righteousness* is not a word we ordinarily use. We would be more apt to talk in terms of the character of God, what God is like. But if we did, we would miss much of what Paul meant. The term *righteousness* in the Scriptures has two sides to it. On one side, it means the final, ultimate right. It is the absolute truth to which everything else is relative. It is like those weights and measures preserved in airless immutability at the Bureau of Standards. It is the basic, unchangeable standard of the right and the true—complete rightness.

But there is another side to it, for this absolute standard of rightness is not simply an object, a perfect yardstick lifeless and passive; there is an activity connected with it. Righteousness seeks to make everyone and everything like itself—that is, to make everything right. There is an aggressive side to righteousness, an ability to initiate right action. It is not satisfied to remain impeccably right itself. It imaginatively seeks to transform. We name this activity the love of God and, when successful, call it salvation.

It is this righteousness that is manifest, shown, in Jesus Christ. He accurately revealed and demonstrated to us the nature of God. But he was not simply God on display, a kind of museum piece for us to admire, measure, and perhaps paint pictures of. He actively, aggressively, imaginatively sought to bring us into a positive relation with God—that is, he sought to impart righteousness to us. Christ was not an elaborate exhibit to show what God was; he was the righteousness of God on the move, seeking to spread that righteousness deep into our lives. He was truth, but he was also love, seeking to save that which was lost. Through Christ we know that God is both absolute truth and seeking love. The first by itself would be icy and cold and remote; the second in isolation would be sheer sentimentalism.

Nietzsche emphasized the idea living truth rather than merely intellectually understanding it. He essentially held that all truth should be faced with the question "Can one live it?"* Well, we

---

* I am summarizing content found in Nietzche's philosophical novel, *Thus Spoke Zarathustra*. Friedrich Nietzsche, *Thus Spoke Zarathustra* (Berlin: Contumax, 2015), 114.

must see the righteousness of God like that, not as an abstraction or a subject for a philosopher to exercise his wits on. It has been lived, manifested in Christ. It is the Creator and Sovereign of the universe expressing himself to us in love, seeking to draw us into participation in his righteousness.

And this, of course, is the theme of the letter to the Romans, the good news that God seeks to saves us—and Jesus Christ is the proof. In Paul's words, "it is the power of God unto salvation to every one that believeth" (Romans 1:16, KJV).

We can go back to the two tramps we started out with. They shared, you remember, a double problem. They were disturbed by the absence of Godot but even further disturbed by the anticipated presence of Godot, for what if they should miss him when he came? The tramps were waiting, but there was no serenity, no hope, and no joy in their waiting. And the tramps are a parable of us.

Does God show himself? And if he does, how do we recognize it? Paul said, "Yes, he does, and we recognize him when we look at Jesus Christ." God does show himself; that is his splendor. And that splendor is defined as the righteousness that we see in Jesus Christ. Paul called this good news, and it certainly is for all of us who have ever pondered God's presence and our own relation to it.

The relation of our lives to what Paul preached, and what has since become the center of Christian teaching about God, will depend at least in the first place on the kind of attention we give to it. It needs and deserves adult attention.

J. B. Phillips observed that a vast number of people have never given the thinking of Paul the benefit of their adult attention.* They quit thinking about Christian claims when they gave up coloring pictures in Sunday school or when, intoxicated by sophomore omniscience, they tossed all religion into a Freudian wastebasket.

---

* J. B. Phillips, *New Testament Christianity* (New York: Macmillan, 1956), 6.

The writings of Paul and the truths of Christianity deserve more from us than that. They deserve the sustained, disciplined attention of our adult minds. Paul's witness that God has definitively shown his truth and his love to us in Jesus Christ has won the minds and lives of attentive, listening men and women in every century. It can win and transform ours.

The righteousness of God has been manifested in Christ.

Amen.

Getting It Straight, Keeping It Simple

After this I will return,
and I will rebuild the dwelling of David, which has fallen;
I will rebuild its ruins,
and I will set it up,
that the rest of men may seek the Lord,
and all the Gentiles who are called by my name,
says the Lord, who has made these things known
    from of old.

—Acts 15:16–18

Being a Christian means living comprehensively, vastly, soaringly—living at our human best, dealing with all that we have been, all that we are, and all that we can be. The life of a chipmunk is a lot easier than the life of a human. A chipmunk deals basically with matters of food and drink and shelter and dodging the predatory talons of hawks. Human life is far more complex: a far wider range of experience to master, relationships to develop, and skills to acquire. But even this complex, intricate life of a human being is simpler than the life of the Christian, for the Christian enters into volitional participation with God, whose will permeates everything, and accepts membership in a community in which every man and woman is a brother and sister. Life is suddenly far, far more complex, for in addition to the material, animal, and political world that constitutes our basic environment, we find ourselves in a spiritual creation, in a God world, that greatly multiplies the dimensions of reality with which we must deal.

It's easier to be a good chipmunk than to be a Christian. It's easier to be a good American than to be a Christian. It's easier to be an adequate human than to be a Christian.

That is why our lives often become more difficult when we decide to follow Christ. And that is why life in a Christian church places higher demands on us than membership in the Lions Club or the Audubon Society. The demands aren't radically different externally—matters of dues and duties—but they are radically different internally: faith, the unrelenting attention to the invisible hope, the courageous pushing into the future, and love, the sacrificial and affectionate involvement of the self with others.

As a pastor of a Christian congregation, I have a responsibility for representing this reality and interpreting it, dealing with people's expectations, illusions, and needs in this context.

I think this is a wonderful life. I want everyone to get in on it. I don't want anyone to live minimally, as chipmunks or as mere humans. In my enthusiasm, I sometimes leave out the hard parts, the way advertisers do. But then I read Scripture and see again how this was lived by our ancestors; I pray and experience again the slowness and slipperiness of my responses to God; and I converse with you and realize the pain and devilry that daily interfere with your responses to our Lord.

This usually happens several times a day for me—this forced honesty, this recovery of reality. And it happened when I read Acts chapter fifteen and began to prepare this sermon.

We are getting used to this, I think: this careening of the church from one difficulty to another. There are moments of sheer ecstasy in this story: the praise of God, the sharing of all goods in common, the surprised discovery that God is making all things new. But they are mixed with periods of muddle and mess: quarreling over discriminatory practices, the ugliness of greed, fraud and hypocrisy, apparently unanswered prayers, the triumph of violence over love.

We are also getting used to the poise and perseverance of this assembly of Christians—they don't quit. They don't wring their hands in self-pity. They don't feel sorry for themselves or each other. They don't walk off the job. They continue in faith and love. They work through their difficulties, praying to God and conversing with each other until they find the nature of God's will being worked out in them. And then they are off again, into the next leg of the journey, the pilgrimage that we are continuing.

So, we are not unduly alarmed when we turn the pages of our Bible to Acts chapter fifteen and find the church in bad trouble. A problem had surfaced that threatened to destroy the church.

What had happened is this: The Jerusalem church, the original congregation, was basically Jewish. Jesus was a Jew, the twelve apostles were Jews, and virtually all the first-generation converts were Jews. They knew the Hebrew Scriptures and had assimilated the two thousand years of stories and customs and rituals of the Hebrew past. They experienced the life of Jesus as fulfilment of that past. Peter and James were the leaders in Jerusalem.

The Antioch church, a mission congregation located three hundred miles north, was a mostly Gentile congregation. These were Greeks and Syrians, Turks and Egyptians, Europeans and Asians— they came from a variety of pagan backgrounds. They experienced the life of Jesus as a rescue from superstition and tyranny. Paul and Barnabas were the leaders in Antioch.

They were agreed on one thing: Jesus Christ is Lord and Savior.

The Christian message and the experience that confirms its truth is that God actively loves his creation, his people, every last one of us, and shows and implements that love by embracing our human condition in Jesus Christ and saving us. Salvation takes place not in the realm of idea or art but in flesh and blood, in every last detail of the human condition. God's love and will are worked out first in the body and brain of Jesus and then also in ours.

That's it. We don't live very long before we find that we can't live the human condition completely or wholly on our own. We need help. The Christian experience is that God is our help and that the way he helps is shown in Jesus Christ. The Jesus story clarifies our stories. The Christ experience heals and fulfills our experience. Everything gets connected. Meanings emerge all over the place. We get a glimpse of our purpose, our destiny.

That is what the Jews experienced in Jerusalem, the Gentiles in Antioch, and what we experience in Bel Air.

But then the glory of their common experience was clouded over by a quarrel. A group of zealous Jerusalem Christians took it upon themselves to make that three-hundred-mile trip to Antioch to announce that it was not enough for these Gentile converts to accept Christ; they had to accept the entire Jewish way also—circumcision, kosher cooking, the works. In other words, if you were going to be a Christian, you had to first be a good Jew.

The Antioch Christians protested: "That's not the way we heard it. That isn't what Paul and Barnabas preached to us; they told us that Jesus was the way, period. We were told that God has no favorites and that there are no preconditions to fulfill. Repent, believe, and be saved. No strings attached."

The Jerusalem concern was that we get the story straight, and how can you get the story straight if you don't start at the beginning? You don't get an accurate understanding of a person in a single conversation; you need to know about that person's ancestry, childhood experiences, adolescent development, work history, and family dynamics. And if this is true of any one of us, how much more is it true of Jesus? No one can understand Jesus without a thorough immersion in the stories and practices to which he is the fulfillment. Jesus is the blossom; Judaism is the stem and leaves, root system and soil.

The Antioch concern was that we keep the story simple—and how can we keep the story simple if we insist on bringing out all those photograph albums and making people look at those old pictures and hear stories of what cousins, grandparents, uncles and aunts, and town characters did in the old country? The genius of the Christian gospel is that Jesus takes me right where I am and creates a new story out of the materials of my life.

Both concerns were legitimate. The problem was that all each party could see was its own legitimacy. They argued. They debated. Peter, a Jerusalem leader, made a speech for the Antioch side, and things began to open up a bit. James listened to the passionately voiced concerns from Jerusalem and Antioch. He listened, he pondered, and he prayed. And he worked out the solution that continues to guide us.

What his decision came down to is this: We need each other, but we will not impose ourselves on each other. Christ is the center. Jerusalem is not the center; Antioch is not the center. Christ is the center.

Amen.

Christir in Our Work

❋

Whatever you are doing, put your whole heart into it, as if you were doing it for the Lord and not for men, knowing that there is a Master who will give you your heritage as a reward for your service. Christ is the Master.

—Colossians 3:23–24, NEB

About the year 1666, an eighteen-year-old young man in France was converted to Christianity. His name was Nicholas Herman. He had been a footman and a soldier at that time and described himself as "a great awkward fellow who broke everything."* He went to a monastery to work, hoping to do something useful with his life, but because he was unskilled and illiterate, he was given the most menial tasks around the place. He finally became the cook to the monastery and remained so to his death. He never graduated from his servant status. In the monastery, he was known as Brother Lawrence.

The reason that we, three hundred years later, still know about Brother Lawrence is that in a most remarkable way, he succeeded in turning the world of work into a world of worship. His kitchen was a cathedral. In very ordinary circumstances, endowed with very mediocre talents, Brother Lawrence learned to practice the presence of God "in his work." He said that "he was pleased when he could take up a straw from the ground for the love of God,

---

* Brother Lawrence, *The Practice of the Presence of God* (Ada, Mich.: Baker, 1967), 14.

seeking Him only, and nothing else, not even His gifts." "The time of business," he said, "does not with me differ from the time of prayer; and in the noise and clatter of my kitchen, while several persons are at the same time calling for different things, I possess God in as great tranquility as if I were upon my knees at the blessed sacrament."* We get the picture of this big, clumsy man turning pancakes for the glory of God and washing the dishes as natural adoration.

Brother Lawrence realized in his life the rule that St. Paul set down in his letter to the Colossians: that everything in life is sacred. There need be no division between work and worship; the time we work is God's time, and the major portion of life that we spend on our jobs is a strategic time for discovering Christ— "whatever you are doing, put your whole heart into it, as if you were doing it for the Lord and not for men, knowing that there is a Master who will give you your heritage as a reward for your service. Christ is the Master" (Colossians 3:23–24, NEB).

This is clearly the teaching of all of Scripture. Psalm 90, one of the great psalms of the Bible, concludes, "Let the favor of the Lord our God be upon us, and establish thou the work of our hands upon us, yea, the work of our hands establish thou it" (verse 17). You will note that this psalmist does not pray for deliverance from work or grace and strength to keep at work as if it were a distasteful occupation. The prayer is for God's confirmation and establishment that it might be good work, blessed by God.

Jesus was a carpenter. He spent a good many more years at carpentry than in his public ministry of preaching, healing, and teaching. His public ministry at the most was three years and might have been less; his years in carpentry added up to about eighteen at a minimum, and perhaps more. St. Paul was a tentmaker by trade and, as far as we know, kept at the trade all his life. Without question, he spent more time making tents than he did writing the letters that are in our New Testament. And there is not a single

---

* Brother Lawrence, *Practice of the Presence*, 16, 31.

hint that he begrudged the time spent at the tents, as if it were less important or less pleasing to God.

But we must admit that the church has not always acted as if it understood this doctrine of work. There has been a division between religious work (which meant work done in the church) and secular work (everything else). Even if no one said it, there was an unmistakable implication that God's work was done in the church. A person called of God went into the ministry, but whoever heard of God calling a person to be an engineer? The church allowed work and religion to become separate departments. As a result, those engaged in so-called secular work find much of the church work irrelevant and uninteresting, for how can it interest them if it does not even affect nine-tenths of their lives?

Dorothy Sayers once wrote,

The Church's approach to an intelligent carpenter is usually confined to exhorting him not to be drunk and disorderly in his leisure hours, and to come to church on Sundays. What the Church *should* be telling him is this: that the very first demand that his religion makes upon him is that he should make good tables. Church by all means, and decent forms of amusement, certainly—but what use is all that if in the very center of his life and occupation he is insulting God with bad carpentry? No crooked table legs or ill-fitting drawers ever, I dare swear, came out of the carpenter's shop at Nazareth. Nor, if they did, could anyone believe that they were made by the same hand that made heaven and earth.*

Pierre Teilhard de Chardin, a French Jesuit priest who at the same time became the world's leading paleontologist, attacked this whole problem of modern humanity and their work in relation to God. He seemed to me to be the closest thing in the twentieth century to what Brother Lawrence was in the seventeenth. He had a

---

* Dorothy Sayers, *Creed or Chaos* (New York: Harcourt, Brace and Company, 1949), 56–57.

vision of the total divinization of a person's life, whether that meant digging a ditch, organizing office personnel into a better routine, putting numbers in order as an accountant, preaching a sermon, searching for reasons as a philosopher, or examining the nature of things as a scientist. But while having the vision, he also recognized that we are a long way from realizing it. He categorized our failures of letting Christ be Master in our work into three types of people: the distorted, the disgusted, and the divided.

Distorted people try to put the world of things and of work behind them. They feel that since God is a Spirit, they will try to be spirits too. By repressing all that seems of this world and excluding as much of the physical world as possible, they force themselves to center their interests only on purely religious objects. "How can the man who believes in heaven and the Cross continue to believe seriously in the value of worldly occupations?"*

Disgusted people are those who become harassed by the inward conflict of feeling that they should do one thing while the world forces them to do another. There is the churchly counsel to be spiritual, but there is the economic necessity to be material (they have families to support). So they end up tossing over the spiritual and living completely human lives.

Divided people—and this is the most usual case—give up any attempt to understand. They never wholly belong to God and never wholly to things. They are imperfect in their own eyes and insincere in the eyes of others, finally resigning themselves to lead double lives.

We can be confident that Paul's ideal of Christ in our work was not spun during some philosophical reverie. Much more likely, he learned it while hard at work making tents. And he wanted to share it with the distorted, disgusted, divided men at Colossae— and in Bel Air.

The threat to the Christian doctrine of work stemmed from a religious movement that had come into the Colossian church and

* Pierre Teilhard de Chardin, *The Divine Milieu* (New York: Harper Torchbooks, 1960), 51.

was threatening to confuse everything and subvert the gospel. In the ancient world, it was called Gnosticism, and it was already producing distorted, disgusted, and divided people in place of the Brother Lawrences who might have been expected. Gnosticism taught that the physical, material world was evil and that the spiritual world of wisdom and knowledge was good. Because the physical world was evil, it must be avoided—to be a spiritual person, one had to become an initiate of all the secrets of the religious life. There was a complex philosophical rationale to support all this, and it became a serious threat to the church. The practical effect was that since the physical world was considered to be of no consequence in the ways of God and, in fact, unredeemable, spiritual people had no responsibility in it. No ethical norms and no legal codes applied to them. They did their work as quickly and as superficially as possible to get their pay; then they would be off to discuss and participate in the spiritual world with their cultic friends.

This turned out to be a flat denial of the major premise of Christianity: God had become human—actual flesh and blood—to redeem creation. The Incarnation, the doctrine that Jesus was a concrete and specific manifestation of God in this physical and material world, is the promise and proof that everything in this world is touched, loved, and redeemed by God. All creation is under his rule. He is prepared to redeem the totality of it. The gospel writers were quite careful to make it clear that Jesus came into contact with every phase of life and embraced all of nature. All vocations were implicated in his ministry: fishing, tax collecting, medicine, law, the military, politics, and religion.

The message of Christ was that the reality of God could and did become realized specifically in the everyday, material, twenty-four-hour-a-day world in which each person lives. There is no secret club that you must get into to experience God; there is no special vocation that you must join to do his work. He is everywhere, and he wills to become visible and manifest in both people and things. If someone says that she can serve God better as chair of a church worship committee than doing her job at work, she is denying the whole purpose of Christ for our lives, which among other things can be stated as "Christ in our work."

But an inferior doctrine of work is not all the fault of bad religion. Much is the result of bad work. How can we divine thoughts about work when we are given dull, monotonous, boring, and meaningless work to do? How can we put our "whole heart into it" when the work is not worth doing? What if this "whatever you are doing" includes work that exacts no pride, needs no intelligence, and has no good purpose? Much of modern work has this character. We work in isolated units for large corporations or perhaps for the government, and we rarely see any relation between what we are doing and the finished product. A study is made, research is done, equipment produced, and that is the last we see of it. It is hard to get excited about such work. And that is why modern work places such a large emphasis not on the work itself but on working conditions, benefits, and leisure. The work itself is not exciting, so we attempt to cram excitement into the fringe areas and into our free time.

There is much written about this in contemporary sociological and economic literature, and one might easily suppose that the first-century advice of St. Paul would be quite out of date for this modern problem. But just as we say the religious situation in relation to work has an ancient parallel, so does this problem of boredom in work. A closer look at Paul's passage on work shows that he was writing this particular section to slaves. Now, no work could be quite so uninteresting, and in some cases actually repulsive, as slavery. Slaves were kept solely for their economic value, and their relation to work was to get it done. There was no consideration of their talents or their qualities as individuals, and of course they received no sympathy or compassion for their ideas of worthwhileness or meaning in the work. The slave who was a Christian would have faced a great temptation to find his sense of worth and meaning in life quite apart from his work—in his religion. With his mind filled with the secrets of God and the rewards of heaven, he would not have his mind on his work. He could easily excuse any poorly done work with the Gnostic doctrines that the work was evil anyhow and that there was no reason for doing a good job at an evil task that would only increase the evil.

Paul reminded the slaves that work is God's. Christ is the Master whose central work is incarnation—that is, embodying the spiritual love of God in the material and physical world of people and things. If individuals were unfortunate enough to be slaves, they still might redeem even that plight by being Christian slaves and using their work as material to embody and act out God's love. "Put your whole heart into it," said Paul.

Dr. David Read, a Presbyterian pastor in New York City, wrote,

> When I was a university chaplain I found difficulty in persuading students who had been captivated by the Christian Gospel that their service and witness were not uniquely in arranging meetings, promoting crusades and discussions, but also in the "daily stage of duty"—in other words, their studies. Every one of us here is called to worship God not only in the high and holy moments when we are on our knees, or in church together, or carrying through a program of evangelism, but in "the daily stage of duty" whereby we earn our living, or look after a house. . . . The Christian life is worked out at the typewriter, the store-counter, the desk, and the kitchen sink as surely as in our moments of inspiration and spiritual adventure.*

One small parenthesis: When Paul said that God "will give you your heritage as a reward for your service," he was not just promising them heaven if they would put up with their poor lives long enough. Christianity is not a religion of rewards. Rather, Paul was saying that the only way to work is to work for God. No work is sufficient in itself to satisfy a person, but all work is the occasion

* David H. C. Read, *I Am Persuaded* (New York: Scribner, 1961), 65–66.

for a materialization of the love and purpose of God. Christ in our work is a witness to God's love in history, our history. And this is our heritage. The heritage is not a reward that comes in the form of a paycheck, achievement, or success or by increasing one's economic value. It is a heritage of God that promises not only a new heaven (though it does promise that) but also a new earth—that is, the redemption of the material and physical so that God's love will be seen and experienced by all people.

I do not say that this is an easy command to follow. On the contrary, I think that it may be the hardest we ever set ourselves to. But I also think that it, more than anything else in Scripture, may be the most important and have the most practical effects and the largest-range of influence on our lives. If that "great and awkward fellow," Brother Lawrence, could practice the presence of God in his kitchen so joyfully and successfully; if Teilhard de Chardin as a paleontologist and priest could discover God divinizing all his work and all the world; if St. Paul, tentmaker and pastor to slaves, could say, "Whatever you are doing, put your whole heart into it, as if you were doing it for the Lord and not for men . . . Christ is the Master," then we should not hesitate to make it the goal of our lives that Christ should be in our work, "working in [us] that which is pleasing in his sight" (Hebrews 13:21).

Amen.

ABOUT THE AUTHOR

Eugene H. Peterson, translator of *The Message* Bible, wrote more than thirty books, including *Every Step an Arrival, As Kingfishers Catch Fire, Run with the Horses,* and *A Long Obedience in the Same Direction.* He earned a degree in philosophy from Seattle Pacific University, a graduate degree in theology from New York Theological Seminary, and a master's degree in Semitic languages from Johns Hopkins University. He also received several honorary doctoral degrees. He was founding pastor of Christ Our King Presbyterian Church in Bel Air, Maryland, where he and his wife, Jan, served for twenty-nine years. Peterson held the title of professor emeritus of spiritual theology at Regent College, British Columbia, from 1998 until his death in 2018.

"This hunger for something radical—
something so true that it burned in his bones—
was a constant in Eugene's life. His longing for
God ignited a ferocity in his soul."

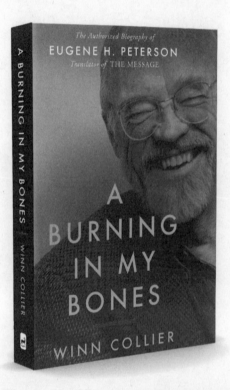

A Burning in My Bones is the essential authorized biography of
Eugene H. Peterson. Winn Collier, through exclusive interviews
and access to Eugene's personal writings, artfully reveals the
dreams, struggles, and spiritual life of the iconic American
pastor and beloved translator of *The Message*.

WATERBROOK

Learn more at
WaterBrookMultnomah.com

The Definitive Collection of Eugene H. Peterson's Teachings

Through the life and words of Eugene H. Peterson, one of the most renowned pastors and theological teachers of our time, you'll see Jesus and every aspect of your life with new eyes.

WATERBROOK

Learn more at WaterBrookMultnomah.com